THE POLITICS OF BUREAUCRATIC CORRUPTION IN POST-TRANSITIONAL EASTERN EUROPE

Using a mix of ethnographic, survey, and comparative-historical methodologies, this book offers an unprecedented insight into the corruption economies of Ukrainian and Belarusian universities, hospitals, and secondary schools. Its detailed analysis suggests that political turnover in hybrid political regimes has a strong impact on petty economic crime in service-provision bureaucracies. Theoretically, the book rejects the dominant paradigm that attributes corruption to the allegedly ongoing political transition. Instead, it develops a more nuanced approach that appreciates the complexity of corruption economies in non-Western societies, embraces the local meanings and functions of corruption, and recognizes the stability of new post-transitional regimes in Eastern Europe and beyond. This book offers a critical look at the social costs of transparency, develops a blueprint for a "sociology of corruption," and offers concrete and feasible policy recommendations.

MARINA ZALOZNAYA is Assistant Professor of Sociology at the University of Iowa. Born and raised in Crimea, Ukraine (now Russia), she received her MA in Sociology from the University of Wisconsin and her PhD in Sociology from Northwestern University. Her research on informal economies, corruption, and political transformations in non-democratic societies has been supported by multiple grants, including from the Open Society Institute, the National Science Foundation, and the U.S. Department of Defense. Her work has also been featured in a number of key sociology and interdisciplinary journals.

CAMBRIDGE STUDIES IN LAW AND SOCIETY

Cambridge Studies in Law and Society aims to publish the best scholarly work on legal discourse and practice in its social and institutional contexts, combining theoretical insights and empirical research.

The fields that it covers are studies of law in action; the sociology of law; the anthropology of law; cultural studies of law, including the role of legal discourses in social formations; law and economics; law and politics; and studies of governance. The books consider all forms of legal discourse across societies, rather than being limited to lawyers' discourses alone.

The series editors come from a range of disciplines: academic law, socio-legal studies, sociology, and anthropology. All have been actively involved in teaching and writing about law in context.

Series editors

Chris Arup *Monash University, Victoria*

Sally Engle Merry *New York University*

Susan Silbey *Massachusetts Institute of Technology*

A list of books in the series can be found at the back of this book.

THE POLITICS OF BUREAUCRATIC CORRUPTION IN POST-TRANSITIONAL EASTERN EUROPE

Marina Zaloznaya
University of Iowa

CAMBRIDGE
UNIVERSITY PRESS

CAMBRIDGE
UNIVERSITY PRESS

University Printing House, Cambridge CB2 8BS, United Kingdom

One Liberty Plaza, 20th Floor, New York, NY 10006, USA

477 Williamstown Road, Port Melbourne, VIC 3207, Australia

4843/24, 2nd Floor, Ansari Road, Daryaganj, Delhi – 110002, India

79 Anson Road, #06–04/06, Singapore 079906

Cambridge University Press is part of the University of Cambridge.

It furthers the University's mission by disseminating knowledge in the pursuit of education, learning, and research at the highest international levels of excellence.

www.cambridge.org
Information on this title: www.cambridge.org/9781107184312
DOI: 10.1017/9781316875582

First published 2017

A catalogue record for this publication is available from the British Library.

Library of Congress Cataloging-in-Publication Data
Names: Zaloznaya, Marina, author.
Title: The politics of bureaucratic corruption in post-transitional Eastern Europe / Marina Zaloznaya, University of Iowa.
Description: Cambridge, United Kingdom ; New York, NY : Cambridge University Press, 2017. | Series: Cambridge studies in law and society | Includes bibliographical references and index.
Identifiers: LCCN 2016046812 | ISBN 9781107184312
Subjects: LCSH: Political corruption – Europe, Eastern. | Bureaucracy – Corrupt practices – Europe, Eastern. | Post-communism – Europe, Eastern.
Classification: LCC JN96.A56 C693 2017 | DDC 364.1/3230947–dc23
LC record available at https://lccn.loc.gov/2016046812

ISBN 978-1-107-18431-2 Hardback

To Tommy, Valentina, and Lex
Like everything else I do, this book is for you.

CONTENTS

TABLES

ACKNOWLEDGMENTS

This book is inspired by stories of my childhood friends, who have navigated the exchange economies of universities in our native Ukraine with admirable grace and resilience. Conceived as a dissertation project at Northwestern University, the research described in the following chapters evolved into a book during my first few years as a faculty member at the University of Iowa. *The Politics of Bureaucratic Corruption* is a product of a long, challenging, and ultimately very satisfying intellectual journey, during which I benefited from the assistance and support of many wonderful people and institutions.

I start by expressing my heartfelt gratitude to hundreds of welcoming and generous Ukrainians and Belarusians who opened up their homes, classrooms, and friendship circles to help me understand local informal economies. It is to their trust and generosity that I owe my ability to write this book. Among them, five people deserve special recognition. First, I thank Alesia Rublik, a giving and devoted friend, who helped me learn the ropes and acquire my most useful contacts in the city of Kiev. Second, I thank Oleksandr Yudenko, whose assistance and friendship made my ethnographic observations both possible and enjoyable. Third, I thank Vera, Rhaisa and Natalia Smolskaya for putting up with my months-long presence in their Minsk home and helping me meet many important respondents.

With gratitude, I also note that my multiple international research trips were made possible by generous funding from the National Science Foundation, Roberta Buffet Center for International and Comparative Studies, Northwestern University Sociology Department, and the University of Iowa College of Liberal Arts and Sciences. Although *The Politics of Bureaucratic Corruption* does not reflect the official views of these institutions, their support was crucial for my research.

While writing this book, I have benefited tremendously from the assistance of many talented social scientists who read my drafts and provided critical feedback. The two sociologists who have made the biggest impact on my thinking about corruption, and whom I am honored to call my mentors and friends, are John Hagan and Mark Suchman. I am greatly indebted to my wonderful dissertation chair John Hagan for sharing his vision, encouraging me to ask big questions, and being an enthusiastic cheerleader through the good and the bad. To my first and longest-serving mentor, Mark Suchman, I am deeply grateful for inspiring my interest in socio-legal studies, teaching me how to think about the law and lawbreaking critically, and for being incredibly generous with his time and much-needed advice.

I also extend a warm thank you to three other members of my dissertation committee, Laura Beth Nielsen, James Mahoney, and Bruce Carruthers, as well as my postgraduate collaborators, William Reisinger and Matthew Light. These amazing scholars took time to read, and reread, my manuscript and offer invaluable suggestions for its improvement.

Additionally, I am grateful to a number of other academic colleagues and teachers who have looked through, thought about, and discussed parts of my book with me, including Elizabeth Onasch, Michael Sauder, Kathryn Hendley, Elisabeth Anderson, Ivan Ermakoff, Ted Gerber, Kim Schepple, Vicki Claypool, Andrew High, Freda Lynn, Karen Heimer, Kevin Leicht, Gabriel Abend, Brian Sargent, Amy Myrick, Diana Rodriguez Franco, and Natalia Forrat. I also thank the two anonymous reviewers and the editors from the Cambridge University Press series "Cambridge Series in Law and Society" for their wonderful suggestions. Finally, I extend my gratitude to the anonymous reviewers and editors of the *Law & Social Inquiry* and *Crime, Law, and Social Change* journals that have previously published some data analyses featured in this book. These scholars' intellectual investment in my book has turned it into an undeniably better piece of scholarship.

In preparing *The Politics of Bureaucratic Corruption* for publication, I have also benefited from the guidance of my inspiring academic friends and colleagues, including Michaela DeSoucey, Lauren McCarthy, Mitra Sharafi, Elana Buch, Ellen Berry, Emily Wentzell, Jennifer Cyr, Jessica Robbins-Ruszkowski, and Nicole Van Cleeve, who generously shared with me their own experiences, connections, and clever tips.

Over the years, parts of this book have been presented at many conferences and invited talks, including multiple American Sociological Association and Law and Society Association meetings, the Kennan Institute at Woodrow Wilson International Center for

Scholars, the Comparative-Historical Workshop at Northwestern University, the LSA Graduate and Early Career Workshops, the Max Planck Institute for Study of Societies, the University of Iowa Sociology Theory Workshop, UI Social Science Interdisciplinary Group, and the UI Anthropology Department, Center for Russia, East Europe and Central Asia at the University of Wisconsin-Madison, and the Centre for Criminology at the University of Toronto. In each of these venues, audiences have me asked thought-provoking questions and offered useful suggestions.

In addition to professional assistance, I have also benefited tremendously from the backing of caring family and friends who know little about sociology or corruption but a whole lot about unequivocal support. Specifically, I am deeply grateful to my loving parents, Valentin Zalozniy and Lina Zaloznaya, who have always encouraged me to do things that I did not think I could do, and my wonderful father- and sister-in-law, Thomas and Antonia Lalagos, who, without judgment or questions, have stepped in to help with the kids during my research trips.

While friends whose personal support has been vital to me are too numerous to name here, I must acknowledge my best friend Liz Onasch, who has kept me sane and grounded while I was working on this book and simultaneously dealing with challenges of new motherhood. From lending a critical eye to my drafts to cooking, babysitting, and sharing countless glasses of tea and wine, Liz has been an incredibly capable and reliable one-woman support system to me through the years.

My biggest gratitude, however, is to my husband Alexei Lalagos, whose unwavering support, intellectual feedback, and unconditional confidence in my abilities have made this book possible. From the time he secretly read my dissertation proposal in preparation for our first date, to the time when he took the "night shifts" with our infant twins so that I could write in the mornings, he has been my bedrock. It is to him and our spunky and clever twins, Valentina and Tommy, that I dedicate this book.

INTRODUCTION

From the Arab Spring and the Occupy Movement to the Saffron Revolution and Euromaidan, prodemocracy protests worldwide are calling to end corruption. Commonly defined as "abuse of public office for private gain," corruption is an impediment to meritocratic competition in business and government and a cause of rising inequality around the globe (Lambsdorff 2005; Mauro 1997; Shlapentokh 2013). Every year, the international community spends millions of dollars to fuel anti-corruption campaigns by civil society actors, national governments, and transnational and intergovernmental organizations (Rose-Sender et al. 2010; Sampson 2010).

Despite these colossal efforts by the international community, scholarly knowledge about the causes of corruption remains limited. Thus, two decades after the fall of the Soviet Union, social scientists continue to think of the widespread corruption in Eastern Europe as a side effect of tumultuous democratization. Such dominant theories tie corruption to the allegedly ongoing political transition, with an implication that corruption will subside and ultimately disappear as democratic governance in the region matures.

The Politics of Bureaucratic Corruption challenges this transitional paradigm in the study of post-Soviet corruption. A carcful mixed-methods investigation at the heart of this book reveals that bureaucratic corruption has little to do with political transitions that are, for all intents and purposes, over. Rather, everyday illicit exchanges between ordinary people and bureaucratic service providers are shaped by new hybrid regimes that have emerged in the region since the demise of the Soviet Union.

The Politics of Bureaucratic Corruption compares the corruption systems of post-Soviet Ukraine and Belarus. Over the past two decades, Transparency International, the largest global anti-corruption watchdog organization, has consistently ranked Ukraine and Belarus in the twentieth percentile of the most corrupt nations in the world (Appendix I, Table 4). Based on these rankings, many scholars and policy analysts conclude that under-the-table transactions between service providers and their clients, such as petty bribery, gift giving, and "string pulling," are ubiquitous in both countries. Petty bureaucratic corruption is also believed to go hand in hand with illegal business practices, grand corruption in politics, and state capture by criminal-economic interests (Holmes 2012; Kostadinova 2012; Ledeneva 2006). As a result, in the Western popular imaginary, Ukraine and Belarus have emerged as interchangeable examples of states that are endemically and hopelessly riddled with corruption.

In contrast to this dominant view, the following chapters show that bureaucratic corruption is far from ubiquitous in the two countries. While many Ukrainians and Belarusians regularly resort to bribery and nepotism in their dealings with street-level officials, others avoid such transactions as inappropriate or unnecessary in ways that current theories of corruption fail to explain. Moreover, despite their nearly identical rankings on Transparency International's and other corruption indicators, Ukraine and Belarus are characterized by different patterns of distribution of informal economic activity across local bureaucracies. While Ukraine has more and less corrupt organizations in different bureaucratic sectors (e.g., more and less corrupt universities and hospitals), in Belarus some sectors (e.g., higher education) are entirely free of corruption, while others (e.g., health care) have relatively high corruption levels.

The primary goal of this book is to explain such within- and across-country variation in bureaucratic corruption in light of the dissimilar political development of the two countries since the fall of socialism. Over the past quarter century, Ukraine has oscillated between the pro-Western and pro-Russian political trajectories, while Belarus reverted to semi-authoritarian governance under the idiosyncratic president Aleksandr Lukashenka. The argument of *The Politics of Bureaucratic Corruption* links these macro-level processes to the unique landscapes of petty organizational corruption in the two countries.

At the heart of the inquiry that unfolds over the next five chapters lie firsthand accounts and ethnographic observations that reveal how ordinary Ukrainians and Belarusians understand organizational corruption systems, navigate conflicting institutional demands, and choose between legal and extralegal ways to obtain bureaucratic services. These data reveal that citizens' corruption conduct is contingent on their interactions with other organizational members and shaped by informal norms of different bureaucracies. In turn, such organizational dynamics are a function of macro-level political processes. Through concrete reforms and policies, as well as through less tangible changes in the living conditions of the citizenry, political transformations affect organizational environments, which then affect citizens' engagement in corruption. By tracing the institutional histories of local universities and linking them to political processes in the two countries, the book reveals that *the rate of political turnover* – the frequency of change in political leadership and orientation – has had a strong impact on the distribution of corruption across the street-level bureaucracies of Ukraine and Belarus.

METHODOLOGICAL NOTE

The Politics of Bureaucratic Corruption employs a methodological approach that differs from that of existing comparative work on corruption. To capture ordinary people's journey between the legal and extralegal worlds of local organizations, I had to employ a wide gamut of methodological techniques and resort to some creative solutions. In an effort to learn about the practices and meanings of illicit exchange, as well as their distribution across local bureaucracies, I conducted interviews with ordinary Ukrainians and Belarusians, ethnographic observations in local universities, a survey of Ukrainian students, an analysis of online discussion forums, and an overview of local mass media reports and relevant polls.

The primary institutional focus of this book falls on higher educational establishments (HEEs).[1] For most Eastern Europeans, the undergraduate years mark their first and, arguably, most formative engagement with bureaucratic corruption. Comparative cases are

[1] HEEs include universities, institutes, colleges, academies, and other local institutions that issue state-backed diplomas of completed higher education (equivalent to Western bachelor of arts or science degrees).

based on hospitals and secondary schools, which are also frequented by most local citizens.

Between 2006 and 2013, I made four research trips to Kiev and Minsk, the respective capitals of Ukraine and Belarus.[2] In each city, I spent approximately four months teaching English, observing, and taking part in the formal and informal lives of two HEEs that represent the major types of post-Soviet institutions of higher education. The first type of institution I observed in each city was a large public university that hosted departments in a wide range of disciplines and specializations. Universities of this type generate the bulk of local academic scholarship, employ the most prominent intellectuals, and offer highly prestigious diplomas to their graduates. The second type of HEE I observed in each country was a smaller, specialized institute that offered in-depth instruction in a specific field. Such institutes specialize in subjects such as law, linguistics, economics, transportation, environmental sciences, and so on; they vary in their prestige levels and can be either private or public.[3]

In each of the four HEEs, I spent between fifteen and twenty hours a week teaching English lessons, helping instructors with class preparation, and holding individual and group tutoring sessions. During recesses and after class, I spent time in faculty lounges and offices, attended extracurricular events (such as presentations and exhibits), participated in faculty meetings, observed in common student spaces (such as corridors and canteens), helped students with homework, and attended social gatherings.[4] In the course of this fieldwork, I was able to learn about the official and unofficial ways that the universities operated, become familiar with interactional patterns among their different members, and discover how local cultures shaped these members' perceptions of the importance, stability, and permeability of administrative and legal rules.

[2] I focused on the capital cities for several reasons. First, both countries have high levels of administrative centralization. Their capitals host the vast majority of higher education establishments, ranging from the most prestigious old HEEs to the newest and the least recognized schools in each country. Second, while HEEs in other cities serve mostly local populations, Kiev and Minsk universities and colleges attract students from all over Ukraine and Belarus. These two cities offered access to a geographically diverse student body. Student respondents came from all over the two countries, including other large cities, smaller towns, and rural regions. Third, the two cities are comparable in their administrative and political functions, social class structure and in the ethnic composition of their populations.

[3] In 2010, Kiev hosted sixteen HEEs of this type, while Minsk had twelve.

[4] I took extensive field notes and used a voice recorder to record some classes, focus group discussions, and conversations.

TABLE 1 Interviewees by type

	Ukraine	Belarus
Students	35	28
Alumni	5	7
Parents of students[a]	20	11
Instructors[b]	27	18
Experts[c]	16	15

[a] Parents of university students tend to be deeply involved with university corruption. At the time of admissions and in the early years of their children's studies, parents often arrange and carry out illicit transactions with university instructors and administrators. In later years, students tend to take over the arrangements and actual exchanges but often continue to use their parents' money. This group included parents of student interviewees and parents of students who had not been interviewed for this project.
[b] The interviews conducted in Ukraine in 2010 were complemented with twenty interviews (with ten students, five instructors, and five parents) that I had carried out in Kiev in the winter of 2006. These interviews are included in the general count.
[c] This group of interviewees consisted of experts on corruption, economic development, higher education, and human rights (such as journalists, NGO workers, political activists, and incumbent officials in the government).

During my time at the local HEEs, I was also able to recruit a diverse sample of students, parents, and instructors for in-depth, semi-structured interviews (see Table 1).[5] I asked students and parents for their opinions on the state of higher education in their respective countries, their experiences with specific universities, their direct and indirect encounters with corruption, and their visions of their own

[5] To gather my sample, I employed a variety of recruiting techniques targeting different respondent groups. I recruited most students and parents through snowball sampling. Because their acquaintances had "vetted" me, these respondents felt relatively comfortable discussing the sensitive topic of corruption. Snowball sampling is widely used in studies of illegal and stigmatized activities to reach hidden populations and increase participation rates (Osipian 2009). In each city, I started with personal or professional contacts (mostly those I made during fieldwork) who then introduced me to the next wave of respondents; second-wave interviewees introduced me to the third wave, and so on. To recruit university instructors, I relied on formal channels as well as the introductions of previous interviewees. I identified contact information of the instructors and experts online and contacted them by email, phone, or in person to request their participation. These respondents included instructors as well as professors and varied in gender, age, specialization, and tenure in their respective HEEs. Please see Appendix II for more information.

professional trajectories.[6] I also invited instructors to share their opinions about the strengths and weaknesses of local higher education institutions; relationships among students, instructors, administrators, and parents in their respective HEEs; and their personal experiences with bureaucratic corruption.[7] Finally, I complemented these interviews with informational discussions with a number of oppositional activists, NGO officials, journalists, and politicians who study, write about, or work on eradicating corruption in their respective countries (see Appendices II and III for more information on interviewees).

In addition to ethnographic fieldwork and interviews, I also analyzed more than a dozen online discussion forums that were affiliated with either unofficial university websites or education and youth portals. It is a common practice among students of Eastern European HEEs to launch chat rooms to exchange information on different courses, offer paid assistance with assignments, share and sell class notes, and discuss instructors.[8] Other non-university websites, dedicated to educational issues and similar topics of interest to the youth, also have discussion forums where students, alumni, and the general public share their thoughts about local higher education processes (see Appendix III for the list of discussion forums).[9] On these discussion forums, I identified and coded stories of illicit exchanges as well as accounts of actors' relationships to one another and their HEEs. These websites offered an invaluable source of data, since they contained direct "conversations" among ordinary Ukrainians and Belarusians and were full of narratives of corruption uncolored by the presence of a researcher.

To build my understanding of local higher education policy and trace the institutional history of select HEEs, I also collected and analyzed relevant primary organizational and governmental documents, such as decrees from Ukrainian and Belarusian Ministries of Education, independent evaluations by local and Western NGOs, reports by government subcommittees, organizations' mission statements, and internal quality assessment briefs, among others. I complemented this analysis with a survey of local media reports and scholarship on Ukrainian and

[6] Interviews lasted from thirty minutes to two hours.

[7] These interviews lasted between half an hour and two and a half hours.

[8] Sometimes, instructors and administrators contribute to these discussions, but their involvement is generally limited.

[9] While other sources of data collected for this book pertain exclusively to Kiev and Minsk HEEs, contributors to these informal forums were affiliated with a variety of institutions throughout the two countries.

Belarusian politics in the post-Soviet era (see Appendix III for more information on primary sources).

Finally, to increase the reliability of my findings and gather quantitative evidence to assess the trends emerging from my ethnographic and interview data, I carried out a survey of 193 students from four Kiev HEEs.[10] The questionnaire presented student respondents with the names of eight departments across eight HEEs and asked students to rank these departments' levels of corruption, quality, and prestige[11] on a scale from 1 (representing the lowest value) to 5 (representing the highest value).[12]

To sum up, this book brings together a mixture of unique qualitative, quantitative, and documentary data on corruption and its political roots. To reconstruct relevant social processes on macro and micro levels, I combined the information gathered through several media – interviews, direct observations, official documentary reports, unmediated interactions among local actors, the press, expert and academic analyses, and a survey. On a micro level, these diverse data shed light on the actual processes of corruption "on the ground." They allow me to identify different types of corruption and establish patterns of cross-organizational variation in informal economic processes. On the macro level, these data shed light on specific ways that hybrid political governance structures the formal and informal lives of local bureaucracies. Importantly, a mixed-method investigation is also key to identifying mechanisms that link the micro and macro levels of social life in post-transitional societies. Ultimately, what makes this book unique among works of comparative corruptology is its focus on causal chains that connect the corruption behavior of individual actors first to organizational structures and then to larger governance processes.[13]

STRUCTURE OF THE BOOK

The Politics of Bureaucratic Corruption opens with an argument that a new theory is needed to explain bureaucratic corruption in countries

[10] Based on my interviews, I had established that two of these universities were widely perceived to have high levels of corruption, while the other two were considered relatively non-corrupt. In each, I recruited respondents from two departments – the reportedly high and low prestige ones.

[11] Prestige was defined as "value that other students and employers ascribe to educational experience and diplomas from the specific institution."

[12] See Appendix I for descriptive statistics.

[13] The term *corruptology* refers to a large body of research on corruption across – social scientific disciplines.

that, like Ukraine and Belarus, combine elements of autocratic and democratic governance. Chapter 1 lays out three theoretical principles that guide the book's inquiry and underpin a causal account of corruption that breaks out of the dominant understanding of informal economic systems as products of political transition.

The first two empirical chapters, Chapters 2 and 3, paint an "on the ground" picture of corruption economies in Ukrainian and Belarusian universities, respectively. In these chapters, I explore when, how, and why ordinary citizens resort to corrupt transactions in their dealings with university officials and administrators. Chapter 2 examines the motivations of ordinary Ukrainians engaged in corruption and describes how such transactions actually happen. Chapter 3 also discusses two comparison cases – Belarusian hospitals and secondary schools – that feature corruption processes that differ from those of local universities.

Chapters 4 and 5 link micro-level accounts of bureaucratic corruption in universities, schools, and hospitals to the recent political history of Ukraine and Belarus. In Chapter 4, I argue that independent Ukraine's continuous fluctuation between more and less democratic forms of governance in the post-Soviet period resulted in the fragmentation of its bureaucratic landscape into more and less corrupt subsectors. Chapter 5 focuses on the political trajectory of post-Soviet Belarus. It shows that the consolidation of power in the hands of President Lukashenka was achieved through political repression, which greatly, even if unintentionally, decreased corruption in select institutional sectors.

The concluding chapter, Chapter 6, summarizes the main principles of the sociological study of corruption in post-transitional hybrid regimes presented in this monograph. It debunks the myth of nationwide corruption cultures and stresses the anti-corruption potential of small-scale organizational interventions.

CHAPTER ONE

BEYOND TRANSITION: POLITICAL TURNOVER AND BUREAUCRATIC CORRUPTION IN HYBRID REGIMES

In early spring of 2010, after several months of fieldwork in the Ukrainian capital city of Kiev, I took a sixteen-hour train ride to Minsk to start my research on Belarusian universities. As the train pulled into Minsk Central Train Station, I could not shake the feeling that I had travelled back in time. Once "brotherly peoples" (братские народы, in Russian), present-day Ukrainians and Belarusians live in remarkably different social worlds. Brimming with commercial and artistic activity, Kiev is home to countless private businesses, a vibrant art scene that features performances by local and international artists, and a wide array of European and American stores and global restaurant franchises. In contrast, Minsk appears stern and regimented. With a meager selection of dining, entertainment, and retail venues, its streets are clean, its public transportation is on time, and its police (милиция, in Russian) are everywhere.

The distinct appearance of the two cities belies fundamental differences in the political and economic makeup of post-socialist Ukraine and Belarus. The two closest satellites to the Russian Republic during the Soviet era, these countries have followed dissimilar developmental trajectories after gaining national independence in the early 1990s. Although Ukraine's political history is marked by pendulum-like swings between more and less democratic governance, Western analysts tend to categorize Ukraine as a new democracy (Barrington and Herron 2004; Karatnycky 2005; Sasse 2001; Wolczuk 2000). Following prescriptions of the international community, over the past two decades, Ukraine introduced competitive elections, adopted a number of democratic political institutions, liberalized its currency, and opened its economy to global trade. In contrast to the Western sweetheart Ukraine, post-Soviet Belarus is denounced by the international community as "the last dictatorship in Europe" (Amnesty International 2015). After a brief period of liberalization, in 1994 Belarusians elected an idiosyncratic president, Aleksandr Lukashenka, who has maintained an isolated authoritarian regime through falsified elections, prosecution of political opposition, and systematic restrictions on citizens' expression and mobility (Allison, White, and Light 2005; Korosteleva 2012; Silitski 2005).

My fieldwork in Ukrainian and Belarusian universities revealed that differences in the formal makeup of the two countries go hand-in-hand with significant differences in their informal economies. In both Ukraine and Belarus, some people engage in bureaucratic corruption on a nearly daily basis, while others never resort to bribes, gifts, or favors to obtain bureaucratic goods and services. Yet, who partakes in petty corruption, in what situations, and for what reasons, differs strikingly across the two countries. Some but not all Ukrainian university students pay bribes and bring presents to their professors in exchange for satisfactory grades or assistance on examinations; some but not all also pay bribes in secondary schools and hospitals. By contrast, my interviews and observations did not reveal a single instance of petty corruption in Belarusian universities. Yet, many Belarusians complain about having to pay bribes in secondary schools and hospitals to receive proper treatment from teachers and doctors.

Such systematic differences in bureaucratic corruption patterns across the two countries are surprising in light of their shared legacy of Soviet informal economies. Historical accounts reveal that during the socialist era, Ukraine and Belarus had identical corruption systems based on in-kind delayed-reciprocity exchanges called *blat*. *Blat* allowed citizens to temporarily "lend" to one another the access and privileges stemming from their employment or social networks. For instance, hospital workers ensured that their friends and family could see good doctors without having to wait in long lines; university employees helped their friends' children gain admission by calling on favors from their colleagues. In return, the beneficiaries of *blat* helped their benefactors when the latter needed something that they could access through their own jobs or friends (Ledeneva 1998).

Analysts agree that *blat* allowed ordinary citizens to fulfill their everyday needs in the context of consumer scarcity, pervasive red tape, and other pitfalls of planned economy (Rehn and Taalas 2004; Sampson 1987a). In both Ukraine and Belarus, it constituted the primary mode of bureaucratic corruption for a good part of the twentieth century (Lennhag 2011; Williams et al. 2013). Stark differences in the corruption systems of the two countries emerged only after the demise of the Soviet Union in the early 1990s.

In this chapter, I argue that social scientific literature on corruption fails to explain exactly how the divergent political trajectories of Ukraine and Belarus shaped their respective corruption systems. Besides referencing the shared legacy of *blat*, most accounts attribute widespread bureaucratic corruption in the region to the tumultuous transition to democracy that created opportunities and incentives for petty law breaking (Libman and Obydenkova 2013; Pathak, Xavier-Oliveira, and Laplume 2015; Stefes 2007). Although intuitive, such a "transitional paradigm" cannot account for systematic differences within and across the corruption systems of postcommunist societies. In the following sections, I explain the failure of dominant theories and outline the bases of an alternative theoretical approach to corruption in non-Western societies.

POLITICAL TRANSITION AS A CAUSE OF BUREAUCRATIC CORRUPTION

Why do social scientists equate widespread corruption with political transition? Transitional corruptology developed in the context of the global social movement against corruption. Academics and activists alike recognize corruption as an impediment to meritocratic competition in business and politics and a root cause of inequality and underdevelopment worldwide (Ades and Di Tella 1997; Gupta and Abed 2002; Gupta, Davoodi, and Alonso-Terme 2002; Mauro 1997, 2004; Tanzi 1998). As such, corruption constitutes a prominent target for intergovernmental organizations, national governments, local politicians, and civil society groups across the globe (Sampson 2010). Over time, the anti-corruption efforts of the international community have crystalized into a global regime, with its own funding mechanisms, institutional frameworks, policy scripts, and enforcement strategies.

One outcome of this worldwide mobilization against corruption was the collection, and wide dissemination, of cross-country indicators of corruption (Davis, Kingsbury, and Merry 2010; Doig, McIvor, and Theobald 2006; Kaufmann 2006; Sampford et al. 2006). Originally intended to mark the danger zones for international business, such indicators are compiled by international organizations such as the World Bank, Business International, Transparency International (TI), and Political Risk Services, among others. As a rule, they take the form of two-digit numbers based on surveys of local and Western experts and business people (Knack 2006; Treisman 2007).

Since comparative data on corruption are difficult to collect, social scientists eagerly embraced these indicators, despite their well-documented reductionism and inconsistency (Blake 2009; Kaufmann 2006; Knack 2006; Urra 2007). Using these data, scholars revealed strong statistical relationships between corruption indicators and various indices of countries' economic and political performance, such as GDP, the Economist and Freedom House democracy indices, the Freedom of Press Index, the Economic Freedom of the World Index, and others (i.e., Ades and Di Tella 1997; Ali and Isse 2003; Brunetti and Weder 2003; Fisman and Gatti 2002; Herzfeld and Weiss 2003; Jong-Sung and Khagram 2005; Lalountas, Manolas, and Vavouras 2011; Paldam 2002; Park 2003; Shen and Williamson 2005; Sung 2004; Xin and Rudel 2004).

Most importantly for the purposes of this book, these cross-national studies revealed that societies that had recently adopted democratic electoral systems suffer from significantly higher rates of corruption than all other political systems, including autocracies (Bohara, Mitchell, and Mittendorff 2004; Montinola and Jackman 2002; Treisman 2000). Corruption scholars explained these post-democratization spikes in corruption with a reference to institutional disarray and economic hardship that accompany political transitions. Since mature democracies are the least corrupt political systems, the increase in corruption that immediately follows democratization is seen as a temporary side effect of political evolution. By framing corruption as a nonpermanent affliction of transitioning societies, dominant theories imply that it is bound to disappear as democratic governance stabilizes and matures over time (Johnston 2005; Moran 2001; Treisman 2007; Zakaria 2003). Consider, for instance, the following account of postcommunist corruption by Levin and Satarov:

> Corruption, its scale, dynamics, and specific features, is a consequence of the general political and socioeconomic problems of the transition from socialism. Historically, corruption has begun when a country enters in a period of modernization and change. The stories of the robber barons of

> US are well known. It is understandable in a historical context that negative features of radical change should be present in Russia. Russia in the transition underwent a radical renovation of its public, state and economic foundations. (2000: 114)

Transition-focused theories make an important contribution to our understanding of the political causes of corruption. It is indisputable that economic recession, legal ambiguity, and rapid institutional change that accompany political transition bring about growth in economic crime and corruption. At the same time, these explanations do not reveal the actual mechanisms whereby different political processes in post-authoritarian, "transitional" societies translate into citizens' decisions to resort to corruption. Without a clear understanding of such mechanisms, it is impossible to explain persistent differences in the corruption economies of allegedly transitional societies. While we know that Ukraine and Belarus are quite distinct in both formal and informal makeup, current theories cannot explain how these two levels of social organization are linked in each of the two countries.

A THEORETICAL ALTERNATIVE TO THE TRANSITIONAL PARADIGM IN CORRUPTOLOGY

In this book, I develop a theoretical alternative to the dominant transition-focused explanations of the political roots of bureaucratic corruption in post-Soviet societies. Three principles of inquiry allow me to break away from the dominant framework: letting go of the assumption of transition, distinguishing between different corruption types, and paying attention to within-country distribution of informal economic activity across different organizational sectors.

Principle 1: Letting Go of the Assumption of Transition

A central assumption of transition-focused theories of corruption is that formerly authoritarian countries are gradually remaking themselves into mature democracies. However, the empirical evidence in support of this assumption is sparse. In many cases, the third wave of democratization – a series of prodemocratic uprisings that shook up Eastern Europe, Latin America, and Africa in the second half of the twentieth century – did not lead to the anticipated democratic consolidation. In fact, in the decades following the deposition of autocratic governments, most countries have struggled to establish a functional infrastructure and maintain transparent governance (McFaul 2002; Rose and Shin 2001). For instance, despite the celebrated triumph of democracy at the end of the Cold War, a number of former Soviet Republics are as far from the democratic ideal today as they were in the late Soviet years, and some are, arguably, even further. Over the past two decades, some former republics, such as Russia, Belarus, and Azerbaijan, partially liberalized their political and economic systems only to revert to largely nondemocratic governance, whereas others, such as Turkmenistan, have not experienced even brief periods of liberalization.

Given the contradictory evidence from all over the world, the theoretical framework that maintains that post-authoritarian countries are transforming into mature democracies has fallen out of favor with many political scientists. Instead, analysts argue that alleged new democracies are better described as hybrid regimes that combine elements of autocratic and democratic governance in unique yet stable configurations (Carothers 2002; Diamond 2002; Levitsky and Way 2010; Wigell 2008). Hybrid regime theory lets go of the assumption of linear progress toward a more desirable political order and embraces the variation in the developmental trajectories of post-authoritarian nations. According to this theory, formerly authoritarian societies adopt unique governance systems that are neither fully autocratic nor completely democratic; the characteristics of these hybrid political systems vary based on political and cultural legacies, foreign influences, and historical contingency. Despite the wide acceptance of hybrid regime theory in political science, many students of corruption in the Global South continue to operate under the assumption of linear democratization (Boskholov 2003; Dryomin 2004; Round and Williams 2010).

Although corruption scholars usually categorize both countries as "transitional," Ukraine and Belarus have undergone different political transformations in the post-Soviet era and have developed distinct preconditions for corruption as a result. Since the election of President Lukashenka in 1994, Belarus has grown progressively less free. Although its constitution declares the country a democracy and sets up a number of democratic institutions (including a presidential electoral system, a separation of powers, and a multiparty parliament), the country's political process is marred by persistent suppression of opposition, large-scale capture of power by Lukashenka's cronies, and the state's excessive control over the economic and social lives of citizens (Bennett 2011; Korosteleva 2012; Way 2005a). In contrast, independent Ukraine has oscillated between more and less democratic governance over the course of recent decades. It has a generally competitive electoral system, with only occasional "manipulation of voter lists, ballot-box stuffing, and/or falsification of results" (Levitsky and Way 2010: 8), as well as a fairly liberalized albeit flailing economy (Hoffmann and Möllers 2012; Schnytzer and Andreyeva 2002). Ukraine has also developed all the formal democratic institutions of a representative presidential republic. Yet, under some presidential administrations (such as Kuchma's and Yanukovych's), Ukraine experienced significant setbacks to its democratic development as a result of embezzlement and self-dealing by political elites and restrictions on citizens' freedoms (Darden 2001; Kuzio 2011; Protsyk and Wilson 2003; Shelley 1998).

Ukraine and Belarus offer just two examples of different political pathways that transition from communism actually entails. In fact, there are as many models of transitional political processes as there are postcommunist nations – and most of them culminate in regimes that are only partially (sometimes to a rather small degree) democratic. The following chapters shed the assumption of ongoing political transition in Ukraine and Belarus. Instead, I identify the specific characteristics of their hybrid political systems that are linked to systematic cross-country differences in the incidence and distribution of corruption in local bureaucracies.

Stepping out of the convenient yet largely inaccurate transitional paradigm, I connect the actual processes of hybrid political governance to corrupt transactions between street-level bureaucrats and their clients. Drawing such "micro–macro" connection is a two-step analytical process. First, I explain ordinary citizens' corruption-related choices in light of the structural and cultural pressures and incentives they encounter in service-provision organizations. Then, I consider how political developments in each country have influenced the evolution of these organizations and given rise to such pressures and incentives.

One specific feature of hybrid regimes that emerges as consequential for bureaucratic corruption is political turnover – the variability in the country's domestic and foreign policy, usually associated with changes in political leadership. In the following chapters, I argue that high rates of such turnover in hybrid regimes result in the coexistence of different cultural and institutional logics, some of which are favorable to corruption while others are unfavorable. Individual organizations align with one of the two logics by creating local environments that encourage or discourage corruption via cultural pressures and material rewards and punishments. Ukraine is a case of high political turnover. In contrast, low political turnover in hybrid regimes, which, by their nature, tend toward political oscillation, is, usually, an outcome of targeted repression of politically noncompliant groups. Such repression often happens through close governmental oversight of select organizational sectors, which, in turn, eradicates most organizational rule breaking (including corruption) within these sectors. The Belarusian case illustrates the effects of low political turnover. Later in this chapter, I discuss in more detail how low political turnover in hybrid Belarus and high political turnover in hybrid Ukraine created systematic differences in their bureaucratic corruption systems.

Principle 2: Distinguishing between Political, Business, and Bureaucratic Corruption

To link political governance in post-transitional Ukraine and Belarus to the informal economies of their service provision organizations, this book distinguishes among various types of corruption that afflict these societies. In this section, I argue that the distinction between political and bureaucratic corruption, often muddled in the literature, is particularly important for understanding the macro social roots of illicit exchanges between ordinary citizens and bureaucrats in hybrid political systems.

Political corruption refers to the abuse of political power through nondemocratic means such as oppression, economic control, rigged elections, and self-interested manipulation (Amundsen 1999). It represents a violation of the trust with which the populace endows the ruling elites. Corrupt political leaders make resource allocation decisions through national policies that serve their power-preservation goals rather than the interests of their constituents (della Porta and Vannucci 1997; Jain 2001: 73). Such corruption is facilitated by insufficient separation of powers and absence of checks and balances (Persson, Roland, and Tabellini 1997). In contrast to bureaucratic corruption, immediate and singular economic gain is not the primary goal of political corruption. Even though political power often generates material spoils, the latter constitute additional benefits rather than the primary goal of such corruption. Importantly, political corruption often occurs through systematic modification of rules that goes beyond their simple evasion or abuse. The advantages stemming from political corruption are systematic and cumulative, as the system itself is subverted and adjusted to the benefit of political actors.[1] Most hybrid regimes, by definition, suffer from political corruption.

In both Ukraine and Belarus, academics and journalists document political corruption. In Belarus, it takes subtle as well as very blunt forms. To maintain their control over the country, Lukashenka and his cronies amended the constitution, removing temporal limitations on presidential terms, changing the makeup of other political institutions, such as the Parliament, and purging all pre-Soviet cultural symbols that could encourage nationalist dissent (Korosteleva 2012: 43–44). In more open acts of authoritarian subjugation, the presidential elections of 2001, 2006, and 2010 were followed by waves of arrests and exile of opposition leaders who protested the large-scale electoral fraud that had left the incumbent president with upward of 80 percent of votes (Ash 2015: 1030–32). In Ukraine, both pro-Western president Viktor Yuschenko (in power from 2005 to 2010) and his pro-Russian successor Viktor Yanukovich (2010–2014), along with their respective governments, were allegedly involved in political corruption. For instance, Yuschenko's prime minister, Yuliya Tymoshenko, was charged with intended bribery of the Supreme Court justices and convicted of abuse of office during the 2009 gas dispute with Russia (CNN 2011). Corruption accusations against Yanukovich's government were even more extensive. From pressing Ukraine's Constitutional Court to rule in favor of his protégés to extending Russia's control over the Black Sea fleet in the Ukrainian city of Sevastopol in exchange for cheaper gas and, allegedly, political patronage, Yanukovich and his Party of Regions were mired in corruption scandals throughout the president's incomplete term (Kuzio 2015: 93–95).

Political corruption is distinct from *bureaucratic corruption*, which entails abuse of office for economic gain by citizens without access to political decision making. Bureaucratic corruption involves singular, even if frequent, sidestepping of formal rules for personal gain rather than the manipulation of these rules for long-term and systematic benefit. Bureaucratic corruption occurs when officials take advantage of their professional privileges to receive unsanctioned compensation

[1] The system is usually subverted by the falsification of elections, the suppression of oppositional elements, and the nationalization of industries that would have otherwise exercised significant political clout.

for performing their job-related duties or for extending additional, extralegal benefits to a payer (Jain 2001: 75). Such corruption includes petty bribery, "greasing" of bureaucratic wheels, kickbacks, "protection payments," and so on (Humphrey 2002; Smith 2010; Zaloznaya 2012).[2] According to prior research, bureaucratic corruption is commonplace in the former Soviet Union, and a part of daily life for many local citizens (Karklins 2005; McMann 2014). It happens in a variety of organizations, including hospitals and clinics (Rivkin-Fish 2005), universities and secondary schools (Osipian 2009), police control posts (Gerber and Mendelson 2008), and private firms (Round, Williams, and Rodgers 2008). While many such exchanges result from either direct or implicit extortion from bureaucrats (Tavits 2010: 1270), many also happen on the initiative of the clients. Studies suggest that ordinary citizens often fear that if they do not offer corrupt compensations, they will receive suboptimal services (Polese 2008: 54); use bribes and gifts to speed up or otherwise improve the cumbersome bureaucratic process (Karklins 2005: 21); or simply feel grateful or sorry for the severely underpaid service providers (Miller, Grødeland, and Koshechkine 1998: 289).

Empirical evidence reveals that bureaucratic corruption is widely normalized in the post-Soviet countries: local citizens believe such transactions to be a rule rather than an exception, and many consider them a justifiable strategy for obtaining bureaucratic services (Ledeneva 1998; Miller et al. 2001: 136–40; Tavits 2010). Yet, it is important to keep in mind that such normalization does not mean that ordinary citizens consider widespread bureaucratic corruption either a positive or a desirable phenomenon. In fact, Kelly McMann writes that before many citizens of the region (she focuses on Central Asia, specifically) turn to corruption, they seek legal ways to satisfy their needs, such as assistance from family, licit market exchanges, or formal governmental programs. For local citizens, corruption is, in McMann's words, "the last resort" (2014: 1–3). In her monograph on corruption in postcommunist societies, Rasma Karklins argues that people are "frustrated ... because they feel helpless ... Many cynically believe that in order to get along they have to 'play the game' – that 'the system' compels them to do so" (2005: 3). Similarly, in his

[2] Politicians may also engage in bureaucratic corruption: for instance, they may allocate contracts in ways that benefit their protégés or use insider knowledge to gain economic advantage. This informal activity is different from political corruption because it does not modify the "rules of the game" or extend the political power of a corrupt actor.

book on inequality, trust, and corruption, Eric Uslaner notes that "While people don't see petty corruption as moral, they 'adapt' to it because they see no way out" (2008: 11). Writing about Ukraine specifically, Morris and Polese also suggest that informal payments to street-level bureaucrats are premised on shared beliefs about fair compensation in the space left vacant by the dysfunctional state. In this way, authors suggest, "a sense of shared obligations and an acute sense of the incommensurability of needs and means, come to the fore in such encounters" (2014: 12). Such moralization of informal exchanges allows citizens to cope with the stigma and negative implications of behavior that is antisocial and illegal, yet, for many, also unavoidable.

Bureaucratic and political corruption also differs from the large-scale *economic* and *business corruption*, documented widely in both Ukraine and Belarus. This third type of corruption entails efforts by those with access to large-scale economic resources to illicitly enrich themselves and their cronies. In public procurement, according to Rasma Karklins, such corruption often takes the forms of diversion of "public funds for civil servant spoils," "mismanagement and profiteering from public resources," and "malpractice and profiteering from privatization and public procurement" (2005: 23–28). In Eastern European business, such corruption involves kickbacks (откат, in Russian), clientelism, pressure on entrepreneurs, tax evasion, fraudulent accounting practices (двойная бухгалтерия, in Russian), and other financial schemes (Kaufmann et al. 2000; Markovska 2007). According to Alena Ledeneva, in post-Soviet Russia, economic corruption also assumes a number of country-specific manifestations, such as blackmail with the use of compromising material (компромат, in Russian) and "shadow barter" (2006: 58–91, 115–42).

As this non-exhaustive discussion suggests, economic and business corruption usually involves complex coordination among multiple actors. As a result, they often span the analytical category of organized crime and overlap with political corruption (Shelley 1998). In fact, many consider Ukraine an "oligarchic state," in which the powerful interests, stemming from pervasive economic corruption, strongly impact the political landscape (Puglisi 2003b). Similarly, in reference to late-Soviet and post-Soviet Russia, Solomon and Foglesong note the emergence of "partnerships involving entrepreneurs ... criminal organizations, and government officials" (2000: 74). Others also acknowledge state capture by criminal-economic groups – the so-called criminal-political nexus – throughout the region (Gerber 2000; Jamieson 2001; Shelley 2006).

Despite huge differences in the nature, causes, and consequences of political, business, and bureaucratic corruption, the Transparency International Corruption Perception Index and other numeric indicators of corruption do not systematically differentiate among them. Most such indices combine expert perceptions of business corruption, self-dealing by politicians, and bureaucratic corruption into a single two-digit number (Galtung 2006; Knack 2006).[3]

The conflation of different types of corruption makes these data inappropriate for studies of its political roots. The independent variables that are often used in indicator-based studies (measures of political regimes) also partially reflect the degree to which politicians abuse their office to maintain power. In fact, political corruption – the capture of political power through suppression of opposition, modification of the "rules of the game," and insufficient separation of powers – is a core characteristic of nondemocratic political systems (Amundsen 1999: 4). Thus, the Economist Democracy Index, the Democracy Barometer, Polity Indices, and the other regime indicators that these studies use as independent variables inevitably incorporate some measures of political corruption. The simultaneous presence of the latter on both sides of regression equations leads to circular conclusions about positive and linear associations between nondemocratic governance and corruption.

Moreover, when various illegal practices are lumped into a catchall category of corruption, the important linkages and relationships among its different manifestations, as well as between them and various political processes, may be lost, even in studies that avoid the circularity described earlier. To protect against this risk, *The Politics of Bureaucratic Corruption* carefully distinguishes between different types of corruption. Specifically, I rely on distinct data sources to assess the extent and patterns of political and bureaucratic corruption in Ukraine and Belarus. I analyze bureaucratic corruption on the basis of interviews with ordinary citizens, online discussion forums, and observations in universities. I document political corruption, by contrast, through

[3] For instance, TICPI measures "corruption which involves public officials, civil servants or politicians. The data sources … include questions … on: bribery of public officials, kickbacks in public procurement, embezzlement of public funds, and on questions that probe the strength and effectiveness of anti-corruption efforts in the public sector. As such, it covers both the administrative and political aspects of corruption" (TI 2011).

interviews with oppositional activists, analyses of reports from international nongovernmental organizations, and a survey of local media publications. Using these nuanced data, I explain ordinary citizens' corrupt behaviors in reference to specific characteristics of the organizational environments within which they interact with officials. In turn, I show that political turnover, strongly impacted by political corruption, shapes such cultural and structural characteristics of local bureaucracies.

This book's careful separation of different types of corruption pays off: besides revealing the link between bureaucratic corruption and political turnover, my analysis also unveils an inverse relationship between political and bureaucratic corruption that is often obscured by indicators and other synthetic measures of corruption. Data from Belarus, for instance, suggest that the decrease in bureaucratic corruption in local universities was an outcome of political corruption of the country's president. This inverse relationship, in turn, provides clues as to why new democracies often score higher on corruption indices than authoritarian regimes.

Principle 3: Exploration of Within-Country Variation in Corruption

Many existing studies fall back on the generalization that in postcommunist societies, corruption is so common that it is endemic. Frederiko Varese's piece on "Pervasive Corruption" (2000) illustrates the dominant black-and-white thinking about corruption in the former Soviet bloc. Using the Transparency International Corruption Perception Index, Varese concludes that countries that rank low on this index (for TICPI, lower rankings indicate more corruption) are "trapped in the sub-optimal equilibrium" (2000: 11) of pervasive corruption. In such societies, he argues, "the cost of identifying a willing partner to a corrupt exchange is virtually zero" (2000: 1), "corruption comes to be considered as the normal state of affairs" (2000: 7), and social norms support corrupt rather than honest behavior.

However, the assumption of ubiquitous spread of corruption and corruption-favorable norms in low-ranked TICPI countries has little empirical ground. In a recent poll in Belarus, only 28 percent of citizens reported having given bribes to officials in the course of the preceding year (FindTheData 2016). In Ukraine, the portion of people who reportedly paid a bribe during the same period is larger: 40 percent, according to a recent study by Kiev International Institute of Sociology (2016). Yet, even if we assume that these estimates are conservative and allow for the bias associated with reporting illicit activity, such polls reveal that claims of endemic corruption are exaggerated. Large portions of both populations effectively avoid under-the-table transactions with bureaucrats: corruption is not a part of their daily lives.

Let us consider the example of Ukraine, the country that Varese invokes repeatedly. Another recent public opinion poll reveals that while 59 percent of Ukrainians acknowledge widespread corruption in local organizations, only 3 percent describe it as "natural and obvious," and more than half favor harsher punishments for its perpetrators (Vgorodok.com 2015). Moreover, extensive survey evidence suggests that corruption is not distributed evenly across Ukrainian organizations. Thus, Miller, Grødeland, and Koshechkina find that ordinary Ukrainians encounter corruption to different extents, depending on which organizations they frequent. According to the authors, citizens are more likely to face corruption in health care institutions than in courts or customs offices, for instance (2001: 256–58). Similarly, a 2015 survey of Ukrainian business leaders reveals that while as many as a quarter of respondents paid bribes in local tax administrations, only 2.8 percent encountered corruption in courts, and less than 2 percent encountered corruption in the municipal government (Glavpost.com 2015). A number of other studies also show that, although common, corruption is not ubiquitous but, rather, distributed in differentiated and systematic patterns across local organizations (Miller et al. 2001; Zaloznaya 2012).

The lack of attention to within-country variation is largely a product of the methodological nationalism in the comparative research on corruption. Since most such studies use cross-country indicators, the nation-state constitutes their primary unit of analysis. To allow for an easy comparison across nations, TICPI and other indicators of corruption overlook the complexities of corruption distribution within individual countries and do not distinguish among its different types. Such oversimplified treatment of informal economic processes within nation-states, paired with direct comparison across tens or hundreds of countries with vastly different cultural and socioeconomic profiles, creates an unfortunate tendency toward the reification of local corruption landscapes and obscures the mechanisms that link corrupt behaviors of ordinary citizens to macro-level political processes.

Methodological nationalism undermines our understanding of the political roots of corruption in Ukraine and Belarus. Without sufficient attention to within-country variation in corruption patterns, cross-national corruptology is unable to offer more discerning conclusions than the ones that attribute allegedly pervasive corruption in these two countries to underdevelopment, poverty, ineffective law enforcement, and other manifestations of political transition (Fisman and Gatti 2002; Treisman 2000; Van Rijckeghem and Weder 2001).

In contrast, this book shows that subnational and, specifically, organizational variations in corruption are key to understanding the political roots of informal economies in Ukraine and Belarus. Qualitative research, time and again, reveals that bureaucratic corruption is a profoundly organizational phenomenon. Organizations create structural incentives, generate opportunities, and erect barriers to corrupt transactions. They also develop local cultures that serve as a lens through which their members imbue corruption with meaning and interpret its feasibility and appropriateness (Ashforth and Anand 2003; Jackall 1988; Zaloznaya 2012). It is therefore not surprising that the ethnography of bureaucratic corruption in Ukraine and Belarus, presented in the following chapters, reveals that systematic patterns of informal economic activity emerge at the level of bureaucratic organizations.

In addition to structuring citizens' engagement in corruption, organizations themselves are directly shaped by political processes in their respective countries. The makeup of organizations necessarily reflects the policy choices of former and current political administrations and the economic profiles and cultural legacies of their home societies. In other words, organizations mediate between macro-level political processes and micro-level corruption behaviors. As the rest of this book demonstrates, the inquiry into the organizational variation in corruption effectively leads to the discovery of its political and economic determinants in hybrid regimes.

CHAPTER-BY-CHAPTER OUTLINE OF THE ARGUMENT

Following these three theoretical principles, *The Politics of Bureaucratic Corruption* argues that rates of political turnover in hybrid political regimes shape the distribution of informal economic activity across local service-provision bureaucracies.

Chapter 2 reveals the intricate workings of the bureaucratic underbelly of Ukrainian universities. Using data from interviews, observations, and informal discussion forums, this chapter explains how ordinary Ukrainians decide to engage in corrupt exchanges, choose appropriate amounts and modes of delivery, approach potential transaction partners, and carry out various informal deals. In addition to describing the vibrant off-the-books economies of local universities, this chapter also explores the central role that organizational cultures play in shaping bureaucratic corruption. The analysis suggests that citizens decide to engage in university corruption based on untested assumptions that they acquire by interacting with and observing their organizational peers. The Ukrainians' likelihood of engaging in corruption is, therefore, constructed in interactional settings within specific organizations, rather than determined by countrywide cultures or individual sociodemographic characteristics. Chapter 2 concludes that (1) informal environments of Ukrainian bureaucracies vary in how conducive they are to corruption, and (2) the extent to which local citizens engage in corruption depends on which organizations they frequent.

Chapter 3 offers a micro-level analysis of the informal lives of Belarusian universities. This chapter opens with a vignette from the field notes that describe my first day of work at a local HEE. The description of its subdued and regimented life presents a stark contrast to vibrant entrepreneurial atmosphere in Ukrainian universities. In fact, the ethnographic and interview data discussed in this chapter suggest that under-the-table exchanges between students and instructors are extremely rare in present-day Belarus, as both cultural and structural environments of local universities strongly discourage informal economic activity. The interviews with Belarusian instructors reveal strict controls and accountability requirements, tightly integrated hierarchies, and an absence of bureaucratic discretion; students, for their part, report heavy ideological pressures and restrictions on their geographic mobility. While these organizational processes are not conducive to "horizontal" transactions between students and instructors, they allow for a different type of bureaucratic corruption: "vertical" exchanges between higher- and lower-level university officials, whereby university instructors and administrators carry out illicit requests from their superiors to hire, fire, admit, or expel certain students and employees. At the same time, the data, presented in this chapter, also reveal that Belarusian secondary schools differ strikingly from local universities: horizontal corruption involving bribery and nepotism between officials and their clients permeates these organizations.

Chapter 3 shows that, like fellow Ukrainians, Belarusian citizens decide whether to carry out or avoid corrupt exchanges based on their informal knowledge about specific organizations. Yet, in contrast to Ukraine, some organizational fields in Belarus remain entirely free of bribes and favors between officials and their clients, while others embrace high levels of horizontal corruption. Together, Chapters 2 and 3 open the black box of bureaucratic corruption in the region, revealing complex social dynamics behind illicit exchanges that it entails, a varied universe of ways in which these exchanges occur, and a range of meanings that they carry.

Chapter 4 links informal exchanges in Ukrainian bureaucracies to the country's hybrid political governance since independence. This chapter opens with the story of Liza, who received her first bachelor's degree from a highly corrupt Ukrainian university and her second from an institution where illicit transactions were fairly infrequent. A survey of Ukrainian students, reports from local news sources, and discussion forum entries confirm the coexistence of more and less corrupt HEEs in contemporary Ukraine. These data set up the main puzzle of the chapter: why are some Ukrainian organizations more conducive to under-the-table transactions than others?

In search of an answer, Chapter 4 discusses a survey of Ukrainian university students that reveals that there is no statistically significant relationship between perceived corruption and prestige levels of local HEEs. This finding implies that high- and low-corruption universities do not operate in the same educational market – rather, they align with one of two separate bureaucratic spheres that coexist in present-day Ukraine. The first bureaucratic market is characterized by corruption-conducive institutional logics; the second market prioritizes transparency and is unfavorable to corruption. Moreover, each of these two subsectors brings together prestigious and non-prestigious HEEs. The rest of the chapter demonstrates that this fragmentation of the higher education sector into high- and low-corruption segments is a product of frequent political turnover in post-Soviet Ukraine. First, Ukraine's oscillation between Russian-style authoritarian leadership and pro-Western political orientation facilitated the coexistence of corruption-favorable and corruption-unfavorable definitions in its cultural repertoire. At the same time, the high rates of political change generated opportunities as well as pressures for local HEEs to adopt institutional logics of either one or the other type. These structural "push" and "pull" factors arose from inconsistent and poorly implemented reforms, partial preservation of Soviet educational models, and under-regulated denationalization of higher education. Based on this analysis, Chapter 4 concludes that in hybrid political regimes, high political turnover is likely to generate cross-organizational variation in bureaucratic corruption.

Turning to structural causes of cross-sectoral variation in corruption in post-Soviet Belarus, Chapter 5 traces the institutional history of local universities through documentary and interview data. This analysis suggests that before the year 2000, Belarusian higher education contained vibrant informal economies of exchange, similar to those of hospitals and secondary schools. By 2005, however, universities assumed their current "clean" state with a near absence of horizontal corruption. This chapter brings together a range of evidence to argue that this decline in informal economic activity reflected the consolidation of autocratic governance over higher education. The data reveal that students' low levels of support for Lukashenka's candidacy in the election of 2001, as well as the growth of oppositional youth movements, attracted Lukashenka's attention to local HEEs as threatening to the stability of his regime. In retaliation, the president tightened his grip over universities, unintentionally eliminating favorable preconditions for horizontal corruption. Chapter 5 concludes that hybrid regimes with low political turnover are likely to generate cross-sectoral variation in bureaucratic corruption through targeted suppression of political opposition.

THE MAIN TAKE-AWAY: EFFECTS OF POLITICAL TURNOVER ON BUREAUCRATIC CORRUPTION IN HYBRID REGIMES

The comparison of bureaucratic corruption systems in post-Soviet Ukraine and Belarus reveals significant and systematic differences despite the two countries' similar rankings on corruption indices and their comparable treatment in corruptological literature. In Ukraine, the variation in corruption is cross-organizational: its bureaucratic sectors are fragmented into more and less corrupt segments with which individual organizations align by adopting corresponding institutional logics. In Belarus, the variation in bureaucratic corruption is cross-sectoral: horizontal corruption permeates some local organizational fields, while others are free of corrupt exchanges between bureaucrats and their clients but abound with vertical informal transactions.

Historical process tracing indicates that rates of political turnover in the two countries are, in large part, responsible for this distribution of petty bureaucratic corruption. In Ukraine, high rates of change in political leadership generated a variegated cultural landscape that accommodates corruption-conducive and non-conducive cultural schema. At the same time, the inconsistency of the local policy landscape, erratic reforms, and lack of effective regulation gave rise to opportunities and pressures for local organizations to adopt either corruption-favorable or corruption-unfavorable institutional logics. In Belarus, in contrast, low political turnover was possible, to a large extent, because of the repression of oppositional groups, targeted through their membership in specific organizational sectors. Political pressure on these sectors, then, brought about their horizontal transparency (absence of horizontal corruption) amid widespread bureaucratic corruption elsewhere.

In this book, I argue that hybrid political regimes are likely to generate systematic within-country variation in rates and patterns of bureaucratic corruption. By definition, such regimes combine diverse political institutions that range from liberal-democratic to authoritarian and totalitarian. Their cultural repertoires, therefore, tend toward multiplicity reflective of such variegated political landscapes. This coexistence of democratic and nondemocratic political structures gives rise to more and less corruption-favorable ways of thinking, while the rates of political turnover impact the distribution of these different logics across local institutions.

In hybrid governance systems, high rates of political turnover indicate low levels of state capture by incumbent elites and significant political freedoms for the citizenry. The lack of systematic ideological pressure from the state, in turn, allows for an uninhibited organizational alignment with different institutional logics. As a result, such regimes are likely to have cross-organizational variation in bureaucratic corruption: their bureaucracies adopt either corruption-favorable or corruption-unfavorable institutional logics, depending on the specific structural constraints and opportunities they face.

In contrast, low political turnover in hybrid regimes, which by their very nature tend toward different political systems, is often a sign of targeted repressions by the incumbent political elites. To maintain their grip over the government and to decrease the risks of political turnover, such leaders engage in systematic oppression of oppositional citizens – often through surveillance and control of the bureaucratic sectors with which the latter associate (Allina-Pisano 2010). The outcome of this selective pressure from the state is cross-sectoral variation in bureaucratic corruption: political repressions decrease horizontal corruption in the affected organizational fields, while other bureaucratic sectors preserve high levels of informal activity typical of lenient nondemocratic governance.

Like the arguments of other comparative-historical studies, this book's argument is open to scope and generalizability critiques. Quite fairly, readers will wonder whether the proposed relationship between bureaucratic corruption and political turnover holds across all hybrid governance systems. The answer is not necessarily. While the very nature of hybrid regimes inclines them toward corruption distribution that reflects the frequency of their political turnover, the specifics of this relationship may differ across individual nation-states. Thus, in Ukraine and Belarus, this relationship was impacted by the countries' unique history, the idiosyncrasies of local politicians, and pure chance. If, for instance, President Lukashenka had chosen to suppress political opposition though direct punitive methods (i.e., by throwing its members in jail) instead of organizational repressions, there would have been no structural pressure to eradicate horizontal corruption in universities and other politically noncompliant sectors. Similarly, the remarkable degree of oscillation between democratic and autocratic governance in post-Soviet Ukraine stemmed from the country's unique geopolitical location and historical legacy. Critics might argue that the fragmentation of organizational fields into corruption-favorable and corruption-unfavorable segments could only happen in Ukraine's exceptionally fluid political system and would not be feasible in systems with lower political turnover.

Yet, despite some limitations to the scope of the book's country-specific conclusions, its broad arguments are generalizable. First, *The Politics of Bureaucratic Corruption* underscores the significant and systematic differences in when and how the citizens of hybrid political regimes break the law in local organizations. Second, it reveals that specific combinations of autocratic and democratic governance in such regimes have a strong effect on the rates and patterns of bureaucratic corruption. Finally, the argument suggests that as a correlate of unique combinations of democratic and autocratic governance in hybrid regimes, political turnover impacts the distribution of bureaucratic corruption within individual countries.

CHAPTER TWO

THE SECRET LIFE OF UNIVERSITIES IN POST-SOVIET UKRAINE

Liza, a good friend of mine who holds two bachelor's degrees from top Kiev universities, was most helpful as an initial connection to several faculty members and many university students in Ukraine. When I first told Liza about my book idea, she exclaimed, "You can probably write three whole books about corruption in universities in this country! There's just so much of it, I don't know if you can even cover it all – it's everywhere!" [USt3].

Liza's reaction reflects a common sentiment among my Ukrainian respondents. Most parents and instructors I interviewed acknowledged the magnitude of the problem and expressed personal chagrin about the negative impact of corruption on Ukrainian higher education. Some, in contrast, insisted that ubiquitous under-the-table exchanges in local universities made their lives significantly easier. Regardless of their personal stance on the issue, however, most interviewees agreed that economic deviance was omnipresent and largely expected in Ukrainian HEEs.[1] They described university corruption "a rule, rather than an exception" [USt37], "a fact of life" [UPa5], and "a reality that we cannot escape" [UPr16].

Local news media and online discussion forums confirm this popular sentiment. For instance, between September 2011 and September 2013, Osvita.ua, a leading online educational portal in Ukraine, published more than a hundred articles discussing university corruption

[1] Seven out of twenty-seven interviewed professors insisted that corruption was rare or nonexistent in Ukrainian universities.

(Osvita 2014g). These articles range from sensationalized accounts of high-profile scandals, such as bribery incidents involving the president of the National University of State Tax Administration (Osvita.ua 2014a, 2014b), the chair of the Law Faculty of one of Lviv's HEEs (Kontrol'naya Rabota 2014), and the vice president of Uzhgorod National University (Odarenko and Anramovskaya 2013), to discussions of pros and cons of various anti-corruption policies (Osvita.ua 2014a, 2014c, 2014d, 2014f) and students' graphic descriptions of their HEEs' vibrant informal exchange economies (Osvita.ua 2014a, 2014e). Osvita.ua is just one of many popular websites that cover the topic of university corruption. Discussions of types, causes, and consequences of corruption are pervasive in local media (e.g., Argumentua.com 2014; Ekzamen.Kiev.ua 2014; Euroua.com 2014; Informatsionniy Tsentr 2013).

Like the stories told by university-affiliated Ukrainians, the popular press paints a gloomy picture of a profoundly corrupt, non-meritocratic higher education system. For instance, a recent article on Gotostudy .com.ua, an online portal for college applicants, reads: "it is with great sadness that we conclude that, in its current state, [Ukrainian] public system of higher education . . . is a centralized system of corruption, within which professionalism, quality of instruction, and unbiased science lost their importance. Corruption in education resembles a cancerous growth paralyzing the brain of our nation" (Antonovich and Merezhko 2014). An article featured in Reporter.ua claims:

> Possible legal punishment for bribery does not stop either students or instructors. Bribery in higher education flourishes throughout the country and takes a variety of forms, from "gifts" of candy and cognac to the "sale" of actual diplomas. The fact is, it has become a norm that if a student does not have sufficient knowledge, he can always "arrange" to get a grade by other means. (Narbut 2012)

Several survey-based studies support this popular pessimism about the spread of corruption in higher education. According to a 2011 representative survey of Ukrainian university students, carried out by the Demographic Initiatives Fund and the Ukrainian Sociology Service, 62.3 percent of Ukrainian students come in contact with corrupt transactions at least once during their undergraduate studies. According to this survey, students' likelihood of involvement in university corruption increases with each additional year of enrolment (Onischenko 2012). Other studies offer even higher estimates of students' involvement in university corruption. A 2012 survey of more than two thousand students, conducted by Kharkiv Institute of Applied Humanities Research, found that 73 percent of respondents had personally encountered informal economic activity in local universities (Ryabchun 2012).

Another way to assess the magnitude of informal economies in Ukraine's higher education is by estimating the revenue that they generate. According to the Kharkiv Institute study, an average higher education institution of five thousand students, located in a medium-size or large Ukrainian city, produces as much as USD $2 million in annual corrupt exchanges (Ryabchun 2012). Based on the estimates of the former vice president of the Ukrainian National Bank, quoted in the popular online periodical *Tema*, the total volume of informal economic markets in Ukrainian higher education exceeds USD $3 billion each year (Odarenko and Abramovskaya 2013).

Western social scientists also acknowledge pervasive educational corruption in the post-Soviet Ukraine. Ararat Osipian of Vanderbilt University has published a series of articles that discuss the widespread and popular normalization of corrupt exchanges in Ukrainian academe (2007, 2008b, 2009, 2012). Based on countrywide representative surveys, William Miller and his colleagues suggest that higher education is the second-most corrupt organizational sector in the country (after health care) (2001: 258–60); Abel Polese ranks universities among the three most corrupt Ukrainian bureaucracies (2008: 47). These scholars confirm popular perceptions regarding the extent of university corruption and problematize its social consequences.

GETTING IN

In 2005, then president of Ukraine Viktor Yuschenko signed a series of laws requiring all Ukrainian HEEs accredited by the Ministry of Education to adopt the standardized system of university admissions testing, known as External Independent Testing (EIT or ZNO, in Ukrainian). Like the Scholastic Aptitude Test (SAT) in the United States, EIT is administered by an independent agency, the Ukrainian Center for the Evaluation of Quality of Education,[2] without any direct involvement of high schools or HEEs. The summer of 2008 marked the first admissions period when all governmentally accredited colleges and

[2] In Ukrainian, Український центр оцінювання якості освіти (the center's website can be accessed at http://testportal.gov.ua).

universities in Ukraine used EIT to select their students (Lunyachek 2011).

In part, EIT reform was a response to popular disgruntlement with the declining quality of the Ukraine's higher education and its outdated Soviet-style methods of instruction and evaluation (Maina 2013)[3]. In part, the adoption of EIT also reflected the overall trend toward the Westernization of higher education that had been taking place in Ukraine and some of its neighboring countries in recent years (Gleason 2001; Kremen, Nikolajenko, and Stepko 2006). Mainly, however, EIT was the government's response to endless reports of corruption in the old system of university admissions. Prior to its introduction, individual HEEs could administer their own enrollment exams, many of which were oral, unsupervised by unaffiliated monitors, and otherwise resistant to transparency (Kachur 2014; Kursor 2014; Ukrainskiy Tsentr Otsinjuvannya Yakosti Osvity 2014).

My interviews suggest that before the adoption of EIT, bribery and nepotism were rampant in university admissions. Students report that in high-status HEEs, enrollment spots went up for sale months before the admissions examinations were set to take place. The sums that guaranteed admissions varied widely with the prestige of an institution and the popularity of the specific major. Evgeniya, a mother of two university alumnae, told me a story of admissions corruption, different versions of which I later heard from other respondents:

> I knew she [the respondent's daughter] wanted to go to this particular school [but] the university is very prestigious, and we were afraid we just wouldn't have the money to get her in ... I don't think anybody gets in there without a bribe! ... I called the mother of her friend who was attending this university and found out which dean I could talk to about prices ... I met with that dean, and she told me that the price was usually three thousand dollars but that all seats were already filled ... But, if we could pay $4,500, maybe ... So, I just met with that woman-dean again and gave it all to her, and she said she'll pass it on where it's supposed to go. [UPa 21]

A number of respondents also agreed that in many prestigious universities, money was not enough to ensure admissions. In such HEEs, social capital was a precondition for using financial resources: one had to know the "right" people to just have a chance to submit

[3] Interview with Natalia Shulga, Kiev, 02/11/2010.

a bribe. According to Kirill, a student of chemical engineering, "Simple mortals couldn't even think of these places. No one 'from the street' (с улицы, in Russian) got in there. You had to be a diplomat's daughter or someone like that to have any kind of chance" [USt12]. The interview accounts by Kirill and other respondents suggest that during the 1990s, traditional elements of Soviet *blat* practices merged with monetary transactions in a new type of hybrid post-Soviet informality that drew simultaneously on participants' social and economic resources.

In many medium- and low-prestige HEEs, however, a modest under-the-table payment or an informal, often indirect connection to a faculty member sufficed to procure the applicant some unsanctioned assistance. As a rule, informal transactions took place before admissions exams and came with an implicit promise of assistance during the testing period. The weight of the guarantee varied according to the amount of payment and the intimacy of the relationship between an applicant and the university employee. The returns on admissions bribes ranged from an opportunity to take the entrance exams ("After paying, I knew they would not fail me right away but actually look at my test" [USt26]) to a guarantee of a specific grade ("My parents bought a 4 [B] for the Ukrainian literature exam" [USt35]) or an assurance of admission ("She knew she would get in because she paid, so she was not that nervous at the exam" [USt27]). According to some interviewees, instructors often "reserved" a number of positions in the incoming cohort for their informal protégés, significantly limiting the number of seats open for competition: "Though nobody knows this, for those who have not paid, the competition is really for a small portion of spaces, like one-fifth of whatever it is of spaces that they are told they are competing for" [USt3].

Sometimes, admissions bribery also entailed private lessons with admission committee members or other influential instructors. Parents could locate willing tutors through personal networks and, in exchange for a generous payment, expect these tutors to "pull the necessary strings" [UPa7]. Though unspoken, the expectation of patronage was shared, as suggested by the unusually high fees that professors charged for these private lessons. In some instances, the practice of preadmissions tutoring was institutionalized on the organizational level: some universities offered entire series of overpriced preparatory classes. According to all three groups of respondents – students, parents, and instructors – enrollment in these classes carried with it an unofficial promise of assistance during the entrance exams, though interviewees disagreed about the weight of that promise.

While the introduction of EIT made admissions corruption more challenging, it did not eradicate it altogether (Shkolota.net 2014). According to the survey by the Democratic Initiatives Fund, 28 percent of Ukrainian university students believe that informal exchanges persist at the enrollment stage (Kontrol'naya Rabota 2014). For one, the independent testing has not absorbed all the discretion of university personnel. Thus, some universities combine standardized tests with department-specific supplementary exams in subjects that are not easily testable in a multiple-choice or essay format (such as fine art; acting; graphic design; and other artistic, performance-based, or skill-based disciplines), and bribery and nepotism allegedly continue to flourish in these departments. Moreover, even when no discipline-specific tests are used to supplement EIT, parents often arrange for their insider connections to "put in a good word" [UPa16] or explicitly ask for their child at the time of admissions. It is not clear how much these nepotistic requests actually help the protégés, but many interviewed parents insisted that based on what they had heard from others, seen on TV, or observed in other organizational settings, "it is better to give, just in case" [UPa5].

Local media reports confirm these parents' intuition. For instance, a journalistic account by Alex Ravchev reveals a number of schemes whereby university employees can influence the admissions outcomes of the applicants. Ravchev writes that according to the Ukrainian Ministry of Education regulations, high school graduates can apply to several HEEs at the same time by submitting multiple copies of their application materials. Yet, only the applicants who submit the original application packet to a specific HEE can, by law, enroll in the tuition-free track (бюджет, in Russian) during the second and third waves of admission (after all the applicants with scores that make the cut are already admitted). According to Ravchev, for a monetary compensation, university administrators are willing to overlook this requirement (Ravchev 2013).

Alternatively, some prestigious HEEs "mistakenly" post incorrect lists of admitted students that omit the names of several successful applicants. In the following few days, most omitted applicants (who are usually very good students and, therefore, receive multiple admissions offers) accept offers from other, less prestigious institutions, freeing up the spots for several students with lower scores. By the time the corrected enrollment lists are made public, qualified applicants are committed to other institutions. As a rule, less qualified students pay sizable bribes in exchange for this enrollment opportunity (Ravchev 2013).

A different scheme involves the university-administered preparatory courses. The Ministry of Education allows some departments to add extra points to candidates' EIT scores for taking these expensive classes. Journalists document multiple cases of students buying the certificates of completion from university administrations and receiving extra credit without attending actual classes (Kontrol'naya Rabota 2014). Lastly, unofficial university websites are full of offers from current and former students willing to take the EIT for someone else in exchange for a relatively modest monetary compensation (the offers start at five hundred grivna or slightly more than $60USD) (Kontrol'naya Rabota 2014).

With the introduction of standardized testing, some admissions corruption was also pushed out of universities into hospitals, social security offices, and secondary schools. During the transition to EIT, the Ministry of Education mandated that HEEs have two admissions standards: one for the general applicant pool and one for the so-called quota applicant pool, for which the cut-off scores are either lower or nonexistent. Quotas are allocated for students with disabilities, select ethnic minorities, and doctor-certified victims of the Chernobyl catastrophe (Ministerstvo Osviti ta Nauky, Molodi ta Sportu Ukraini 2014). To help their children get into prestigious universities, Ukrainian parents often procure fake medical notes (**медицинские справки**, in Russian) or counterfeit birth certificates through informal connections or bribes to doctors and passport officials (Ryabchun 2012). As a result, the number of students eligible for quotas has skyrocketed in recent years. According to an instructor of Russian philology at a prestigious public university, "Everybody has some sort of disability these days. All but a couple of students admitted last year were quota students, for instance. So when you look around these hallways, you can't help but wonder, 'How come everyone looks so healthy and happy?' My guess is that their disabilities just disappeared when they were admitted" [UPr18].

Additionally, students and professors alike insisted that introduction of EIT had an adverse effect on corruption in Ukrainian high schools. Before 2008, students' high school grades did not play a major role in admissions decisions that were based primarily on entrance exams.

In the reformed system, however, applicants' grades are taken into consideration alongside their EIT scores. As a result, bribery, nepotism, overpriced tutoring, and purchase of credentials in Ukrainian high schools have reportedly increased significantly over the past five years (Kontrol'naya Rabota 2014). In the words of Egor, a sophomore in a journalism department, "All that corruption that used to exist at the time of entrance exams, it did not go anywhere ... it just moved. Schools used to be somewhat corrupt, but now it's a complete circus because there people can still improve their chances of getting into a university by buying grades" [USt9].

PASSING THE TEST

According to interviews and media reports, corruption ramps up significantly once the admitted students begin their studies. As new enrollees join the student community, they encounter the intricate organizational traditions and norms regulating informal exchange markets of their HEEs.

My data suggest that corruption is particularly common during tests and examinations. Stories of current and former students, print and online newspaper articles, and online discussion forums reveal multiple ways in which these informal transactions occur. For instance, exam corruption may entail the acquisition of grades in exchange for an in-kind favor or financial compensation. Students usually deliver an individual or collective bribe to an intermediary, who passes it to an instructor before the exam. The story of how Nastya got a B on her English exam paints a typical picture of the mediated delivery of a bribe before an exam:

> Well, it was very simple. Toward the end of the semester, I started asking around about what I needed to do to get a good grade in English. Someone told me they had paid a certain sum to get the grade I wanted, so I knew what to expect and started getting the money together. The last step was just to figure out how to get the money to her [the professor]. Again, another friend of mine suggested I try going through the departmental secretary. So I breathed in deeply and approached that lady a couple of days before my exam, which I was sure to fail otherwise ... And indeed she just took my money as if it's supposed to be like that and assured me it would get to where I want it to go. It was one of my first times, and I was of course nervous, but it turned out there was nothing to be worried about. [USt27]

Alternatively to money-for-grade transactions, corrupt exchanges may also entail non-monetary compensations for more ambiguous promises of assistance. Sometimes a phone call from a superior, a promise of a future favor, or even a friendship bond is what obliges an instructor or administrator to extend unsanctioned help to a student. Such help may range from prompting correct test answers to raising students' grades, covering up their absences, or keeping them enrolled.

My interviews, observations, and analyses of media and discussion forums suggest that the ways that informal compensations are delivered to faculty vary significantly from one university (and even one department) to another. The only persistent commonality is that face-to-face exchanges between students and professors are relatively rare. Instead, different universities (and departments within them) develop and institutionalize mechanisms that facilitate small-scale corruption without direct contact between the exchange parties. For instance, some departments have designated intermediaries who serve as go-betweens for bribe givers and bribe receivers; others have a tradition of bribery by mail whereby students send instructors money in their grade books (зачётки, in Russian); yet other departments develop price lists that specify appropriate amounts for different subjects and grades.

Table 2 offers an extended, albeit not exhaustive, list of common corruption mechanisms in Ukrainian universities. These mechanisms decrease the ambiguity associated with choosing an exchange partner, alleviate the discomfort of guessing the appropriate compensation amount, and ensure that everyone is on the same page about the goal of the transaction. They also permit the parties to completely or partially avoid personal contact, making corruption less risky and less psychologically taxing.

Emergency tutoring, for instance, is a common bribery mechanism whereby an instructor gives students individual lessons before an exam in exchange for a compensation that significantly exceeds the market rates for tutoring. Emergency tutoring usually entails an implicit promise of assistance during the exam. Liza's story illustrates how this mechanism operates:

> We had this professor of philosophy ... He took bribes in a very interesting way. He was a Soviet instructor, profoundly honest – someone you could not buy under any circumstances [chuckles and winks]. So he found some original ways to be someone he did not want to be – a corrupt bastard. So the first batch of people he ripped off were students who did

TABLE 2 Corruption mechanisms in Ukrainian universities

Type of Exchange	Mechanism	Facilitating Effect
Mediated Exchange	An intermediary names the price and passes on the bribe	Avoidance of contact between participants in bribery exchanges
Bribes by Mail	A student sends a bribe with a friend or through the mail and does not show up for the exam	
Group Bribing	A group of students designates one representative to deliver a collective bribe	Minimization of contact between participants in bribery exchange
Price Lists	Administration unofficially announces the bribery rates for different subjects	Avoidance of negotiation between participants in bribery exchanges
Public Good Collections	Professor or staff member collects donations for textbooks, repairs, activities, etc.	Denial of corrupt exchange (enactment of cooperation for the common good)
Exam Celebrations	Students bring treats/gifts/flowers to professors during the exam; organize a celebration with food and drinks right after the exam.	Denial of corrupt exchange (enactment of a personal relationship and gratitude)
Direct Service	Students provide services directly to an instructor (e.g., update her computer, arrange for a free appointment with a beautician, help find cheap airline tickets) during the semester and are later rewarded with an inflated grade.	

> not attend his lectures . . . he just basically did not let them take exams due to poor attendance. So they came to him: "What should we do? What do you want?" And he's like, "I am sorry, but I am afraid I can't help you. You have to read the textbook, all three volumes of it too, but there is of course all the info that I gave when you were not there that might also be on the exam, but it's not in the book." "So what should we do?" And he's like, "Well, I guess I could give private lessons. But I don't do group ones, only individual." His lessons cost twenty bucks – insane money at that time. Students were like, fine, fair enough – we could have had it for free. [USt3]

Another common corruption mechanism involves collective bribing, whereby several students taking the same exam or facing the same issue deliver a collective payment. Lena, a management student, gave me an example of a "group exchange":

> They wanted to transfer us to another dorm, and we were really opposed to it. So someone suggested we bring a "package" (пакет) and talk to the dean's assistant about it. It was three of us . . . We decided it's fair to do it together. . . we were so horribly awkward – we were just standing there, not knowing what to do. So, anyway, my friend says, "Do you think you can do this and that for us, and we'll thank you?" And the dean goes like, well, let me do that first, and the gratitude will come later. So my friend, dork that she is, says, "Well, this package is pretty heavy – do you mind if I just leave it here instead of dragging it back and forth?" [laughs]. He's like, "Okay, okay, you can leave it here," and hid it in his cabinet! Just like that! [USt22]

Intermediaries often facilitate informal exchanges by providing the involved parties with information and helping them avoid uncomfortable face-to-face interactions. Alla Igorevna, who teaches sociology at two Kiev HEEs, explained the function of intermediaries as follows:

> In a university where I worked for a couple years, instructors were connected to the administration, so they were bold, and they would just go ahead and . . . ask their students, "So, are we going to take this exam alternatively or no?" "Alternatively" (альтернативно, in Russian), of course, means with bribes . . . But the next place I worked, instructors and students were a little afraid. They would act through староста [the student leader of a group] or the people in the department who knew about the tariffs, like secretaries and lab assistants. [UPr16]

Interaction between intermediaries and students is usually concise and formulaic. In response to a direct request, intermediaries name the price without further ado. This standardized exchange allows ordinary Ukrainians to engage in a widely stigmatized activity with minimal discomfort – in a way that practically negates the act itself. When asked whether it is uncomfortable to bribe, one student told me, "Not really. It's not like some criminal operation ... You just go to the dean's assistant, 'explain your situation' ... Then she just tells you how much you need to pay" [USt20].

Despite the proliferation of monetary exchanges in higher education, *blat* and nepotism continue to play an important role in the informal economies of Ukrainian universities. Here is what Olga Genadievna, an instructor of art history, told me about her HEE: "I am 95 percent sure that it's not bribes that matter here ... but, rather, good relationships, long evenings over an opulent dinner table, holidays – Student's Day today, Teacher's Day tomorrow – some drinks, some snacks, maybe an occasional present, but mostly niceness and brotherhood. A lot of times, it's these relationships that decide everything" [UPr2].

Blat and nepotism are so common that most student respondents could easily recount instances when someone they knew had benefited from connections to influential people. Katya, who studies German philology, told me one such story:

> There is this girl who got in because her aunt was teaching at our university. The level of her English, let me tell you ... and English was the second main subject in our major! ... During our first class, the instructor asked us to write something about ourselves, and she wrote, "Hello, my name is Natasha, I live in Kiev." And then she turned to me and asked if I could help her write something else. I mean, then I was just surprised. And years later... we were taking a master's exam together that was supposed to qualify us as teachers of English. It was difficult – several stages, difficult topics ... I overheard Natasha answering, because I was in the room preparing to answer next. Anyway, Natasha was asked something real basic. And Natasha goes, like, "I don't understand question." Literally! And the whole answer was in this vein ... And ... surprise, surprise! I leave the room with a B and Natasha with an A." [USt11]

DOING THE HOMEWORK

In addition to informal transactions that accompany admissions and final exams, corruption also pervades the preparation of research and term papers, labs, problem sets, and other homework assignments.

Besides plagiarism, the most common form of homework-related informality entails outsourcing its production to an independent business or a freelancer. According to my interviews, informal forums, and media reports, Ukrainian students often pay someone else to complete their assignments. Out of forty students I interviewed, eleven reported outsourcing all or most of their homework, nineteen claimed that they did most but not all of it themselves, and only nine reported personally completing all their homework.

In many Ukrainian cities, bus stops, university buildings, libraries, and park benches are covered with flyers that feature offers to complete assignments, write term papers, solve problem sets, and prepare senior, master's and doctoral theses for students of local colleges and universities. A quick Internet search also yields a variety of options for anyone interested in this kind of service (e.g., VIPDiplom 2012 [with an ironic marketing slogan of "Quality, Service, Honesty"], Ekzamen.Kiev.ua 2014, and Kursovik.com.ua 2014, among dozens of others). Student forums have entire sections featuring offers of assistance from different organizations and individuals. The announcement that follows appeared on the informal forum of a technical institute in the southwestern city of Vinnitsa:

> The "Academy" is an agency that offers you help in preparing different types of student works, including theses (bachelor's and master's) along with all accompanying documentation, term papers on various topics and of various difficulty levels, take-home tests and quizzes (of theoretical and practical nature), research reports on different subjects and of various difficulty levels, essays, and individualized assignments. We guarantee the quality of the work!!! All the assignments are prepared by qualified specialists (NOT STUDENTS)[Capitalization in the original]. The work is tailored individually, to satisfy your needs, and relies on an extensive library base and experience (NOT INTERNET). We also offer pre-prepared papers that have already been successfully defended, at affordable rates. We supervise the assignments till final submission, and all the required corrections and adjustments are made free of charge!!! If you need to submit quality work on time, you can turn to us any time" [A mailing address and phone numbers follow]. (Hardtechno.ua 2014)

Most assignment-preparation agencies, like the "Academy," employ current and former HEE instructors, graduate students, upper-level undergraduates, and even schoolteachers. They charge according to the difficulty of the assignment and the deadlines. Following is an account of a student's collaboration with one of these agencies:

> I bought my senior thesis. I was working two jobs, and somehow the time escaped me . . . I think it was around April that I realized I wouldn't be able to prepare it in time for my defense in May. So I decided to go to these people. I don't even remember where I found them – through an ad in a paper or on the subway. So I went there; they had a small office. Mainly senior theses are written either by current instructors – these are good ones – or retired instructors – these are bad ones, because many are stuck in the communist way of thinking . . . they use their old textbooks too . . . I never talked to someone who actually wrote it. I talked to the guy who was working there for at least an hour though – he was some sort of [an] intermediary. And he essentially wanted to know what school I was writing for, what the requirements were, if there were any mandatory sources . . . In a week or so, I got a call from him, went back, and he gave me the basic outline of the paper. I read it and gave it to my advisor. She looked over it, made her comments, which I took back to the office. And voila! In two weeks I had a completed paper. I got an A . . . Plus it was relatively cheap, eight hundred grivna or so [around $150 USD at the time]. The price depends on the school. My university is the most prestigious one in the country, so they would not have asked less. But, anyway, as I suspected . . . the paper had references to Stalin and Lenin! I had a bit of suspicion, actually, that the prof who was grading it was actually the same as the one who wrote it! [laughs] . . .
>
> I: How did the people at the office talk to you about it? Was it awkward?
> R: Awkward? Not at all! It's strictly business. Nothing else. It's like if you go to a plastic surgeon, pay them loads of money, and get a third breast. They're not interested in why you need a third breast . . . All they want is your money. [USt3]

Students may also choose a less formal route by either buying a completed assignment or ordering to have it completed by another student in their HEE. Online discussion forums are filled with offers of services and requests posted by students in need of help. The following examples of such solicitations come from the informal site of Kiev National University of Construction and Architecture:[4]

> I offer help with any problems you might have with construction mechanics ("Stroymeh"): I can solve problem sets, help you pass exams, and make arrangements with the prof. [Followed by contact information]," and "Will complete labs, tests, and term papers in engineering geodesy (1st–5th years). Any level of difficulty. Fast. High quality. [Followed by phone numbers and name]

[4] Accessed online January 10, 2012, http:// kisi.com.ua

Many students also find clients and service providers by word of mouth. For them, personal connections and shared experiences in the same HEEs serve as informal guarantees of quality, timeliness, and discretion. Nastya, a political science student, explains her preference for personally vetted individual providers over the agencies that offer similar services:

> I don't like these firms. It's simply too much. You have to go to some office, talk to someone you don't know – what for? When right here, right under your nose, there are plenty of people who would be very pleased to help you out. First of all, they have been through the exact same classes themselves and know the material well. Why risk in vain? Plus, they usually don't charge as much if they know you. It's a sort of mutual help. [USt27]

CORRUPTION IN OTHER AREAS OF HIGHER EDUCATION

While bribery, nepotism, and homework outsourcing are the most common types of informal exchanges in Ukrainian higher education, under-the-table transactions also take a number of other forms. For instance, students often sell their cheat sheets (шпаргалки, in Russian) through unofficial university websites, hire fellow students to take tests and exams in their stead, and devise various collective schemes to obtain unsanctioned assistance in exchange for money or favors. Most often, these transactions span the boundary between academic dishonesty and outright corruption or fall into the undefined, grey zone of informal activity between the two. The following story by Tanya, who studies tourism and recreation in a major Kiev university, shows student ingenuity in devising ways to bypass formal rules:

> Once we had this super difficult math professor, with whom we really had trouble – he treated us as if we were all math majors . . . so during the test my friend and I sneaked out and ran to the math building, stopped two random guys, and asked them to help out . . . We paid them something, but really not that much. It took them like ten minutes to solve the problems for us, but many people do it in a more organized way. You can find people on forums or through acquaintances – usually those are all-A's students from upper classes. They have fixed prices and, what's awesome, they guarantee a grade – or your money back! [USt19]

Another common informal transaction in Ukrainian universities involves an outright purchase of bachelor's, master's, and doctoral degrees. Ukrainian interviewees repeatedly told me that students who have large sums of money at their disposal could completely bypass going to college and get straight to the holy grail – the diploma in hand. Nataliya, a mother of a current university student, described the two ways that Ukrainians can buy a university diploma. In the first scenario, an interested buyer hires an agency that takes care of all the logistics. The buyer's input, in this case, is limited to the choice of school, department, the year of graduation, and sometimes the selection between a regular and a "red" diploma that indicates an excellent academic record. This method of diploma acquisition is relatively inexpensive but does not come with a guarantee of a permanent record: a customer literally buys a diploma – a fake form filled out with fake information. In this scenario, the official degree rosters at the Ministry of Education remain unchanged and bear no mention of the diploma recipient.

Like offers of assignment preparation, ads for agencies offering diplomas for sale are ubiquitous in Kiev. Flyers listing prices and proclaiming the speed and safety of diploma purchases are posted in local subway trains and circulated on street corners, at street markets, and near local schools and universities. Such services are also aggressively advertised online.

By contrast, the second method of diploma acquisition comes with a record in the Ministry of Education register – the country's primary database of educational credentials. Thus, if an employer has any suspicions about the validity of a potential employee's diploma, her doubts can be easily assuaged with a reference to the ministry's archives. Nataliya herself had used this second safer and more expensive method of diploma acquisition. In an interview, she told me how she had bought a fake degree in psychology from the Ministry of Education several years earlier:

> When I was young, I didn't finish my studies because I got married and left for Germany. And then for a long while I forgot all about studies because I was actively working and didn't really need any credentials . . . but years later . . . when I wanted to work, I was told I had to have a diploma . . . I was told, "We are not interested in where this diploma comes from, but we need to have it" . . . So I decided to buy the diploma and started to ask my acquaintances if anyone knew how to do this. So they introduced me to some students who knew. The students told me

about the different kinds of diplomas I could get . . . There are those that are not registered, so literally, just blanks that are filled in . . . This means that the blanks are real but if someone decides to check with the actual university, where they have their lists and archives, your name won't be there . . . I think those are the majority of bought diplomas. But then there are also diplomas that come with your name being registered everywhere. With those, I know that if you do it through a university, you'll have one price, and if you do it through the Ministry of Education, the price is different. That's what I did – I went through the ministry.

I: So that person who told you all of this, how does he know?

R: He is a relative of a woman who works in the ministry . . .
The diploma has to match the time when you would have been in school and obviously have the format that they had back then . . . but it's actually cheaper to get the older format one. I think because old archives are not checked as much . . . I never really saw or talked to the woman who helped me, so I don't know what her position is in the ministry. All communication was through her grandson . . .
It took a week and two thousand dollars to get my diploma. Not cheap, of course, but I think that if I actually went through and paid for every exam and every paper, it would actually be more expensive and take longer . . . Of course, the guy who helped me, he is a friend of friends, so there is a certain assurance there that if something is wrong, I can locate him . . . Kiev is a big village, and if that's his business and he's interested in me spreading word about him, it's in his own interest. In that way, it seemed trustworthy for me.

I: So, how did he talk to you about it? Did he worry about confidentiality?

R: Yes, I think he must have been nervous about it, but of course it was all done in friendly tones. So he knew people who vouched for me, and I knew who I was contacting. We both knew what we would be talking about, so it's not like he was looking over his shoulder. [UPa5]

Last but not least, university corruption entails a variety of schemes by administrators and other university employees that do not involve horizontal exchanges with students. While these informal arrangements are not the primary focus of this book, it is important to acknowledge their frequency and variety. They create a backdrop and, in many ways, a precondition for the proliferation of transactions between university bureaucrats and their clients. For instance, the accreditation of educational institutions by the Ministry of Education, mandatory for all HEEs that issue state-approved diplomas, is a common nexus of large-scale bribery and fraud that does not involve students directly

(JAE 2012).[5] In exchange for hefty bribes, many HEEs without adequate resources, sufficient teaching personnel, or satisfactory curriculum obtain licenses from the Ukrainian Ministry of Education (Yavorskaya 2009). A member of the ministry's accreditation committee described to me one of many ways that departments get around various licensing requirements:

> For instance, accreditation requirements mandate having two or three full professors in each department. So all these new departments just go around hiring people – whoever they can afford. They usually get someone with academic cache, nice-sounding credentials, like some old professor emeritus, pay him off to show up there once a month . . . Not only does he not know anything about the current state of scholarship, he's not fit to teach outside of the Marxism-Leninism framework in general! Plus, his actual contribution to the department is close to zero.[6]

Other ways to bypass the official accreditation demands include forging inventory documents, paying off various ministry inspection committees and outside reviewers, decoupling the curriculum "on the books" from what actually goes on inside the classrooms, and maintaining very low de facto standards for admission and certification of students. By contrast, some university administrators insisted that even when all the official accreditation requirements are properly met, it is often impossible to obtain or keep the Ministry of Education licenses without hefty under-the-table payments to ministry officials. They insisted that bribery was not a choice when it came to accreditation by the ministry: rather, given the singular importance of accreditation for any HEE, Ministry of Education officials are in a unique position to extort bribes and impose informal tariffs in exchange for their services [UPr21; UPr11; UPr16].

When asked about other types of corruption in Ukrainian universities, many respondents suggested that employee hiring and retention practices were also riddled with informality. For instance, many recent PhDs receive positions in their degree-granting departments because "the chair and senior instructors like them" [UPr7]. Absent the tradition of open competition in hiring, many faculty members are protégés of various university administrators who treat their positions as

[5] Most local employees do not recognize university diplomas that are not approved by the Ministry of Education. As a result, HEEs that do not offer state-backed degrees struggle with attracting potential students.

[6] Interview with author, Sept. 30, 2010

privatized sources of income, using university property and professional privileges to generate additional unsanctioned profits (i.e., Gadyatskiy 2009; Kontrol'naya Rabota 2014; Obozrevatel.com 2012; Round, Williams, and Rodgers 2008).

Finally, rampant corruption reportedly permeates scientific research, publishing, academic tenure, and promotion. Such corruption entails bribery of journal editors to secure scholarly publications, informal payments to Ministry of Education officials in exchange for textbook certification, pressure on students to buy various instructional materials, and a variety of other informal practices. My interviewees recounted stories of corruption in dissertation preparation and defenses [UPa2], in the certification of educational materials by the state [UPr1], in promotion [UPr21], and in academic publishing [UPr1]. Local newspapers also abound with accounts of large-scale embezzlement of funds intended for the purchase of laboratory equipment (Hrabro.com 2014) and rental of research facilities (Antikorruptsionniy Portal 2014); acquisition of tenure through nepotistic connections (Antonovich and Merezhko 2014); purchase of doctoral dissertations (Euroua.com 2014); and kickbacks for government contracts to supply public HEEs with food, lab equipment, and office necessities (Sovsun 2013).

VARIATION IN THE CORRUPTION BEHAVIOR OF ORDINARY UKRAINIANS

Lacking the systematic and nuanced data on educational corruption, many journalistic and academic accounts imply that most Ukrainian students and professors partake in bribery and nepotism in their HEEs. The emerging image of a profoundly corrupt system of higher education resonates with the popular idea that the transition from socialism caused a fundamental breakdown of organizational processes in Ukraine and other former Soviet republics.

What most accounts of higher educational corruption overlook is the systematic variation in ordinary Ukrainians' participation in the informal economies of local colleges and universities. In fact, a closer look at the available statistical and ethnographic data suggests that not all students pull strings or pay bribes to get ahead academically. These data also show that not all university instructors and administrators demand or accept bribes from students and their parents. For instance, the same 2011 study by the Democratic Initiatives Fund and the Ukrainian Sociology Service that is commonly cited in local media as evidence of ubiquitous corruption in higher education suggests that out of 62.3 percent of students who have "come in contact with bribery or nepotism in universities," only 33.2 percent were directly involved in informal exchanges. The remaining 29.1 percent have only heard about university corruption from someone they know. And, of course, this leaves 37.7 percent of students who have neither heard of nor taken part in corruption personally (Onischenko 2012). Similarly, an earlier poll by the Ukrainian Ministry of Internal Affairs shows that 29 percent of Ukrainians pay bribes in various bureaucratic settings on a regular basis, 19 percent do so occasionally, and 17 percent refuse to pay bribes altogether (Bova and Valliere 1999: 9). A 2006 survey by the Ukrainian Ministry of Education also offers evidence of significant variation in corruption conduct, revealing that only 20 percent of Ukrainian university students know about instances of bribery and only 13 percent admit to personal involvement (Osipian 2007: 1). In relation to bureaucratic corruption more broadly, Miller and colleagues (2001: 72, 104) find that informal economic behavior of citizens is only loosely related to their reported beliefs about the spread of corruption. While 81 percent of their Ukrainian survey respondents believed that citizens needed to offer an expensive present or money to obtain a bureaucratic service, only 33 percent reported actual participation in bribery.

My data also testify to significant variation in ordinary people's engagement in university corruption. Although most of my interview respondents were confident that corruption was ubiquitous in Ukrainian higher education, only about half of students (twenty-two out of forty)[7] and roughly one-third of instructors (eight out of twenty-seven) reported personal engagement in informal exchanges at some point in their academic careers. Beyond doubt, the discrepancy between perceptions of ubiquitous corruption and rates of personal engagement is largely due to biased self-reporting of illegal activity. My analysis, however, strongly suggests that it also reflects systematically differentiated patterns of corrupt behavior among ordinary Ukrainians: while many people resort to bribery and nepotism in universities, many also abstain.

[7] In my research, the portion of students who reported personal participation in corruption was higher than in other studies (half versus one-third, approximately). The overrepresentation of subjects with corruption experience in my study may result from the small size of my interview sample. It is also possible that respondents were more likely to report personal engagement in an informal interview with a researcher they knew and trusted personally than in an anonymous formal survey.

In my interview data, two patterns point to this conclusion. First, the respondents reported significant variability in the corrupt engagement of their friends and acquaintances. In other words, all interviewees agreed that other students and professors differed notably in how much corruption they committed. To illustrate this variation, a student of public relations and advertising from a specialized institute in Kiev told me in an interview, "Among my friends, there are those who have not passed a single exam without a bribe or a present, and then there are those who have never done anything of the sort. To me ... these people are the same" [USt8].

Second, the majority of respondents who insisted that they had never participated in university corruption readily admitted to having been involved in corruption in other organizations. Such unselfconscious confessions suggest that these interviewees were not trying to conceal involvement in the informal economies and, therefore, had no reason to misrepresent their participation in university corruption. Consider the following quotes from a medical radio-physics student and an instructor in a psychology department at a large university:

I: *Would you ever give a bribe to a professor?*

R: *No, not a professor. I definitely have given a lot of bribes in my life, but not to professors* [USt17].

P: *Well, when I was a student in my hometown, [at] a small school without many rich people, I never really faced it ... not once in five years ... But as an instructor here, I can see it ... basically, I can't deny that it happens here, it would be dishonest.* [UPr10]

Furthermore, availability of different bribery mechanisms in Ukrainian universities suggests that their members choose from a range of possible ways to engage in informal economies. Other studies also support this finding. For instance, Caroline Humphrey's work on the former Soviet Union, distinguishes between multiple modes of participation in corruption, including "transactional bribes," "greasing," and "local tariffs" (2002: 130–40). Hallak and Poisson (2007: 30–31) further differentiate between the bypass of criteria, the capture or leakage of funds, bribery, favoritism, nepotism, fraud, influence peddling, and other corrupt acts. Writing specifically about Ukrainian universities, Osipian maintains that "forms of corruption include bribery, embezzlement, extortion, fraud, ghost instructors, abuse of public property, nepotism, cronyism, favoritism, kickbacks, cheating, plagiarism, and research misconduct" (Osipian 2009: 106). Media accounts also reveal the wide variety of informal economic behaviors in Ukrainian universities. A simple Google search yields a range of news stories about different corruption scenarios, including accounts of nepotism during admissions (Sidorchenko 2011), extortion of unsanctioned payments for tests and examinations (Gavrish 2013), voluntary "donations" from students and their families (Odarenko and Abramovskaya 2013), and purchase of disability certificates or confirmations of minority status (Ryabchun 2012).

In other words, behind the sensationalist media accounts, unsystematic studies, and reductionist numeric indicators lies a complex system of social relations whereby ordinary Ukrainians support one another in the face of economic uncertainty, construct and negotiate the meaning of education, and cope with institutional breakdown. This economy of exchange and support entails different levels and methods of engagement. While some Ukrainians regularly resort to informal transactions, others abstain from unsanctioned economic activity in their universities, time and again. Moreover, among those who do take part in informal economies, methods of participation vary significantly, ranging from immediate monetary exchanges to in-kind support within long-term social networks.

This persistent variation in the informal economies of Ukrainian universities raises an important question: Why do people exposed to the same structural pressures of political and economic instability treat the boundary between the public and private spheres so differently?

Several large-N surveys suggest that sociodemographic and economic characteristics of ordinary Ukrainians cannot predict their engagement in bureaucratic corruption. The 2011 study by the Democratic Initiatives Fund shows that men and women are equally likely to offer or accept bribes in universities (50 percent and 52 percent respectively) (Onischenko 2012). Miller and colleagues find that age, educational background, and income are also not associated with the likelihood of corrupt behavior (Miller et al. 2001: 115–18, 30). Work by Shaw and colleagues (2015) and Frank and Schulze (2000) further confirms that socioeconomic and demographic profiles of Eastern Europeans do not predict their informal economic behavior.

A few studies that suggest potential reasons behind this variation focus on incentive structures and perceptions of individual actors. For instance, Grødeland et al. suggest that citizens' decisions to resort to corruption depend on their perceptions of bureaucrats' goals and the importance of their bureaucratic problem (Grødeland, Koshechkina, and Miller 1998: 664–69). Miller et al. (2001) add that the bargaining power of organizational actors vis-à-vis one another also influences whether ordinary Ukrainians use formal or informal strategies to acquire services in street-level bureaucracies.[8] Čábelková and Hanousek (2004) further argue that people's beliefs about the spread of informal economic relations in particular contexts affect their own participation in illicit exchanges.

Although these studies are revealing, they do not systematically identify the roots of within-country variation in bureaucratic corruption that lie outside any one individual. In other words, they do not shed light on the social processes that create differentiated cultural and structural incentives for corrupt exchanges between ordinary citizens and employees of service-provision organizations. To fill this gap, I trace the micro-level determinants of ordinary Ukrainians' corrupt behaviors and connect them, first, to their organizational and, second, to their broader sociopolitical contexts. My goal is to explain exactly how Ukraine's post-transitional political evolution generated the cultural and structural milieus in local bureaucracies that impact informal economic behaviors of its citizens.

I start at the micro level. In the rest of this chapter, I take a closer look at the stories of university life recounted to me by ordinary Ukrainians. My goal is to understand exactly how different university actors make decisions to engage in corruption, and what characteristics of their organizational environments are favorable to such decisions.

WHY STUDENTS GIVE BRIBES

From multiple conversations with Ukrainian students, I learned that most do not think of university corruption as a matter of personal choice. Rather, the majority of college-age Ukrainians believe that it is impossible to earn a bachelor's degree without making under-the-table payments to professors and administrators. Many argue that informal arrangements are expected by faculty members, embedded in their HEEs' day-to-day routines, and considered normal by their fellow students. Their testimonies suggest that in present-day Ukraine,

[8] Miller et al. (2001: 275–78) also find that perceived economic pressure, type of industry, and occupation affect individuals' likelihood of engaging in bribery.

becoming a college student entails taking on an informal economic responsibility alongside more traditional student duties such as attendance and preparation of assignments.

Young Ukrainians think about university corruption long before they join any higher education institution. According to my respondents, high school students and their parents carefully consider the corruption levels of different HEEs when choosing where to apply for college. The survey of 193 university students that I carried out during my fieldwork in Kiev reveals significant consistency in respondents' perceptions of corruption across local universities. Survey respondents were asked to rank eight departments across eight HEEs in terms of their corruption levels, prestige, and quality on a simple scale ranging from 1 to 5. The distribution of corruption rankings for different HEEs reveals (1) significant differences in perceived corruption levels of different organizations, as well as (2) consistency in the perceived magnitude of corruption within individual universities and institutes. As an example, frequency figures show such distributions for two HEEs. Figure 1 suggests that most respondents ranked Kyiv-Mohyla Academy somewhere between 1 and 3 on the corruption scale (higher numbers indicating higher levels of corruption); Figure 2 shows that the rankings for Kiev State University (Taras Shevchenko University) clustered on the other side of the ranking scale – between 3 and 5.

These data reveal that Ukrainian universities have different corruption reputations: while students believe some to be filled with informal economic exchanges, others have reputations of being moderately or even completely "clean" institutions. Most likely, these reputations originate in student communities and are perpetuated and reinforced by media stories and rumors. Over time, they become a part of local cultural repertoire, easily accessible to anyone with interest in higher education. It is largely on the basis of these informal reputations that families of applicants select their future alma maters. As a rule, choosing a university reputed to be corrupt means that a family is willing and able to take part in its informal economy. Consider the following candid account by one interviewed father:

> When my son was choosing where to study, his ideas were, uhhhmm, I would say, unrealistic. He wanted to apply to some schools where, even if by some miracle, he got in, we would never be able to afford the "payments" (and I am not talking about tuition here) to get him

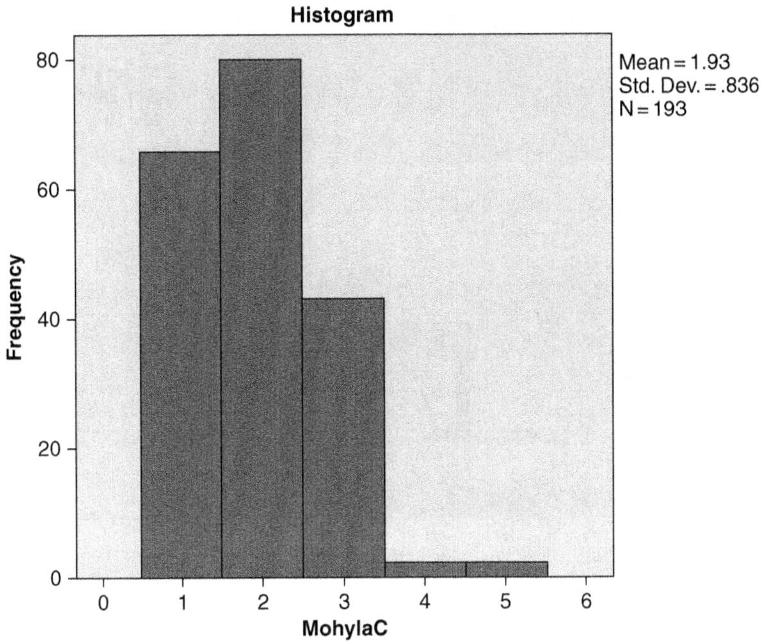

Figure 1 Frequency chart for corruption rankings of Kyiv-Mohyla Academy

> through . . . His mother and I had to be straight – here is what we can pay, so here's what you can count on. He then chose some schools where we knew bribery might have existed but was certainly moderate. [UPa2]

Before the introduction of EIT (the standardized admissions testing), students and parents often conducted significant investigative work on the informal profiles of HEEs during the weeks preceding entrance examinations: the necessity to bribe was imminent. Through informal conversations with friends and acquaintances who worked at or attended specific HEEs, they identified "contacts" who could facilitate informal transactions and learned about the tariffs and delivery methods that were customary in those universities.

Typically, parents carried out the exchanges by meeting "the contact" and giving her a specific sum of money or a gift. Most contact people were intermediaries who passed the illicit compensations to admission committees and other university officials. Administrative assistants, junior instructors, and nonacademic

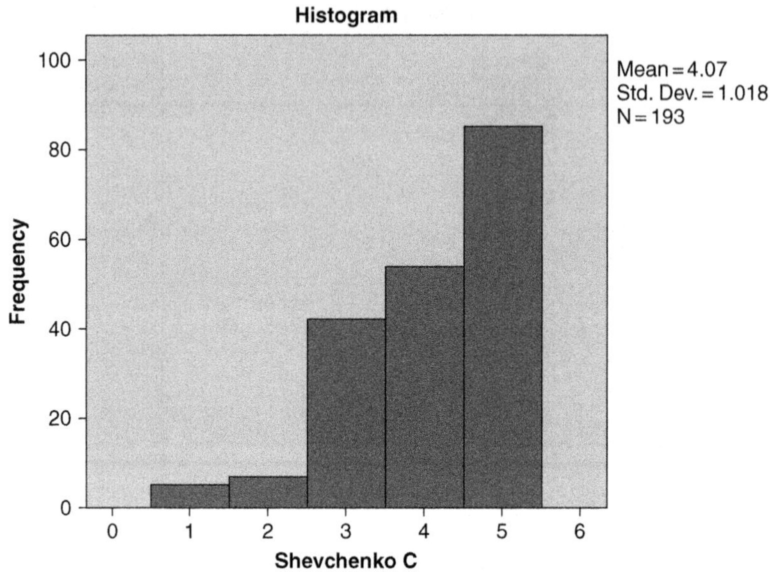

Figure 2 Frequency chart for corruption rankings of Kiev State University

deans usually played the role of the intermediary. Most also took a "cut" for their services.

Parents and students learned about other informal mechanisms for ensuring admissions, such as preparatory tutoring or use of fake disability certifications through "kitchen conversations with friends or neighbors" [UPa13], observations of their peers, and testimonies of those who had already used them successfully: "You simply look around and see what others are doing. Maybe you have someone who's been through all of this and is now at the university in which you are interested. So you ask them, learn what they did" [UPa19].

After admissions, students tend to take over their parents' role as primary "corruptors." Their informal socialization into the inner workings of the bureaucratic underbelly starts promptly after enrollment. During the first semester, in anticipation of term papers and tests, inexperienced first-year students often turn to their more knowledgeable peers to find out whether bribes or presents are necessary, what the going rates are, and how they can arrange for less awkward and risky deliveries in their specific HEEs.

This transmission of expertise among students is fundamental to the organizational cultures of corruption in Ukrainian universities.

An overwhelming majority of my interviewees confirmed that their classmates, as well as more advanced students of their HEEs, were their primary sources of information on the ins and outs of university corruption. The following interview extracts reveal the centrality of informal interactions with university peers in shaping students' corruption behavior. When asked how he decided that he should engage in bribery, Andrey, a former student of marine navigation, told me, "Well, that's easy . . . You talk to upperclassmen, and they tell you who you can make arrangements with and who you absolutely have to bribe. . . . Basically, you go with the flow – do what others do, give when they give – and everything will be just fine" [USt26]. Another interviewee, Valera, talked specifically about new students:

> It's their first task to figure out how things work. It's not generally a secret – you can just talk to any older students or even lab assistants or secretaries. People help each other out, give advice . . . Then, just by hanging around, you hear things, people tell you about their experiences, you watch professors . . . Basically, you collect this information ahead of time so that the exam does not catch you unprepared. [USt31]

In search of information on the "how to" of informal exchanges, students also turn to the Internet. In recent years, the emergence and growing popularity of chat rooms dedicated to university corruption made the transmission of knowledge on corruption logistics easier. Students no longer need to expand significant effort to find out what their instructors expect "under the table": a simple Internet search reveals that most Kiev HEEs have unofficial websites with a variety of informal resources and advice for interested students and parents. Some individual departments develop their own informal sites with more targeted forums, where students can obtain information about the corruption habits of specific instructors and tariffs for grades in different courses. Eighteen out of twenty-seven interviewed students reported visiting these websites and forums on a regular basis. Another four reported doing so occasionally or rarely.

Most informal forums have special sections – entitled "How to Pass an Exam," "Useful Advice," or simply "Bribery" and "Corruption" – where students can share their experiences and ask questions about the safety, necessity, and logistics of informal transactions. The following anonymous interactions, copied from the unofficial website of the National Medical University, offer telling illustrations:

A: *How much does a* "3" [a grade equivalent to a "C"] *usually cost?*
B: *On average, $250 USD per exam.*
C: ...
D: *No, what are you saying??? Only physics and* [another subject] *cost $250 USD. The rest range from 500 to 1000 grivna* [USD $63 to $125].
B: *The biggest bribes are in the English department.*
E: *You don't have to bring to Avrahova ...* [last name of the instructor]

And:

OGOMOR: Are there *so-called voluntary contributions during admissions?*
...
OLTHEA: *Not during admissions but afterwards ... a lot!*
...
INESS: *You have to bring money for flowers, for presents for various administrators, for various books and pens and folders ... and believe me, these are not little contributions ...*
NEUROSURGEON: *And as usual, if you don't pay – you don't get* [what you need] (Bogomolca.com 2014)

On the informal websites of many universities, students rate their professors on a variety of criteria, including their expertise, strictness, sense of humor, and attitudes toward bribes (e.g., Kievskiy Natsionalniy Universitet im Tarasa Shevchenko 2014a, 2014b, 2014c, 2014d; Kneu.ua 2014a; KunbaHelp 2014; StudPortal.net.ua 2014). In addition to a numeric rating on each dimension, visitors can view a brief summary that often mentions the instructor's propensity for corruption (e.g., "limits himself to moderate sums," "can be persuaded to take," "doesn't mind a little extra income," "won't let you go without a bribe") and browse through numerous comments, many of which also reference the instructor's corruption habits. Following are a few examples of such comments: "the only thing that I remember about this prof is the lecture on land property law and that he took bribes" (Kievskiy Natsionalniy Universitet im Tarasa Shevchenko 2014a); "she can take your money and give you a 5 or a 4 but sometimes she'll take and still make you retake the exam" (Kievskiy Natsionalniy Universitet im Tarasa Shevchenko 2014b); and "she grabs what she can ... If you don't bring – you are screwed. Our class though – we all passed without even showing up thanks to our starostsa [group leader], who collected money and brought her various envelopes [with money] and gift bags" (Kievskiy Natsionalniy Universitet im Tarasa Shevchenko 2014c).

A number of my student interviewees also claimed that they learned about the informal expectations of their instructors simply by watching them do their jobs: "I knew they took bribes . . . You can tell they do just by looking at them; it's obvious. I am not sure how, but it's just obvious. I guess their behavior shows that they can take . . . I mean, it goes without saying, they don't hint. Nobody ever makes any direct hints" [USt7]. Other students noticed how their peers handled various situations and imitated those behaviors in hopes of avoiding blunders, embarrassment, and failure. For example, Oleg, a third-year economics student at a large state university told me during an interview,

> I saw for myself that students sometimes put money into the little exam book that we have and hand it to instructors . . . and then the instructor looks to see how much is there and probably decides what grade that money is worth. But these things, they don't just happen . . . You need to ease your way into them, not that I am an expert or anything [laughs] but . . . you need to know who to give to, because someone may get offended, someone might even complain . . . I mean you hear a lot of things, but it is better to double-check before you take the risk, that's for sure . . . And it's good that people share, people want to help each other. . . because how would you know otherwise? [USt10]

Yet others concluded that bribery was necessary from gossip and hearsay in their departments: "When I first came here, I heard about people getting special tutors or mailing their grade diaries . . . I just assumed it was the way to do things, so that's what I did too" [USt4]. Another student, Yara, remembered, "[It was] my first econ exam: I was very naïve and good at economics . . . so I decided there was no reason to pay. But my friend . . . said that most students paid, so I decided to also give the professor a little something extra, just to make sure everything went smoothly . . . I really did not feel like gambling" [USt23].

By paying attention to departmental gossip and observing their peers and instructors, Ukrainian students learn the boundaries of acceptable informal behavior in their respective departments. These strategies allow students to determine exactly how much they can maneuver and what they can get away with in the corruption economies of their HEEs: "A big part of it was always fear. I heard all these horror stories about what happens if you don't offer the money" [USt35], and "I can always tell what's ok and what's not . . . I know I can probably get away with not paying for this subject, but I have to give something for another one" [USt31].

These testimonies suggest that information that students gather through social networks, online forums, and observations of peers and instructors often becomes a source of pressure to take part in the informal markets of their HEEs. Indeed, most student interviewees engaged in university corruption (fourteen out of twenty-two) felt compelled to offer informal compensation to their instructors. Afraid to ignore the informal rules of corruption, most offered bribes and presents, bought assignments, and enrolled in "emergency tutoring" preemptively, assuming that they would not pass an exam, complete an assignment, or graduate otherwise. In the words of Zhenya, a graphic design student, "you either pay and stay, or refuse and go" [USt18].

By talking to their peers and watching their instructors, students also learned which bribery-facilitating mechanisms were available at their universities. Apprehensive of possible academic penalties for "doing it wrong," students follow the existing rules of corrupt engagement. Established exchange mechanisms allow them to avoid unpleasant negotiations and minimize the risks of detection and punishment: "Before my first exam, I asked the lab assistant if she knew of anything my chemistry professor needed ... I knew that's what people did. It was always through this lab assistant. Why would I go straight to the professor and make a fool of myself?" [USt14].

Depending on which corruption mechanisms are available at their institutions, students report feeling more or less pressure to engage in university corruption. For instance, Larisa, a female student whose fiancé attended a university with price lists claimed that he felt more "forced into bribery" than she did in her own university, where mediated exchanges and "editing and ordering" mechanisms were more common [USt16].

While students often feel pressure to bribe their instructors, direct requests for money are rare. Professors or administrators almost never demand bribes during exams or in face-to-face interactions with students. Instead, students tend to deduce the necessity "to give" from informal sources prior to actual encounters with their instructors. As Valera, a law student, told me, "you usually know before you approach a prof whether you'll need to pay ... Going unprepared may end badly for you" [USt31]. Even those few (three out of twenty-two) students who considered themselves victims of extortion were never actually asked for money or presents directly. Here is how Denis, an advanced student of international relations, described his extortion experience: "it was clear from the beginning that that was what she wanted: she looked through her little notebook, where she probably notes who has already given, and then turned to me with this stone face" [USt25].

This finding is consistent with other research on corruption in Ukrainian street-level bureaucracies. According to Miller et al., Ukrainians reported that more bureaucrats "seem to expect" bribes (56 percent) than openly demand them (11 percent) (Miller, Grødeland, and Koshechkina 2001: 85). Similarly, a poll by the Ministry of Internal Affairs of Ukraine suggests that citizens often interpret delays, negligence, or rude treatment in bureaucratic settings as veiled demands for bribes (Bova and Valliere 1999: 9).

It is also important to note that not all Ukrainian students see themselves as victims of corruption. According to the 2011 poll by the Democratic Initiatives Fund, only 50 percent of students consider corruption problematic and lament its wide spread in higher education. The other half is more tolerant of informal exchanges: 20 percent consider corruption "a normal fact of life," and the remaining 30 percent see it as a "solution to problems in student-instructor relationships" (Euroua.com 2014). In my study, eight of twenty-two students who participated in corruption admitted to initiating corrupt transactions because they found them personally beneficial. Students claimed that by paying for a passing grade in subjects that, in their view, were less important or relevant to their majors, they could concentrate on classes they valued, jobs, and family duties: "Certainly, bribery is not right ... but you need to consider the whole situation ... [there are] subjects I really don't care about, so why not bring a bribe, huh? Saves me time, gives them money ... it is convenient for everybody" [USt2].

Or, alternatively:

I: *Is corruption a problem in Ukrainian universities?*

R: *It's there, like everywhere, but whether it's a problem, I don't know ... It makes my life easier, because I don't have to study useless things. I am seriously better off making money.* [USt28]

Some students told me that they used the time they gained by "buying" grades, exams, and assignments to focus on subjects that "are worth something" [USt2] or that "will be useful in the future" [USt33]. Others claimed that they needed time to work to support themselves and their families. Yet others admitted that they paid to be able to enjoy their college years rather than study:

> People buy stuff when . . . they just need a document that shows that they got university education. That's when people buy. I don't want to be disrespectful . . . but, frankly, I am not interested in spending my time learning something I will never use again in my life . . . it is just easier for me to pay money for someone else to do it . . . I am capable of deciding what I need and don't need to know." [USt33]

A student's entry on one informal discussion forum offers a summary: "Corruption is definitely not pretty, but how would thousands of students survive without it?" (Univer-sity.com 2014).

Respondents offered similar arguments in defense of buying completed assignments and term papers from agencies or other students: "Who wants to spend their own time doing all the useless homework? It's so easy to just pay someone else. And then you get to use the time how you want. Not all of us have money, you know. People need to work. Just studying is a luxury that not many can afford" [USt16].

Similar rationales also held for the purchase of diplomas and other credentials. In the context of an oversaturated and non-meritocratic job market, many students believed that they needed multiple credentials to be competitive, while the actual skills that these credentials represent were less important. Many chose to minimize the time that they spend working toward the diploma and dedicate themselves to more profitable or pleasurable endeavors. Consider the following quote, in which Nataliya explains her reasons for getting a university degree: "As I saw it, I had two options. Either I was going to go and pay different people for five years, because I didn't think I would really learn much useful stuff anyway, or I could simply solve this problem once and for all" [UPa5]. Others, such as Olga Evgenievna, rationalize their actions by referencing their employers' demands:

> I've been working at my firm for seven years and had pretty much all the responsibilities of a senior manager – all except the salary. Even though I was obviously qualified, since I was doing all the work by myself, they couldn't give me the title and the money because I didn't have higher education. So here I was, thinking to myself, "You want higher education – I'll get you one." Basically, I asked around and figured out how I could buy the paper they needed so badly. I wanted to really leave them without a choice so that they would pay for my work. [UPa10]

Another common justification for purchasing university diplomas is, ironically, students' desire to save money. According to the following extract from an informal discussion forum, some students believe that bribes for individual exams and term papers are more costly than the wholesale purchase of a diploma: "You must have a lot of money. I don't give bribes – I can't afford that. I just go straight for the diploma" (Univer-sity.com 2014).

WHY PROFESSORS TAKE BRIBES

In contrast to students, the overwhelming majority of Ukrainian professors in my sample (twenty-two out of twenty-seven) emphatically disapproved of university corruption. Two explanations of this difference between students and their instructors are possible. First, as a result of selection bias, only professors who had nothing to hide could have agreed to talk to me about corruption or were comfortable enough to directly address the topic in their answers. In many instances, I did not disclose my interest in university corruption at the outset of the interview; if respondents appeared uncomfortable with questions about informal economic relations in universities, I did not ask about their personal involvement. Moreover, instructors were more likely to lie about their attitudes toward and experiences with corruption because of the risks that such disclosure posed for them.

Despite their strong disapproval and, in most cases, an avid denial of personal engagement in university corruption (only eight of twenty-seven interviewed professors admitted personal experiences with university corruption), many professors were sympathetic to the corrupt behavior of their peers. Several claimed that instructors often have no choice but to seek out bribes and favors from students and their parents because of strong, albeit invisible, pressure from university administrations. My interviewees argued that corruption is often a departmental or university-wide affair, whereby accumulated sums get channeled upward through university hierarchies. They insisted that corruption often happens at the request of influential actors outside universities, such as local politicians or business owners. For individual professors, refusal to accommodate the requests of these powerful people can be risky. Consider the following illustrative quotes by Ukrainian university professors:

> People blame professors . . . way too quickly. Often you have to do things that you really do not want to do simply because you are not your own boss. X has certain lists, which he . . . circulates within the admissions

> committee: . . . these applicants will be admitted regardless of how they do on exams . . . If I want to keep my job, I'd better favor them. [UPr22]

And:

> Sometimes people find someone in the administration to call me. Usually it's either "don't give a grade lower than . . ." or "give this grade" . . . and I just have to do it because it is not really phrased like a suggestion I could deny . . . There are always the protégés of the president [of the university] and of the vice president who I am kind of required to help out. [UPr16]

When questioned about this pressure in more detail, most instructors suggested that it rarely came with any mention of concrete sanctions for noncompliance. As a rule, supervisors frame their informal requests as either favors or matter-of-fact job obligations. One professor, for instance, maintained that no one had told him directly about the consequences of not complying with informal requests of his supervisors, but that he was able to draw his own conclusions:

R: *I get maybe four, maybe five people every year stopping by or calling to ask for such-and-such right before the exam. Usually, it's the department chair, different vice deans, the dean, the vice president . . . you name it. Sometimes, they just want to chat and then, in fleeting, see how some student is doing in my subject. I've learned that this means that I should watch the student's progress and be lenient but not go out of my way. But when a dean calls with a direct request that a certain applicant be admitted, I know that I'd better admit the student, or my contract will not be prolonged.*

I: *How do you know?*

R: *How can one not know? I, of course, don't have hard evidence, but everybody understands that. It was just the way he said it, the words he chose . . . his facial expression too.* [UPr1]

Sometimes, illicit requests from supervisors are also accompanied by monetary rewards. The same respondent continued,

> Just this year, I had the department chair come to me begging that I give this one student a chance. It was right before the exam, and I knew that the student was a complete zero, so I told him, "Viktor Ivanovych, you are asking for the impossible. The kid is not only incapable of passing an English exam, he can't even speak in his native language." But he continued insisting, suggesting that I give him private lessons. Of course, I pushed back – my schedule was already full, and what could I teach him in two hours anyway? He kept insisting. At this point I realized that it must be important, so I agreed to meet the student on Sunday, just mentioning

> that it won't be cheap for him to make me work on my day off. After the lesson, which really was completely useless, as you can imagine, I got an envelope from the student's father. Mind it, the price was never discussed. When I opened it, I almost fainted – a thousand dollars! [UPr 1]

In other instances, informal requests come from other instructors, who, technically, have no power or professional leverage over their colleagues. Yet, my respondents felt compelled to grant these favors out of collegiality:

> A couple of times, my colleagues would ask for a student, and I would always try to help out. This is just how we are in this department – people are friendly and look out for each other. I don't think it's corruption; I think this is just a good working climate. And I don't want to be thought of as someone who does not appreciate good colleagues. [UPr18]

My interviewees also suggested that in some Ukrainian universities, corruption is so normalized that their administrations informally emphasize that monetary offers from students should not be denied. According to Danil, a part-time instructor in a journalism department, some faculty communities develop enduring repertoires of stories and myths about the students' lack of diligence, ability, and intellectual curiosity. This negative image of students serves as a justification for accepting bribes and shifts the blame away from the instructors:

R: *In our department, we – and I'm talking about the faculty here – we have a way of distinguishing between students who are a total waste of our time from those who are worth something. Ask anyone here – I'm sure they'll give you the same names . . .*

I: *So what's really the difference between these students?*

R: *Well, how do I explain? The first type,* балбесы, *as we call them* (good-for-nothings, empty heads, in English), *they are not interested in anything. All they want to do is* зависать (hang out, in English) *and spend their parents' money . . . Nobody wants to waste nervous system on these.*

I: *So how do you deal with them? Professionally?*

R: *I don't know, most people just take their money and give them what they want* [grades]. [UPr11]

Another professor respondent corroborated Danil's account:

> In our university, official and unofficial policies are the same – they are oriented toward . . . fighting corruption, but there are places that on paper are against corruption but in reality don't try to fight it. There,

> bribes are monitored from above and encouraged. I have a friend . . . in her former department, students who offered were considered bad students, so the best you could do was take the money. [UPr12]

Possibly as a result of being exposed to such myths, several instructors blamed corruption directly on students, who they alleged were lazy and willing to do anything in lieu of working:

> These kids just don't want to study! Many believe that it's useless for making money in the future, which is the only standard for them. Those who get in because their father has paid are often simply incapable. Imagine trying to teach them! . . . professors first try to avoid corruption but soon realize that sticking to their principles makes them the biggest fools. [UPr3]

These respondents argued that over time, students' disinterest in studying generates certain expectations among the faculty: "Many begin to expect monetary rewards from students after a while, but it is rarely a sign of greed or low morals; rather it's a disappointment with the state of things, aberrant values in the society . . . many educators accept the money and even expect it as compensation for students' disinterest" [UPr19].

In addition to pressure from higher-ups and shared denigration of students, instructors also learn appropriate corrupt behaviors through hearsay, observations, and informal interactions in their specific organizations. Like students, professors often deduce the necessity to participate in corruption by observing others, hearing gossip about presents and bribes, and encountering institutionalized bribery mechanisms. Afraid to stand out or disobey informal organizational rules, many instructors imitate what they believe to be "normal behavior" in their departments. Consider the following interview quotes that illustrate the dynamics of such informal socialization: "At the university X, they had this practice of tutoring students right before exams. This service was very pricey and had little to do with teaching. It was camouflaged bribery. But I did it, mainly because everyone else did. When you begin working in a place, it's not smart to challenge things" [UPr9]. And, "Previously I worked at another department, which was also not very corrupt: there was some activity, but the less insidious kind – mainly presents here and there, some tutoring. Once I started working there, I knew that it was possible to preserve your integrity" [UPr8].

Moreover, while many instructors lament high levels of corruption in local HEEs, others, reportedly, favor petty bribery and nepotism in Ukrainian universities, since these practices allow them to supplement their meager incomes and procure basic classrooms necessities.[9] After all, most higher education establishments in Ukraine are in dismal economic condition, lacking resources to provide for basic instructional and administrative needs of their members. While most state-owned HEEs receive sorely insufficient and regularly delayed funding from the Ministry of the Education, they are legally barred from growing their budgets in alternative ways. Such fiscal centralization, combined with grossly inadequate funding, results in the absence of basic material comforts and instructional necessities, such as heated classrooms, updated textbooks, and basic lab equipment. University employees throughout the country suffer from wage arrears and insufficient fringe benefits. Even when university salaries are paid on time, they are too low to support even a small family. According to a recent survey by the Center for the Studies of Society, 43 percent of higher education instructors in Ukraine receive a monthly salary that is lower than three thousand grivna (Argumentua.com 2014). While the cost of living in Kiev is more than half that in Chicago (Numbeo.com 2014), three thousand grivna are equivalent to only $375 USD. According to the same survey, only 16 percent of Ukrainian university instructors earn more than 4,500 grivna (roughly equivalent to $562 USD). In such conditions of dire need, many instructors may resort to bribery and nepotism to improve their personal financial situations, create tolerable conditions in their classrooms, and ensure the availability of basic instructional materials.

Yet, it would be misguided to reduce instructors' participation in university corruption to instrumental calculus. My survey data suggest that higher instructor salaries are not, in fact, consistently associated with lower corruption levels in Ukrainian HEEs. Kiev State University, for instance, ranks highly in terms of perceived corruption: with an average corruption score of 4.07 out of possible 5, this HEE has the highest corruption score of eight schools ranked by the survey respondents. Yet, the salaries of KSU instructors are notably higher than the country's average. In late 2012, a full KSU professor earned as much as 11,483 grivna (approximately $1,435 USD) a month, an associate earned 9,754 grivna ($1,219 USD), and

9 My sample did not include any instructors who openly approved of university corruption. Yet many of my interviewees insisted that many of their colleagues favored informal economies in local HEEs.

an assistant professor earned 5,384 grivna ($673 USD) (Pervynna Profspilkova Organizatsija 2013). In contrast, the salaries of instructors in the National Music Academy (The Conservatory), ranked by my respondents as low on the perceived corruption spectrum (with a score of 1.74 out of possible 5), started at only 800 grivna ($100 USD) a month (LB.ua 2014). Thus, while economic need may increase instructors' likelihood of engaging in corruption, objective measures of their economic well-being (as opposed to their perceptions of relative deprivation, constructed within local organizational cultures) cannot predict their corrupt behavior.

Instead, my analysis suggests that instructors' perceptions of students' motivation, as well their ideas of what their colleagues and supervisors expect, are, by far, the strongest predictors of their corruption-related behavior in local universities. Similar to students, professors make decisions about engagement in bribery on the basis of shared institutional myths, tacit norms, available bribery mechanisms, and observations of their organizational peers. Their testimonies, along with those of students and parents, provide robust evidence of the impact that informal organizational cultures have on ordinary Ukrainians' corruption behavior.

CONCLUSION

In social science, the recognition of organizations' potential to shape deviant behavior dates back to the writings of Max Weber (Bendix 1998; Vaughan 1999: 271–72). The most tangible and direct way that organizations affect the behavior of their members is by shaping the costs and benefits of action. Yet, a wealth of empirical research shows that organizations also generate and institutionalize shared systems of meaning that impact the conduct of their members by creating a lens through which individuals interpret these costs and benefits (Alderfer and Smith 1982: 39–40; Fineman 1996; Vaughan 1998: 27).

In this chapter, I presented evidence that organizational cultures strongly affect the corruption behavior of ordinary Ukrainians. My interviews suggest that Ukrainian students and parents usually engage in corruption after talking to "informants," observing peers, and encountering institutionalized bribery mechanisms in their specific universities. Similarly, most instructors choose to pursue or avoid corruption based on what they learn in informal interactions with fellow instructors and students. Informal organizational norms of local universities mediate the university members' perceptions of costs and benefits associated with bribery, gift giving, and nepotism and shape their corruption behaviors accordingly. As a result, whether corruption is an accepted way of getting ahead in a specific university is a much better predictor of citizens' participation in educational corruption than their demographic and socioeconomic characteristics.

But exactly how and why do different ways of thinking about corruption, embedded in organizational cultures, translate into corrupt and non-corrupt behavior by university members? Karl Weick's (1995) notion of "organizational enactment" proves useful in answering this question. Weick suggests that organizational actors comply with informal rules of organizational conduct because they hold untested assumptions about what happens if they renege. Although these assumptions are not based in fact (they are untested), actors enact them out of fear of possible consequences, thereby turning these assumptions into a self-fulfilling prophecy.

In line with Weick's theory, Ukrainian university actors comply with unwritten rules of corruption behavior out of fear of possible consequences that range from expulsion and termination of employment to unfavorable reputation and derision. My interviews reveal that students rarely experience direct extortion. Rather, afraid to ignore the rules of corruption, most offer bribes and presents, buy assignments, and enroll in emergency tutoring preemptively, assuming that without informal compensations they will not pass exams, complete assignments, or graduate. Parents, afraid that their children will fail or drop out, finance their children's bribes and seek out influential connections to plead for their children. Professors, in their turn, experience pressure from their colleagues and superiors, who expect them to assume the duties of bribery collection and nepotistic promotion along with other job obligations. Legitimating mythologies that construe students as disinterested or incapable increase these pressures. Afraid to break organizational rules, embitter workplace relations, or jeopardize their careers, instructors enact the acquired corruption-related definitions.

In short, the evidence, presented in this chapter, suggests that variation in corrupt behaviors of ordinary Ukrainians is better explained by their affiliation with different bureaucratic organizations rather than their individual characteristics. It is, therefore, not surprising that researchers have not been able to identify a profile of a "corrupt student" or a "corrupt professor." The difference is not between individual Ukrainians – it is between organizations that they frequent: some universities in present-day Ukraine are more corrupt than others. In fact, my interviews with Ukrainian students and instructors, analyses of online forums, and a survey of students reveal that Ukrainian universities differ systematically in the extent to which their cultures are favorable to informal economies and, as a result, in how frequently petty corrupt transactions occur between their affiliates. Chapter 4 presents empirical evidence in support of this finding and puts forth an explanation of this cross-organizational variation in light of Ukraine's political trajectory since independence.

CHAPTER THREE

FEAR AND TRANSPARENCY IN THE UNIVERSITIES OF POST-SOVIET BELARUS

Oksana is a twenty-six-year-old language instructor at Belarusian State Agrarian Technical University in Minsk. She is also enrolled in the university's graduate program, but she is not sure that she will ever write her dissertation. She does not like working at the university. According to Oksana, students are not motivated and the department's chair is unnecessarily strict. Because Oksana does not make enough money to support herself, she and her boyfriend share a small apartment with Oksana's mother, with whom she has a difficult relationship. Oksana says that at her current university, no one ever offers her anything "under the table." In fact, she has never seen or heard about students or parents doing favors, bringing presents, or offering money to any instructor. It does strike Oksana as strange that exchanges of bribes and favors between faculty and students are so unusual at her university, particularly because such transactions are common in many other organizations. Half joking, she says that had bribery existed, she would have been able to move out of her mom's apartment and "finally start my life" [Bpr11].

The apparent absence of petty corruption in Belarusian universities, referenced by Oksana, took me by surprise. Coming from an entrepreneurial and vibrant Kiev, where I was immersed in motley informal economies of local universities, I had expected to encounter similar rates and patterns of bureaucratic corruption in Belarusian HEEs. After all, Western social scientists and political analysts often lump Ukraine and Belarus together in the category of pervasively corrupt societies on the basis of their similarly low Transparency International rankings (see Appendix I, Table 4; see Varese 2000 and Vasilev 2012 for examples). Yet, despite my formal hypotheses and informal expectations, my ethnographic observations in Belarusian universities fully supported Oksana's impressions. As a matter of fact, there was practically no corruption for me to observe, as the structural and cultural makeup of Belarusian HEEs turned out to be unfavorable to rule breaking in general and petty informal exchanges between students and their instructors in particular.

THE CLIMATE OF REPRESSION IN BELARUSIAN HEES

My notes from the first day of fieldwork in Minsk testify to stark and clear differences between Belarusian and Ukrainian HEEs:

> Today I went to XXX [the name of the university where I observed] for the first time . . . Things seem really different from how everything works in Kiev . . . The university itself is very monumental, quiet, and not at all chaotic. Clean – in ways that are quite striking, as I am so used to the mayhem, dilapidation, and mess in Ukraine. The campus actually reminded me of a Soviet movie – non-vibrant, "in working order," yet profoundly institutional, void of personality. There were literally no commercial signs around (no ads, nothing for sale, no mention of monetary exchanges in general . . .). Instead, there are Belarusian flags, texts of hymns everywhere (neatly and carefully framed), patriotic poems, and pictures of the president . . . There is a lot of other propaganda on display: various diplomas (mainly issued by the Belarusian government), WWII dedications (it feels like the war ended a couple rather than fifty years ago . . .), patriotic insignia, etc. In fact, one could hardly tell that this is a place where a couple thousand young, creative, energetic people full of hormones, ideas, and ambition come together, interact with each other, and expand their horizons through learning. In the formal space, at least, there is no student art, no signs of rebellion (e.g., graffiti or indecent inscriptions on the walls), no manifestations of deviance and boundary pushing (e.g., no groups of students smoking and no couples making out). What a difference! It really feels like this is a place where one is supposed to "walk the line" . . . Even the hallways are kind of quiet! Who would have thought this possible! It feels like I am in a caricature of a university. And, certainly, there are no doubts of what one is supposed to think of the president and the country . . .
>
> At around 1pm, I sat in on an actual class – an English language lesson taught by XXX [the name of the instructor]. The class was very regimented and seemed more high school–like in terms of

> students' autonomy vis-à-vis the instructor. Students stood up when the teacher entered (!!! There is NO way this would have happened in Kiev). They also appeared more attentive and respectful than students I observed in Kiev. First, it was an 8:15 am class, and a surprisingly large number of students actually showed up (there were only two absences in a twenty-something-person class). No one talked or played on their phone (would not have thought this possible had I not seen it with my own eyes!!!), although a couple of young men were joking around and being a little disruptive in the back row. As the teacher was presenting the material, most students appeared to be focused and attentive. Later on, XXX [the instructor] told me that this was "all for show" and they were not really interested in the material. Quite possible ... but the fact that students feel obliged to self-discipline and feign interest is interesting in and of itself. It certainly goes with the feeling that I got from walking around the university – that this is a place of order, compliance, and hushed tones.
>
> [04/15/2010]

Absence of Academic Freedom

In the months that followed, I collected abundant evidence in support of my initial impression that the organizational climate of Belarusian universities is subdued and almost sterile in its propriety. Traditional academic freedoms are, for all intents and purposes, nonexistent in local universities (Mazurkevich 2015; Spasjuk 2010). In fact, Belarusian law defines the goals of higher education in ways that are largely antithetical to the principles of academic freedom. According to Section 1.6 of the Law of the Republic of Belarus on Education, "education entails instruction and nurturing that aligns with the interest of personality as well as the interests of the society and the state" (EtalonOnline 2011). The emphasis on the interests of the state in the very definition of education goes against the principle of "unrestricted liberty to question and test received wisdom and to put forward controversial and unpopular opinions, whether or not these are deemed offensive," which, according to the Academics for Academic Freedom Association (AFAF), constitutes the foundation of academic freedom (AFAF 2016). In an interview with a local online newspaper, Vladimir Dunaev, a famous critic of contemporary Belarusian education and a prominent oppositional figure in Belarusian politics, stated emphatically, "If university is an organization that guarantees its members a set of academic freedoms, then it is a fact that in Belarus there are no universities" (Ampby.org 2015).

In higher education, the interests of the Belarusian state are carefully guarded by centralized university administrations and a powerful Ministry of Education – the instrumentality of the national government. These organizations closely monitor and censor all research and publishing activity of Belarusian students and faculty members. Special committees within universities and the Ministry of Education carefully vet the topics of BA and MA theses, dissertations, and faculty research projects. Critical analyses in social science are discouraged, while exact, natural, and applied technical sciences receive priority (Antipenko 2006; Mozheyko 2015). According to one instructor I interviewed, VAK (Высшая Аттестационная Комиссия, in Russian, or Highest Committee for Attestation, in English), the branch of the Educational Ministry that issues postgraduate degrees,[1]

> puts forth a gamut of unclear and unnecessary requirements that they can manipulate to filter out undesirable applicants. A lot of these requirements make no sense whatsoever ... For instance, they accept publications in only a few outdated journals, discourage any innovative research, and promote articles that make no real contributions to science but promote the president and his politics ... The topics of scholarly work are strictly monitored and only narrow and non-dangerous theoretical approaches are allowed. [BPr15]

Another instructor, who had a hard time persuading VAK to accept her work as legitimate, corroborated this view:

> The ease of your defense really depends on whether, as a scholar, you are doing what the state wants you to do. Only the work that they think is "necessary for Belarusian society" passes ... What that means is not really clear – they can always use that argument against you, but your chances are better if you stay out of politics completely. And aspiring кандидаты and доктора [the two degrees that are roughly equivalent to PhDs and full professorships in the Western system] know that in

[1] In contrast to the Western system, in which the allocation of postgraduate degrees is the function of autonomous higher education institutions, high-level academic credentialing in Belarus falls under the purview of the state. VAK committee approves the topics of кандидатские диссертации (PhD dissertations, in English) and докторские диссертации (research projects that assistant professors write and defend to obtain the title of full professor). VAK committees allocate postgraduate degrees to aspiring Belarusians based on an application packet containing these two dissertations, the candidate's other published work, and letters of recommendation (peer evaluations) from fellow academics.

> advance and avoid certain topics because they anticipate difficulties during their defense. [BPr8]

Governmental censorship also pervades classroom instruction. Instructors are pressured to closely follow the letter of detailed, centrally prepared teaching plans that strongly discourage faculty initiative and leave no space for experimentation and creative expression. Students, in their turn, have practically no opportunities to select courses, participate in university governance, and publicly express opinions that contradict the official line of the state (Mozheyko 2015; Spasjuk 2014; Spring96 .org 2015). Anton Sergeevich, an instructor of history and legal studies, told me that state-mandated programs and plans "prioritize repetition, memorization, and dependence on somebody else's opinion over independent judgment and authenticity" [BPr12]. Another instructor, Valeriya, actually left Belarus to teach in neighboring Lithuania because in Belarus she "wasn't able to give students the material that's actually appropriate ... and teach them to think for themselves." Valeriya concluded, "I need to have a chance for self-expression as an educator, and I just didn't have it in this country" [BPr8].

Compliance with formal regulations is emphasized in student handbooks and faculty meetings as a central criterion in the assessment of students' and instructors' performance (Ampby.org 2015; Spring96.org 2015). In the words of Slava, an engineering student at Belarusian State Technical University, "if you do what you're told, it doesn't matter how smart you are – you'll do great here" [BSt37]. Other students agreed, telling me that it was not very difficult to get a university degree in contemporary Belarus, as long as one followed the rules. Taras from Belarusian State University explained, "I get up in the morning, I show up, I look like I'm listening, I go to субботники [events dedicated to cleaning public spaces, mandatory for Belarusian students], I listen to teachers ... Anybody who is not a complete idiot could get their diploma with minimum brain effort this way" [BSt20].

A low profile and diligent observation of rules are also key to professional success of university instructors and administrators. Valeriya, who now teaches in Lithuania, explained, "They [the Ministry of Education] create really rigid boundaries in universities that 'must not be crossed.' Observing these boundaries, really, is the main job of Belarusian professors, not their research or teaching. It is what gets them professional recognition, raises, and so on" [Bpr8].

Preservation of the Soviet Educational Model

In many ways, the rule-oriented culture of Belarusian HEEs goes hand in hand with structural stasis in the country's higher education system. More than two decades after the breakdown of the Soviet Union, Belarusian universities continue to closely follow Soviet educational practices (EduBelarus.info 2015a; Charter97.org 2015f). Nata, who is studying to be a teacher, complained that even the most acclaimed Belarusian HEEs were staffed with "old-guard instructors" who continued to "use teaching notes they made in the seventies or eighties" [BSt6]. She insisted that there was little reliance on technology in the classroom and that students had to use terribly outdated textbooks. During my fieldwork, I collected ample evidence in support of Nata's complaints.

The centrally mandated curriculum plans in Belarusian HEEs do indeed closely emulate the Soviet model, which prioritized exact and natural sciences over social sciences and humanities; deemphasized student-centered and interactive instruction; and promoted narrow, technical specialization beginning in the very first year of instruction. In the words of local educational expert Svetlana Matskevich, as in the Soviet era, contemporary Belarusian "instructional process is not really about educating youth, but rather about preparing the workforce" (Mazurkevich 2015). Agreeing with Matskevich, Vladimir Dunaev, an oppositional activist and education reformer quoted previously, suggests that the distinctions between Belarusian and European education "closely parallel the differences between the [local] Soviet-style planned economy and the knowledge-based European economy … The Soviet system of higher education [preserved in Belarus] does not correspond to modern demands and expectations, particularly in regard to the scientific and ethical progress the globalizing world requires" (Amzoomby.org 2015).

As a result of this continuity in pedagogical approaches, curriculum, and instructional practices, the well-oiled wheels of the Belarusian university system spin in much-too-familiar ways that do not leave space for creativity and experimentation. Modernization and liberalization reforms, periodically proposed by progressive educators, are emphatically brushed aside by incumbent politicians as unnecessary and harmful to the Belarusian education system. Lukashenka and his allies see the Soviet roots of the current system as an asset rather than a liability. In the words of Anatoliy Rubinov, the vice head of the Presidential Administration and a famous opponent of change in higher education, "alongside nuclear energy and weaponry, [the educational system] was one of the spheres in which the Soviet Union was a world leader." Rubinov argues that Belarusian "education should align with the conditions and needs of our country, not those of foreign lands" (Rubinov 2008). According to him and other Belarusian cadres, attempts to internationalize Belarusian universities and model educational practices that have been proven to work in Western democracies are both dangerous and misguided. Authorities even frame some progressive calls to adopt Western trends in pedagogy as a betrayal of the "national idea" and obstruction of the "national revival."

Ideological Indoctrination

One important manifestation of continuity with the Soviet educational model is the central role that ideological indoctrination continues to play in the Belarusian university curriculum (Zayats 2015). Local students take classes in "Ideology of the Belarusian State" rather than political science, in Russian and Chinese rather than Polish, Lithuanian, and German, and in physical education rather than sociology, anthropology, and other critical social sciences (Kulyagin 2015). Instead of collaborating with Western institutions, Belarusian HEEs form partnerships with universities in communist China, Russia, and authoritarian Turkmenistan (Sidorchik 2015; Zhegulo 2015). The university buildings themselves reflect the leadership's efforts to indoctrinate and control students' political views. Most HEEs, and particularly flagship universities, are decorated with portraits and sayings of the Belarusian president; Soviet-style placards advertising the pro-presidential youth movement, the Belarusian Youth Republican Front; and banners promoting physical fitness and a healthy lifestyle – personal obsessions of the president.

All Belarusian students and instructors I interviewed for this book mentioned some type of ideological activity that was taking place at their HEE. For instance, Galina, who teaches chemistry at a large state university, talked about so-called informational days, during which instructors "are supposed to discuss certain topics with students . . . particularly, teach everyone how good things are in our country" [Bpr6]. Many respondents mentioned pro-presidential rallies, early voting, "patriotic" concerts, cleaning days, celebrations of Soviet holidays, and a variety of other politically colored events that were mandatory for students and instructors. Consider, for instance, Table 3, which lists upcoming social

TABLE 3 Social events advertised on the website of Belarusian State University

Russian Проекты, конкурсы и мероприятия	English Projects, Contests, and Events
Мероприятия, посвященные 70-летию Великой Победы	Events dedicated to the seventieth anniversary of the Second World War victory
Мероприятия, посвященные празднованию 70-й годовщине освобождения Республики Беларусь от немецко-фашистских захватчиков	Events dedicated to the celebration of the seventieth anniversary of the liberation of the Belarusian Republic from Nazi occupiers
Встреча с начальником следственного управления Следственного комитета Республики Беларусь	Meeting with the head of the Central Investigative Committee of Belarus
Международный студенческий форум "Свет Великой Победы" 2015	International student forum: "The Light of Great Victory" 2015
Международная молодежная конференция «Молодёжь 21 века против войны»	International youth conference: "Youth of the Twenty-first Century Against the War"
Ретро-календарь на 2015 год «Двенадцать Героев Советского Союза»	Retro-calendar for 2015: "Twelve Heroes of the Soviet Union"

events at Belarusian State University – the country's flagship educational and research institution – publicized on its website in 2015[2]:

All six events have clear political undertones: from exuberant celebrations of victory over fascism in the Second World War to the commemoration of Soviet heroes and meetings with officials from criminal justice agencies, each event aims to discipline the youth, influence their political outlook, and intimidate the disloyal among them. Such events instill a fear of local government, portray all non-socialist governance models in an unfavorable light, foster nostalgia for the Soviet past, and promote an inward-looking xenophobic brand of patriotism. Participation in these activities is required for students to maintain enrollment and receive good

[2] I copied this list directly from the university's website. The website's URL is www.bsu.by/ru/main.aspx?guid=11511

grades. Instructors experience similar pressure to participate in and organize ideological ceremonies and celebrations. According to Galina, "evaluation of how effective instructors are at ideological work with students is a basis for the overall assessment of our work, as well as bonuses and promotions" [BPr6].

Such events are a central part of the larger educational project carried out by local universities. This larger project aims to suppress critical thinking; squash students' curiosity about the world outside Belarus; and elicit their unequivocal support for the incumbent regime through a mixture of fear, lack of exposure to alternatives, and carefully nurtured political apathy.

Oversight of Political Activity

As I quickly discovered during my fieldwork, governmental authorities closely monitor the social and civic lives of Belarusian university members. Students who join civil society organizations or otherwise show political initiative are either pressured into curbing their activity or recruited to support the official line of the state (Ctv.by 2015b). Students who exhibit oppositional tendencies experience a variety of pressures, ranging from formal warnings and exclusion from student organizations to expulsion from university, academic probation, restricted geographic mobility, and undesirable job assignments after graduation (Charter97.com 2015d, 2015g, 2015j; Spring96.com 2009, 2010a, 2010b; Shtrahova 2015). Allocation of dormitory space, distribution of residential chores, and periodic searches of students' rooms are also used to reward political compliance and punish dissent among Belarusian students (Shtrahova 2015).

The control of students' physical mobility is yet another tool that the Belarusian state uses to monitor and elicit political docility. While foreign travel is discouraged for everybody, students who express anti-government leanings are often barred from traveling abroad under any circumstances. In an interview with a local newspaper, Marina Shtrahova, the coordinator of the Students' Rights Monitoring Initiative, elaborated:

> It is practically impossible to receive a university president's permission to travel abroad. The most common basis for refusal is the argument that trips tend to disrupt the educational process and, therefore, adversely affect students' knowledge ... which would be a great argument if we didn't have all sorts of mandatory volunteering and political events, to participate in which students are constantly pulled from their classes. And if students did not get a day off for early voting. (Shtrahova 2015)

University instructors are also informally discouraged from engaging in political activism, and sometimes explicitly banned from doing so by the terms of their contracts (Charter97.com 2015e). Independent online news sources periodically feature stories of Belarusian professors and HEE administrators who have been fired for publicly criticizing the status quo (e.g., Belaruspartisan.org 2015b; Nn.by 2015b; Shulga 2013). Instructors' involvement in the "ideological upbringing of students," as well as "the alliance of their own behavior with the foundational principles of the ideology of the Belarusian state," constitute central criteria in retention and promotion decisions (Shik 2012; Sovadmin.gov.by 2013). Informal yet pervasive peer surveillance reinforces these stringent controls from above. Regina, an instructor of Spanish at a large HEE, told me that "people here [at her university] are very careful with what they say out loud, because people tell on each other . . . someone can go report to the chair to be among her favorites" [BPr2].

Effects of the Repressive Environment on the Recruitment of Subjects

Political pressure, indoctrination, and close organizational oversight in Belarusian higher education undermine university actors' freedom of expression and create a culture of fear in local HEEs. The effects of this repressive climate were readily apparent in Belarusians' unwillingness to participate in my research project. According to Vasiliy, who teaches political science, for many university-affiliated Belarusians, "any official actor is a potential agent of the state who can punish people for their thoughts and opinions" [BPr3]. In addition to concrete fears of persecution, ordinary Belarusians I met in the course of my fieldwork often displayed a general apprehension toward all things public and unfamiliar. While in Minsk, I often recalled the words of Igor, one of my first parent interviewee: "Belarusians are always afraid of something: it's our genetic memory . . . we have always been afraid of something. As a people, we do three things best: be scared, tolerate, and adjust" [BPa11].

Conducting research on corruption was particularly challenging in this oppressive environment. In contrast to the skeptical and rebellious Ukrainian youth, young Belarusians were wary of criticizing the government. Initially, most respondents gave me clean-cut, ideologically complacent accounts that extolled the status quo in higher education and in the country in general. It often took extra persuasion and emotional work to get past this façade of satisfaction and political docility. In fact, only a handful of instructors and experts transgressed their original propaganda-based testimony. Although a few Belarusians agreed to discuss bureaucratic corruption, they preferred to do so away from universities and sometimes away from coffee shops and other public spaces. Many were scared to open up even in the privacy of their homes.[3]

When asked about their fears, most respondents hinted at potential trouble with the government, in the form of forgone promotions, lost positions, and other primarily economic disincentives. The following notes describing my conversation with Viktor, a graduate student in philosophy at a large Minsk university, illustrate the resistance that I often encountered when trying to recruit and interview Belarusians. Viktor did not consent to my taking notes during our conversation, so I wrote them up from memory later that evening:

> As we were talking about reforms in higher education, our conversation touched on the role of the state in regulating and controlling universities. V seemed to be quite in favor of the idea. He said that if people don't like the state of things, they are free to move abroad because, after all, "we live in a free country." I was struck by his statement – it sounded like something an American would say . . . and was obviously untrue in the case of Belarus. Carefully, I asked him if he really believed that he lived in a free country. He avoided the answer by saying that for obvious reasons, he would rather not talk about that. Hoping to encourage conversation, I told him that if he didn't want to talk about it, we wouldn't, but that the reasons were actually not that obvious to me. He then said that he would be happy to explain it to me in three to five years, when he is done with graduate school. He thus insinuated that criticizing the government now might adversely affect his prospects as a graduate student. After hearing this, I pushed no further.
>
> [06/02/2010]

[3] As a result of this apprehensive attitude, I did not manage to collect as much interview data in Minsk as I did in Kiev. Thus, I was only able to obtain access to Belarusian universities through close connections with insiders and recommendations from influential acquaintances. In addition to "pulling strings," I had to take part in several formal and informal discussions of my intentions with high-level university administrators who asked me about my "real goals" beyond intellectual curiosity, my funding sources, and my connections to governments of other countries. Furthermore, online forums and publications discussing the informal lives of universities were nowhere nearly as abundant in Belarus as they were in Ukraine. The government imposes stringent restrictions on paper and Internet publications, censoring and shutting down the offices and websites of oppositional and independent publications (Charter97.com 2015j; Golos-ameriki.ru 2015; 3rdway.org 2015).

UNEXPECTED ABSENCE OF HORIZONTAL CORRUPTION

As sites of repression, Belarusian universities are, for all intents and purposes, free of horizontal exchanges between instructors, administrators, students, and their parents. During the entire period of participant observation in two local HEEs, I neither heard about nor observed a single informal transaction between students, parents, and employees. The lack of open discussion of personal experiences, shared myths, gossip, and hearsay about under-the-table economies – as well as a complete absence of any visible manifestations of the relationships and interactions that they entail – marked a striking departure from on-the-ground realities of Ukrainian universities, which bustle with formal and informal discussions of corruption. Following is an extract from my field notes that shows my astonishment at this difference between the two countries:

> It is day seven and I STILL have not seen or heard anything ... This is incredible! I believe that by now I have logged at least twenty stories at XXX [one of the two Kiev HEEs where I carried out fieldwork] alone. I am not sure what is going on. Maybe this stuff is just more hidden and difficult to spot at XXX [the name of the Belarusian HEE where I was conducting fieldwork], but the fact that NO ONE has mentioned anything is truly odd. Is it possible that my presence is simply very disruptive? I guess it is technically possible, but I also feel like people have been getting used to me. Today Agnelina Ivanovna [the chair of the department] yelled at a student who showed up at the faculty lounge in my presence. This is definitely a change from her emphatic politeness and friendliness last week. Also, X (one of the older instructors) returned to the lounge in the middle of a class period to talk on the phone and signaled to me to not tell anyone in a friendly and sort of conspiring way ... so I do feel like people are getting more comfortable and I should be starting to hear comments and complaints about bribes and presents. [04/22/2010]

When I made these notes, I was still expecting that I would soon begin to hear stories of horizontal corruption between Belarusian instructors and their students. My expectations never materialized. Throughout my fieldwork in Belarusian HEEs, I encountered no formal or informal talk about bribes, presents, or favors among students, parents, instructors, and administrators. Even more unexpectedly, I collected practically no stories of corruption through my interviews with Belarusian students, parents, and university employees. By way of comparison, interviews were my primary source of data on the types, patterns, and logistics of corrupt exchanges among university actors in neighboring Ukraine. None of my Belarusian interviewees suggested that they had participated in, observed, or heard about bribery between instructors, administrators, students, and parents in recent years. The following quotes reflect students' typical responses to questions about corruption in their universities: "It doesn't happen in my school . . . I mean, that stuff, it's all over, but our university is an exception really. Professors don't even take flowers" [BSt30]; "I am very sure that in my department, among my professors and my classmates, nothing like that happens . . . no one has ever hinted" [BSt12].

Timur, a student at a small, specialized institute, told me that he wished that bribery was possible:

> It would be nice if there were a way to get out of some crazy, boring classes I have to take. I'd rather pay [laughs], but no, no such luck . . . Believe me, I'm the kind of guy who would know if there were opportunities, so to speak. But my professors . . . they are all prim and proper, not a step out of line. I bet some of them would actually like to make some зайчики [the colloquial term for Belarusian currency] but they are too scared, I think. Or too well trained. Or maybe they are just better people than I am, I don't know . . . [In response to my question whether corruption happens in other universities]: Nah . . . I don't really think that in Minsk that stuff exists many places. If it did some place, you know I'd be there rather than here [laughs out loud]. [BSt32]

Although stories of corrupt exchanges between students and their instructors periodically surface in the local press, they tend to be framed as outrageous and unusual exceptions to the general rule of transparency (EduBelarus.info 2015; Orlov 2014). For instance, an article entitled "Bribery Is Eradicated in Higher Education" maintains that informal economic relationships in local universities are far from systematic or normalized: "bribery does periodically surface in HEEs, indeed. But it is fair to claim that the fight against it is extremely serious" (Orlov 2014). Another article describes a case of bribery in university admissions – the only case identified by criminal justice agents in Belarus during that year's two-month-long enrollment period – as a grave criminal assault (News.tut.by 2015). Yet another news essay mentions a case of diploma purchase that, according to the author, was only the second of its kind registered in the entire country in 2007 (EduBelarus.info 2015). By comparison, in Ukraine, the practice of buying diplomas is so open and pervasive that ads for related services are handed out in subway stations and featured on billboards in Kiev's city center.

Finally, while Ukrainian universities' informal online forums abound with discussions of bribery logistics and feature entire rubrics dedicated to the "how-to" of corruption, their Belarusian counterparts bear very little mention of this topic. For instance, I did not find a single informal forum post describing concrete exchanges of money or favors between Belarusian students and instructors. In fact, only eleven entries mentioned such corruption at all. The first was a question from an applicant to a Minsk HEE whether it was necessary to pay bribes to the HEE's instructors (the question was answered with a resounding "No"). Three other mentions spouted general accusations toward university administrations (not supported by any evidence), while the remainder referenced vertical corruption, discussed in the next section. In comparison, Ukrainian online forums mentioned horizontal corruption more than two hundred times.

The Belarusian government's official statistics on criminal cases involving bribery in universities support these findings. In 2009, only six criminal proceedings were initiated against HEE employees suspected of receiving illegal compensation in the course of their professional duties. In twenty-four additional instances, suspicious activity did not lead to any criminal charges (EduBelarus.info 2015). Even in transparent political systems with an independent judiciary, corruption statistics offer a highly unreliable proxy for the actual incidence of corruption, since most informal exchanges remain undetected. For obvious reasons, Belarusian official statistics are even more problematic: they are compiled within a nontransparent and highly politicized criminal justice apparatus according to a largely unclear methodology. At the same time, a comparison of these statistics with the annual number of criminal cases associated with corruption in other institutional spheres of post-Soviet Belarus is telling. In 2008, for example, 467 cases of corruption were reported in trade, 367 in industry, and 338 in agriculture. The comparatively low number of cases reported in higher education suggests that such horizontal informal exchanges are indeed rare (EduBelarus.info 2015).

WIDESPREAD VERTICAL CORRUPTION

Despite the apparent absence of exchanges between university employees and students, Belarusian HEEs are not completely free of informal economic activity. During my fieldwork in local universities, I did encounter one type of illicit transaction that, in a Western sense, constituted corruption. I refer to such corruption as *vertical* because it is embedded in the relationship between organizational actors and their superiors. In vertical corruption, employees in lower hierarchical positions bypass administrative and legal requirements at the request of someone in a position of power. Such requests typically deal with inclusion or exclusion decisions, such as admitting student protégés or hiring someone's relatives; retaining or giving a passing grade to failing students who have "protection"; or, in contrast, expelling or firing citizens involved in political opposition. During my time in Belarus, I directly observed and heard stories about faculty members being pressured to exercise their professional privileges in ways that benefited somebody "important" (**важный**, in Russian).

For instance, Faina Lvovna, a professor of humanities at a large Minsk university, told me the following:

> "Certain students are so ... important ... that they just can't be expelled." She continued, "for instance, I once had a student who I literally had never seen. He had never attended a class of mine ... But when the time came to give grades, I got a call from the vice president of XXX [a governmental body under the aegis of the Ministry of Education[4]] who pretty much told me to pass this person because, it turns out, his father was someone big. I don't even know who – I don't care." [BPr15]

Ironically, Faina also admitted, openly and with visible satisfaction, that she got her job at a high-status department of a prestigious Belarusian HEE because both her grandmother and father were well-known professors. Faina said that when the time came for her to find employment, "she had her pick" [BPr15].

In the same vein, a language department chair shared with me that although, on paper, she was responsible for recruitment and retention of the departmental faculty, at least half of current instructors had been hired without her input:

[4] I have omitted the name of the organization to protect the confidentiality of research subjects.

> Basically, the way it happens is that I get word – this could be over the phone or in person – that the dean, the rector [the university president], or someone else in the administration would really like such-and-such to be a part of our team. Will I please oblige ... ? Of course, I oblige ... I must say, this has backfired more than once as we then have to deal with workers who are not qualified. But then again, it's the so-called telephone law. Many of us have gotten our jobs that way. [BPr5]

As these interview accounts suggest, vertical corruption in Belarusian universities may be disguised as a request for a favor, a solicitation, or an appeal from an upper-level administrator. At first glance, such framing seems to imply compensation for the executor's efforts. Yet, the compensation for such informal assistance is less tangible than corruption spoils in Ukrainian universities. While some instructors and administrators get promoted or develop friendly relationships with their bosses, most respondents consider such "help" to be a professional obligation.

The following statements by instructors suggest that most of their colleagues have a negative view of vertical corruption:

> These things ... they happen everywhere, I guess. You help me, I help you – that's a part of life. But I think it is a bit different when you are helping your boss rather than your friend. I am always very happy to help a friend, because even if they do not return the favor, so to speak, they treat you with love, and you know you can rely on them. I guess it should be the same with the boss ... except not really. It's not fully voluntary, like a friendly favor would be – I really have no choice but to do what he asks. And even if the boss is nice to me or I get some sort of reward, it is still not voluntary and not, maybe, how I would have preferred things to be." [BPr10]

And:

> Even though the dean asks, we all understand that the dean does not really need to ask ... It doesn't really matter how he puts it to you – he is essentially telling you how it is going to be ... Well, of course, a lot depends on how dependent one is ... For instance, in our department, the chair is retired, so she's really dependent, because she is now on some sort of short-term contract. I am ready to bet that she doesn't say "no" very often. [BPr11]

The obligation that Belarusian university employees feel to carry out the requests of their higher-ups often generates resentment against the administration. Consider, for instance, this quote by Arkadiy

Andreevich, who teaches in a fine arts and architecture department: "I think, except for a few suck-ups or careerists, most of my colleagues hate doing these things . . . As you understand, they involve behavior that does not correspond to standards that one might hold as an educator and, in general, as a moral person" [BPr1]. In fact, while positive rewards are not common in cases of vertical corruption, negative sanctions for avoiding it can be quite weighty. Valeriya, a former instructor of English at a large university who is now working abroad, told me that a couple of times during her time in Belarus, she "refused to do anything [after receiving a phone call with a request to change a student's grade]. Then my last name was mentioned in деканат [the dean's office, in English], and the chair of the department was given a shaking. Of course, she made my life miserable for a couple months" [BPr8].

At the same time, in contrast to horizontal exchanges, commonly recognized as corrupt by local actors, ordinary Belarusians often do not construe vertical informality in HEEs as corruption. My interviews, for instance, reveal that employees who do illicit favors for their superiors generally do not experience the feelings of guilt or shame that are often associated with breaking ethical and legal norms. In the course of my fieldwork, I did not have a chance to speak with anyone who self-identified as a source of such requests, but their recipients were able to absolve themselves of negative moral implications because of their alleged lack of agency. In the words of Anton, a thirty-four-year-old instructor, "you can't blame someone for doing what is required to keep the job, right?" [BPr12]. In fact, while the overwhelming majority of Belarusians recognized horizontal corruption as a violation of formal rules and moral codes, most described vertical corruption in terms of doing "what you are supposed to do" [BPr5], following orders, and adhering to organizational rules.

Soviet Roots of Vertical Corruption

One of the most open and liberal Belarusian instructors I interviewed in the course of my fieldwork, Valentina, offered an interesting take on why vertical corruption is so widespread in local universities:

> All of that happens because of our collectivism – people don't think of their work as their individual responsibility. Rather, they imagine themselves as a part of a bigger whole and look for other parts of the whole to do their job or to cover up for them . . . We still live with a Soviet

> mentality of getting things done through other people. We still depend on each other, and they depend on us and someone else . . . everyone is basically interdependent. And people help each other because everyone is afraid that if something happens to them or their children, they might need help themselves." [BPr4]

Valentina's explanation traces the roots of vertical informality back to the relational corruption of the Soviet era. Under the Soviet planned economy, characterized by an expansive and overbearing bureaucratic apparatus and a shortage of consumer goods, relationship-based transactions, known as *blat*, constituted the primary mode of informal economic activity. Alena Ledeneva defines *blat* as "the use of personal networks and informal contacts to obtain goods and services in short supply and to find a way around formal procedures" (1998: 1). *Blat* is an example of *relational* informality insomuch as it is embedded in personal networks and facilitated by feelings of mutual sympathy and trust. Framing *blat* in terms of support and assistance, Soviet citizens shared goods and services with an expectation of reciprocity as need arose. For instance, hospital workers helped their acquaintances with doctors' appointments, while factory workers procured factory products without sales tax and store commissions for their friends and family. In many ways, *blat* relations created an informal private market within the state-controlled economy: public goods and services were treated as private and exchanged under the guise of friendship and support (Sampson 1987b). At the same time, inasmuch as reciprocity demanded an "adequacy of response, not mathematical equality" (Polanyi et al. 1957, in Jowitt 1983), *blat* "softened out" the harsh realities of the Soviet production and distribution systems.

Vertical corruption in Belarusian HEEs bears a clear resemblance to *blat* in terms of both its discourse of mutual assistance and the type of trust violation that it entails. To start with the latter, vertical corruption usually necessitates the "rental" of one's professional privileges and access (such as one's ability to give a grade, admit a student, or hire an instructor). The language that the parties to such exchanges use is also highly evocative of *blat* discourse: Belarusians describe them as favors, friendly requests, and mutual help. At the same time, a fundamental aspect of *blat*, delayed reciprocity, is, by and large, missing from vertical corruption in local universities. Despite the rhetoric of mutuality, most providers of corrupt favors do not receive additional benefits beyond the retention of employment and consideration for promotions to which they are legally entitled. In other words, while such transactions resemble *blat* in a number of ways, they also carry new and different incentives and meanings for the participating actors.

Vertical corruption in Belarusian universities is an outcome of a gradual institutional transformation that scholars of institutional change refer to as *drift*. In cases of drift, institutions are refocused and recalibrated over time in relation to their changing structural contexts. This type of institutional change is often "masked by stability on the surface" (Streeck and Thelen 2005: 24) that conceals the actual "slippage" between the formal attributes of institutions, which remain relatively stable, and their on-the-ground implementation and functions, which transform over time. While drift has been theorized primarily in relation to formal institutions, the emergence of vertical corruption as the primary modus operandi of the shadow economy in Belarusian universities suggests that it is also characteristic of their informal counterparts.

Political Implications of Vertical Corruption

My data show that vertical corruption is widespread in present-day Belarusian universities. During interviews, at least a third of local students and the majority of instructors mentioned one or more concrete instance of such informality. Ljubov, who teaches musicology, estimated that about 90 percent of personnel at her HEE had been hired through connections and nepotistic channels. Similarly, Faina, who teaches at a large Minsk university, was certain that the entire administration of her institution owed its employment to vertical corruption:

> Just look at the president . . . He works here, his wife does, and so do his niece and the wife of his son, some of his cousins, and so on . . . It's a family enterprise. And on the lower levels, it's even more so, because it's less visible. And they are secure in their positions because they depend on each other and cover up for each other.

Faina continued, "The situation in our university is a small model of the situation in the country in general: круговая порука ('krugovaya poruka' or, literally, circular guarantee, in English)" [BPr15].

Alena Ledeneva, the author of influential scholarship on Soviet informal economies, defines круговая порука as "a situation in which all the members of a particular group or circle are held jointly responsible for the actions and obligations of group as a whole. Under the conditions of круговая порука, the lives and fates of the members of a group are inextricably linked" (Ledeneva 2006: 91). During the Soviet era, круговая порука offered the government a means for "self-defense and a method for suppressing criticism" (Ledeneva 2006: 100). Through the indebtedness of the lower links of hierarchical chains to their superiors, круговая порука guarantees political compliance and provides ample channels for controlling the citizenry.

As Faina suggested in our conversation, in nontransparent societies, the model of круговая порука is adopted within the national government as well as in local political systems, such as organizations. Just like authoritarian governments, organizational leadership circles are bound together by personalistic loyalty; targeted incentives; and, of course, fear. In Belarusian HEEs, круговая порука creates an environment in which lower echelons of the administration are bound to carry out the infringements of law that are necessary for the recruitment and retention of the politically loyal cadres. Paradoxically, then, круговая порука and horizontal transparency have the same roots in Belarusian universities. Both phenomena stem from the autocratic repression of university members' freedoms of thought and political choice.

HORIZONTAL CORRUPTION IN HOSPITALS AND SECONDARY SCHOOLS

My conversations with ordinary Belarusians touched on bureaucratic corruption in other local organizations besides universities. In fact, my interviews revealed that Belarusian HEEs were rather unique in their horizontal transparency: many other Belarusian bureaucracies reportedly abound with small-scale informal exchanges between employees and clients. All but three of interviewed students and parents and almost three-fourths of interviewed instructors admitted to regularly using connections and bribes in their bureaucratic encounters outside universities. These respondents resorted to horizontal corruption to get appointments, ensure good and timely service, and establish rapport with a variety of street-level officials. They mentioned giving bribes and using connections in hospitals, local equivalents of social security offices, kindergartens, secondary schools, and DMVs. The local press reports such exchanges in courts, tax administrations, and various municipal offices.[5]

[5] See, for instance, EduBelarus.info (2015d, 2015e) and Rakova (2008).

Galina, a forty-four-year-old chemistry instructor, told me that when her mother had surgery, their family's main "medical" expenses consisted of bribes:

> Medicine is insanely corrupt. I am now dealing with a sick mom, and I need to pay for absolutely everything! . . . I told her, "Mom, you just have to stay healthy, because I literally cannot afford it!" I had to bring a bottle of expensive cognac to every single doctor's appointment . . . You see, she is an older lady, and they don't care about old people. So I literally had to "sweeten" every single nurse in that hospital by bringing coffee, perfume, and whatnot. [BPr6]

Similarly, Igor, a thirty-nine-year-old banker, complained to me about the difficulty of obtaining zoning permits for the house he was building on the outskirts of the city: "Nothing gets done without someone making a call from up high! At every stage of the process, I've had to look for people to introduce me and to make requests for me. But even with these introductions, I still had to pay imaginary fees that went straight into the pockets of some fat bastard" [BPa11].

When I asked my respondents about the reasons why horizontal corruption was so pervasive in Belarusian bureaucracies, they offered testimonies that closely mirrored the stories of their Ukrainian neighbors. As clients, many respondents saw corruption as the only possible way to get the desired bureaucratic services. As officials, many thought of it as a practical way to complement their paltry, insufficient incomes. The following quote from Ekaterina, a fifty-six-year-old engineer, illustrates both rationales:

> A friend of mine works in a hospital . . . I always turn to her when I need something at the hospital . . . She helped me see this famous surgeon . . . even people with connections have to wait for months to see him . . . but he knows my friend and was willing to see me when she asked. Of course, I also brought [something] . . . I had to thank him, you know.
>
> I: Why did you have to?
> R: . . . I couldn't just wait . . . If I did, I'd never get to see him, I'm sure others with acquaintances would always get in before me.
> I: And why did he take your present? Isn't he famous? Isn't he well-off?
> R: Oh, no, no. No matter how good they are, these doctors don't make any money. He needs to feed his family too. [BPa4]

My interviews also revealed the popular normalization of horizontal corruption in many Belarusian bureaucracies. The majority of respondents understood informal exchanges with street-level officials in terms of etiquette, mutual assistance, and relationship building. They insisted that small gifts (such as flowers, alcohol, coffee, and candy) express appreciation and respect and are, by and large, expected in daily interactions with street-level bureaucrats. While most interviewees agreed that money and more expensive offerings (such as jewelry and perfume) constituted bribes, very few construed them as immoral or ethically unacceptable. The following quote by Nikolai, a forty-year-old, temporarily unemployed accountant, shows a common way of thinking about petty horizontal corruption in street-level bureaucracies:

I: *Would you consider offering a small sum of money or a present to an official?*

R: *Of course I would. I don't really do it often, but it is not because I think there is anything particularly wrong with it. Probably because I just don't have money. We all have to make do somehow . . . It's not a crime to try to get what you want if you have the means.* [BPa6]

Even respondents who complained that widespread corruption made it hard to obtain desired goods and services found ways to justify it. Consider the following statement by Alyona, a student from Minsk Pedagogical University:

> Yeah, that wasn't pleasant, when I was getting my passport and I didn't bring the lady anything because I was not in a hurry . . . so, instead of the one month that it was supposed to take, it took her five or something like that . . . because she kept on doing other people's documents who I am sure actually paid her something . . . But, oh well, I could have paid also, right? I mean if people paid, it must have been important to them. [BSt31]

Horizontal Corruption in Secondary Schools

To collect data on horizontal corruption outside Belarusian universities, I focused specifically on secondary schools, since most of my respondents had had lengthy and recent exposure to the tertiary educational sector, either as students or as parents of students. One of the first Belarusian parents I met during my fieldwork was Dina Stepanovna. A single mother of two, Dina is a schoolteacher at a nonspecialized secondary school in a residential neighborhood of Minsk. Dina did not consent to a formal interview but allowed me to discuss her story in the book.[6] In my field notes from our meeting, I wrote the following:

[6] Because she did not consent to a formal interview, I did not include Dina Stepanovna in the list of Belarusian parent interviewees.

> Dina Stepanovna has been teaching geography for the last ten years – ever since her husband left them. The job is difficult because of the constantly changing curriculum and lack of resources in local schools. She likes her students, though. She says that they are good kids who try hard. She also says that she considers many parents to be her friends. Soon after, she explained that they help her out with a variety of things, ranging from house repairs to difficult-to-obtain train tickets. She's come to rely on their help. For Dina, these gifts and favors signal students' respect. She takes pride in her work. She says that the support of parents (I asked for a clarification and she specified that she was talking about material support) shows that they appreciate her and value the way she treats their children. When I asked if she gives anything in return for such assistance, Dina said that she doesn't do anything out of the ordinary, other than treat her students with extra care and ensure their success. It is not clear to me whether she meant she just roots for her students and assists them within the bounds of the law and school rules or that she goes above and beyond, exceeding her professional privileges. I felt uncomfortable asking any further – Dina so clearly saw these exchanges in a positive light, and they were so clearly central to her identity as a good teacher that I did not want to suggest otherwise.
>
> [04/17/2010]

Based on my later conversations with Belarusian parents and students, however, I became convinced that Dina Stepanovna did repay parents' gifts and favors with services that exceeded the legal bounds of her professional mandate. Horizontal corruption in schools – such as exchanges of money, presents, and services for grades, preferential treatment, and assistance on exams – is so common in present-day Belarus that it is difficult to imagine that Dina's story was about anything else.

In fact, my interviewees largely agreed that the incidence of such exchanges had increased dramatically in recent years. Thus, many university instructors blamed the allegedly falling quality of university applicants directly on the growing "epidemic of lawlessness" in Belarusian high schools [BPr14]. Angelina Ivanovna, the chair of the foreign languages department where I worked and observed, confided in me, "In the years that I have worked at the university, the quality of students has gotten so much worse! School preparation has completely gone down the drain, mainly because now it's necessary to pay money in school" [BPr14].

According to an explanation that my interviewees invoked over and over again, the growing reliance on standardized testing in secondary and higher education is at least partially responsible for the increase in the incidence of bribery and other petty horizontal corruption in Belarusian schools. Angelina Ivanovna explained,

> Corruption in schools is not new in and of itself . . . but how much of it we have in schools now I would say is . . . I would say is unusual. I personally believe that, largely, all the recent changes in schools, the obsession with testing, particularly . . . They are largely at fault. Now everyone has to get a tutor for their kid to pass the tests. And usually, the way it works is you pay, and the teacher works with your kid. Or she doesn't work with your kid but simply helps him out to do well on the test. Either way, the more money you have and are willing to give, the higher the chances that your child will have good grades. The relationship between the two is quite direct. [BPa14]

One parent, Zoya Alekseevna, even suggested that teachers may in fact

> give kids bad grades just so they'll hire them as tutors. And as soon as tutoring begins, they'll start giving good grades, often in a manner that makes it clear that the grades weren't deserved . . . My daughter had this teacher . . . A real hypocrite! I have some choice words for her . . . Basically, she kept giving my daughter bad grades. She used to say, "I worry about your girl so much that I can't sleep at night!" until I gave in and hired her, despite her really high rates. Of course, as soon as she was hired, L.'s [the daughter] grades improved a lot. [BPa3]

In addition to tutoring for money, many respondents mentioned the so-called поборы ("pobory," or collections, in English) as another common way of extracting money from parents of secondary school students. "Collections" happen when a teacher, usually via announcements during parent-teacher meetings or messages sent home with students, requests monetary contributions from students' families. As a rule, teachers claim that these funds will purchase classroom materials, finance field trips, supplement school building repairs, and provide other education-related necessities. Many Belarusian respondents, however, expressed strong skepticism about the veracity of these claims. Some also noted that teachers use academic and disciplinary penalties to punish students whose parents do not contribute, while rewarding contributors with preferential treatment.

Sometimes, school employees do not attempt to conceal the tit-for-tat nature of these allegedly voluntary parent contributions. One mother told me, for instance, that when her son was in high school (a year before our conversation), his class teacher announced at the **родительское собрание** (parent-teacher meeting, in English) that anyone who bought a three-ring binder for the classroom would be rewarded with two tens (A's in the local grading system). She continued, "So I bought the binders for my son – why not? They are not even that expensive" [BPa10]. Similarly, another parent confided in me that his son's home economics grade had been earned by supplying the teacher with "details and wooden panels" [BPa2] – the materials that students work with in their home economics courses.

The local press features a lively discussion of **поборы**. In newspaper articles and TV shows, opponents of this practice claim that "parents attend parent-teacher meetings with only one question in mind: How much?" They write that families often do not know the reason for their contributions and that teachers sometimes increase the legitimacy of extortion by framing it as an initiative of the parent council. To emphasize the negative implications of this practice, articles condemning such collections feature the stories of parents whose children received bad grades after refusing to honor their teachers' requests for money (Ctv.by 2015a; Zn.sb.by 2009). Other articles, however, praise this practice for allowing parents to participate in and improve their child's educational experience:

> If parents, for instance, do not chip in for bottled water or napkins, these things won't just appear on their own. That's a tried-and-true fact. If I don't buy my son a set of advanced English language textbooks, then he will be transferred to the lower-level class. So for some parents, the standards available at schools are a bare minimum. They want to and have an opportunity to provide their beloved little one with something more. Additional textbooks, modern furniture, useful and varied recreation. (Zan'ko 2015)

In addition to tutoring and collections, many interviewees also mentioned bribes, presents, and favors to individual instructors and school administrators. Most parents who admitted to participating in bribery insisted that they had to "give" for their children to do well and receive the necessary help and support in their respective schools: "If I don't give and Masha's mom gives, who do you think the teacher will treat better: my daughter or Masha?" [BPa10]. As this quote suggests, even though such bribes are technically voluntary, concerned parents often believe that not giving them would negatively affect students' academic outcomes. As a result, parents perceive extortion by school employees: "Nobody would ask you explicitly, but they definitely demand ... I mean, I guess nobody is twisting your arm. You don't have to give. But then you have to accept that your kid will pay for that" [BPa11].

According to my interviews, Belarusians are similar to their Ukrainian counterparts in that they tend to consult their friends and acquaintances with inside knowledge and previous experiences when making decisions about the necessity of bribes, their size, and the appropriate method of delivery:

> Usually, parents tell each other when and what is required ... When I was new, I remember asking another mom, with whom we are friendly, how to give a package to a certain teacher and what another teacher liked ... things like that. I asked a lot at first. But after a while, you can just kind of understand how these things are done. [BPa7]

In the words of Zoya Alekseevna, quoted previously, "we rely on one another to warn us about ... what can and cannot or ... maybe should be done. People look out for one another, that's how Belarusians are used to living" [BPa3].

From group collections to overpriced tutoring and bribes, horizontal corruption in Belarusian schools closely resembles the informal economic landscapes of Ukrainian universities. Both exchange systems entail a wide variety of practices and institutionalized facilitative mechanisms. Both also have deep roots in informal socialization systems whereby parents and students learn about the necessity, appropriateness, and logistics of corruption through hearsay, observations, and informal interactions with one another. Like their Ukrainian counterparts, Belarusian interviewees revealed that their knowledge of how much they needed to "bring" and how central their contributions were to their children's academic success were based on what they saw, heard, and deduced within concrete organizational environments.

CONCLUSION

Ethnographic fieldwork in Belarusian universities and interviews with ordinary citizens about their experiences in other street-level organizations reveal a curious mixture of vertical and horizontal bureaucratic corruption in post-Soviet Belarus. Local universities are free from direct exchanges between employees and their clients, yet ripe with vertical informality, whereby low-level officials break the law and organizational rules at the request of their superiors. By contrast, many other bureaucratic sectors of contemporary Belarus are permeated with horizontal exchanges that involve money, presents, and favors; entail extraction as well as voluntary offerings; and reflect the enactment of organizationally transmitted assumptions.

An interesting implication of this coexistence of different types of corruption across the institutional sectors of present-day Belarus is ordinary people's ability to invoke and reconcile different and often mutually contradictory ways of thinking about illicit transactions with bureaucrats. For instance, my respondents often invoked contradictory cultural schema in regard to the acceptability and justifiability of bureaucratic corruption, depending on the type of organization in question. Consider the following extracts from an interview with the same respondent, thirty-nine-year-old Ernest, a small-business owner. Ernest appeared very surprised that I would ask about corruption in universities:

> The things you are hinting at [exchanges of bribes in HEEs], they are nonexistent here, because nobody would think them possible. How can you buy a professor? In general, what is the point of getting an education, then? For instance, how can you become a doctor if you pay bribes in medical school? What kind of doctor would you be? In things like that, there is simply no sense. And in general, professors ... they are noble people. They don't work for money; they work for future generations. [BPa5]

Yet, toward the end of the interview, Ernest was making statements about corruption in secondary schools that directly contradicted the points he had made earlier:

I: *Do you think corruption in schools hurts academic outcomes? In other words, does such corruption undermine students' knowledge?*

R: *I wouldn't say that. I think some people need an individual approach, when it comes to education, so when people bring a little something extra to the teachers, maybe they can spend more time with those students and give them more individual attention. I don't know. I simply think that our system ... it's so ... how do I say this? It's so "iron"* (*железная*, in Russian) [inflexible] *that it breaks people who don't fit ... And things like parents' help to teachers allow ... to maybe hide from that system a little bit. Of course, those who cannot afford to do it, they ... their children won't get anything, but at least some will. Aren't some better than no one?* [BPa5]

Ernest's testimony contains the most dramatic example of contradictory claims from the same respondent that I encountered in my interviews. Many other Belarusians, however, also espoused ways of thinking about corruption that were hardly reconcilable, even if less directly contradictory. For instance, Zhanna, a thirty-eight-year-old housewife, told me that corruption among the police (allegedly absent in Belarus) would be "a sign of the country falling apart," while corruption in hospitals (allegedly pervasive) is "normal for us" [BPa10]. Such contradictions were also visible in how the interviewees thought about horizontal versus vertical corruption in their HEEs. Thus, Antonina Andreevna, an instructor of graphics, thought that accepting money from a student in exchange for a favorable admissions decision would be completely immoral but did not consider admitting an unqualified candidate based on the request of the rector (the university president) particularly egregious [BPr20].

The coexistence of different cognitive schema in regard to corruption is a testimony to the cultural multiplicity in present-day Belarus. As a hybrid regime, Belarus has developed a cultural landscape that accommodates a variety of corruption-favorable and corruption-unfavorable definitions. Ordinary Belarusians adopt different ways of thinking about corruption based primarily on their exposure to different organizations' informal environments. Like their Ukrainian counterparts, Belarusians enact the untested assumptions regarding potential consequences of breaking organizational norms that they pick up from informal interactions with peers, observations, and hearsay. The ethnographic and interview data discussed in this chapter reveal that, as a rule, the organizational cultures of Belarusian secondary schools and health care institutions are conducive to bureaucratic corruption, while the informal environments of local universities tend to discourage horizontal exchanges between bureaucrats and their clients. Chapter 5 explains exactly how the hybrid political trajectory of post-Soviet Belarus has shaped this variation in the informal cultures of different bureaucratic sectors.

CHAPTER FOUR

HIGH POLITICAL TURNOVER AND CROSS-ORGANIZATIONAL VARIATION IN CORRUPTION IN POST-SOVIET UKRAINE

Interrelations between ideologies and alternative narratives are in conflict with each other but they exist rather in parallel realities.

(Zlobina 2007: 95)

Like many young middle-class Ukrainians, my childhood friend Liza holds two bachelor's degrees. When Liza chose her first major – German language and literature – she was a recent high school graduate and did not have a strong sense of what she wanted to study. Her parents suggested German. With new foreign companies opening offices in Kiev each month, majoring in the language of the biggest European economy seemed like a sure professional bet. Yet, while working toward her linguistics degree, Liza realized that her passion lay elsewhere: she loved art. With a new dream of curating an art gallery, Liza enrolled in the Kiev Academy of Fine Arts as a student of art history a year after her first graduation. Liza's experience in the two HEEs could not have been any more different. As part of a prestigious state university, her first department attracted students from well-to-do families who were capable and willing to take part in informal economic exchanges with their professors. The Kiev Academy of Fine Arts, Liza insisted, was different: it brought together students with a passion for art who treasured the opportunity to learn and had little interest in bribes and other informal shortcuts.

Liza's impressions of cross-organizational variation in corruption resonated with many other conversations I had with students, parents, and instructors in the course of my fieldwork in Kiev. Some of my respondents compared corruption levels of universities based on their first-hand knowledge, others on the basis of rumors and hearsay. My survey of 193 students (discussed in Chapter 2) also revealed a broad consensus regarding the rates of corruption in different educational institutions: respondents consistently ranked some Kiev HEEs as more corrupt than others. Furthermore, the local media coverage reflected Ukrainians' shared beliefs regarding the varying levels of informal economic activity in different universities. For instance, I located multiple articles that compare and contrast the country's HEEs in terms of how much bribery and nepotism happen on their premises (Chuhlib 2011; Korrespondent.net 2015b; Politica.ua 2014).

Of course, these data reflect perceptions rather than the incidence of corruption and therefore warrant caution. In an effort to assess students' actual experiences with informal economic activity in different HEEs, I turned to local universities' informal websites, many of which feature entire sections where students rank their instructors on various characteristics, such as knowledge of the subject, attractiveness, rigor, and sense of humor (Kievskiy Natsionalniy Universitet im Tarasa Shevchenko 2014a; Kneu.ua 2014b). In addition to these ratings, students also enter brief comments, many of which reference specific incidents of corruption. To compare frequency of informal exchanges across HEEs, I analyzed these comments on the websites of three large Kiev universities that, according to my other data, have markedly different levels of informal economic activity. I read through the comments about first forty-five instructors on each website (in alphabetic order) and coded them as corrupt if two or more comments referenced specific instances of bribery, nepotism, or string pulling.

In line with my expectations, this analysis revealed significant cross-organizational differences in the frequency of reported informal exchanges. In the first university, students identified twenty instructors, or slightly less than half of all surveyed, as corrupt. The comments under the faculty list of the second HEE featured no references to corrupt activity whatsoever, while as many as thirty-six instructors (about 80 percent) from the third university were linked to corrupt incidents by two or more comments.

ARE CORRUPT UNIVERSITIES BAD UNIVERSITIES?

What explains the coexistence of corrupt and non-corrupt universities in Ukraine? And what kinds of HEEs develop corruption cultures while their counterparts remain transparent? One intuitive explanation is that corruption may be inversely related to the quality of educational services and is, therefore, simply another axis of organizational stratification in the field of higher education. In other words, since bribery, nepotism, exchanges of favors, and other informal practices undermine the educational process and diminish meritocracy in credentialing, is it possible that corruption is simply a characteristic of bad universities?

This explanation of cross-organizational variation in corruption would make perfect sense in a competitive labor market, where the educational credentials of workers offer a proxy of their ability to contribute to a workplace. Such characteristics of HEEs as their selectivity in admissions, research productivity, and tuition prices, then, signal to employers the desirability of their alumni as potential employees. In a system where employers vie for the most qualified labor, graduates of corrupt universities are likely to have poor job prospects. As a result, in such markets, college applicants strive to avoid corrupt universities, raising the competition for admission to less corrupt HEEs. As the best students enroll in the latter, a hierarchy in which corrupt HEEs are relegated to lower status positions is perpetuated ad infinitum.

Yet, academic and journalistic research on employment practices in present-day Ukraine casts doubt on the conjecture that this market mechanism of stratification is actually at play. Many analysts of post-Soviet Ukraine argue that professional placement of local alumni is shaped more by informal and non-meritocratic considerations than by competitive pressures (Martin 2006; Round, Williams, and Rodgers 2008; Williams and Round 2008). My respondents' testimonies further undermine this hypothesis, suggesting that prestige is hardly an indicator of low corruption in Ukrainian universities. For instance, forty-three-year-old Larissa referred to high corruption levels to explain why her daughter had not applied to a very prestigious university: "It's very corrupt because it's real prestigious, so everyone wants to go there, and professors can do whatever they want because they are not afraid of declining application rates" [UPa20]. Another parent agreed: "There are no regular people, like us, at that place. It is definitely elite ... it's not possible to get in there 'from the street.' You have to have connections or pay a lot of money!" [UPa17].

In addition to interviews, I also used a survey and media analysis to assess whether corruption is inversely related to status of different Ukrainian HEEs. I administered the survey to 193 students from four departments of different corruption and prestige levels in four Kiev

HEEs. [1] The survey presented respondents with names of eight departments in eight different universities in Kiev[2] and asked them to rank the departments in terms of corruption, quality, and prestige[3] (see Appendix I for descriptive statistics). A prompt defined university prestige as the value that other students and employers attach to a diploma from that university. Survey results revealed high consistency in how much corruption Kiev students perceive in different HEEs and how much prestige they ascribe to them.[4] At the same time, a bivariate correlation analysis showed no statistically significant relationship between the perceived corruption and prestige of Ukrainian HEEs (see Appendix I, Table 8 for the results). In other words, my analysis indicates that corruption neither lowers nor elevates the status of local universities.

Additional evidence in support of this finding comes from the local media. Many online educational portals, such as *osvita.ua, kursor.org .ua*, and *abiturient.in.ua*, discuss the status of local HEEs, referencing either their own comparative analyses or formal ranking initiatives, such as Top-200 Ukraine (EuroOsvita 2014), Scopus (SciVerse Scopus 2014), Compas (Abitutient.in.ua 2014), and Webometrics (Ranking Web of Universities 2015).[5] Some articles on these websites also compare the corruption levels of different HEEs based on interviews with students and stories published by other media outlets (i.e., Vgorode.ua 2011). A few portals even ask their visitors to rank the corruption levels of different colleges and universities (Kharkov Forum.com 2014; 056.ua 2013). While these ratings are not methodologically sound, they are highly consistent and thus offer additional evidence of cross-organizational variation in informal economic activity.

1 According to my interviewees, two of these HEEs have high levels of corruption, and the other two have low levels of corruption. In each pair, one department is low prestige and the other is high prestige, according to my interviews.

2 I chose these departments because my interviewees perceived different levels of corruption within them. None of the survey respondents attended the HEEs that they were asked to rank.

3 Students could choose a score on a scale from one to five, where one represented the lowest and five represented the highest possible value.

4 According to a within-subjects analysis of variance, the means for prestige scores were significantly different across universities.

5 The *Top 200 Ukraine* rating brings together three compounded indices that reflect the scholarly potential, the quality of instruction, and the level of international recognition (EuroOsvita 2014). The ranking by *Compas*, in contrast, reflects alumni and employers' perceptions of the practical value of various university programs and the correspondence between the demands of the labor market and the preparation that students receive in different HEEs (Abitutient.in.ua 2014).

The juxtaposition of status and corruption rankings in media publications also reveals little relationship between the two. Consider, for instance, a comparison between two highly prestigious (some would argue, the two most prestigious) HEEs in Ukraine: Taras Shevchenko Kiev State University and Kyiv-Mohyla Academy. Their corruption rankings could not be more different. While Kiev State is often described as one of the most corrupt HEEs in the country, Kyiv-Mohyla Academy ranks consistently low on the corruption scale (Politica.ua 2014). Similar comparisons could be carried out for low-prestige HEEs. Among these, some rank highly in terms of corruption, while others are, reportedly, fairly transparent.

The lack of association between the perceived value of diplomas and corruption levels of different HEEs suggests that corruption is not an affliction of "bad" universities. In fact, the coexistence of high- and low-corruption institutions without cost to the reputation of the former implies that they simply do not compete with each other. Rather, these educational institutions operate in two parallel educational markets: a more and a less corrupt one, each of which is also stratified into high- and low-prestige segments. In the rest of this chapter, I argue that the split in Ukraine's higher education is a product of its nonlinear, vacillating political trajectory in the post-Soviet era. Specifically, the high turnover of Ukrainian political leadership resulted in, first, the coexistence of corruption-favorable and corruption-unfavorable institutional logics and, second, structural opportunities and pressures for local bureaucracies to adopt either one logic or the other.

UKRAINIAN POLITICAL HISTORY AND BUREAUCRATIC FRAGMENTATION

Ukraine is a nation at the crossroads of many cultures and ideologies. For centuries, it has been divided and dominated, physically and culturally, by a number of imperial powers, including Russia, Poland, Lithuania, Hungary, and Turkey (Kuzio 1996). In recent years, as a result of its strategic location between Russia and Western democracies, Ukraine has experienced a plethora of cultural influences from the United States, the European Union, Orthodox and Catholic churches, other former Soviet Republics, and neighboring Russia (Magocsi 2010; Reid 2000; Wanner 2010). Analysts agree that because of the weakness of the Ukrainian state in the post-independence period, these new cultural schema did not replace but rather combined with old Soviet ways of thinking, acting, and organizing (Way 2005b). In the words of Tamara Zlobina, "Contemporary Ukrainian culture is an unstable mixture of political ideologies, cultural narratives and subcultural representations ... The absence of the main doctrine has resulted in cultural diversity and transformation processes often inspired by local people" (2007: 96).

Over the past twenty years, Ukraine experienced pendulum-like swings between more- and less-democratic political regimes (Hale 2005; Way 2005a). In the early years of independence (1991–1993), the first elected president, Leonid Kravchuk, prioritized symbolic initiatives in nationalism and state building over consistent economic reform and stabilization (Wilson 2005b). In the context of plummeting living standards and flailing institutions, Kravchuk focused on the adoption of state symbols, encouraged international recognition of the country's statehood, and promoted unity and centrism domestically (Fritz 2007; Kuzio 2002). In 1994, he peacefully conceded power to Leonid Kuchma, the longest-serving Ukrainian president to date (1994–2004).

Kuchma's presidency marked a clear break with Kravchuk's noncommittal stance on the economy and Western orientation in foreign policy. Kuchma's economic approach emphasized free trade and rapid privatization. With funding from the International Monetary Fund (IMF), he lowered taxes, decreased barriers to trade, and shrank social assistance programs. Yet, as a former *appartchik* with strong links to Ukraine's Eastern regions, Kuchma also reinvigorated the country's relationship with neighboring Russia (Puglisi 2003a; Zon 2005). To that end, he reversed the Odessa-Brody gas pipeline to benefit Russian interests and joined the Single Economic Space shared by Russia, Belarus, and Kazakhstan (Kubicek 2005: 277). Under the façade of economic austerity, Kuchma expanded presidential authority and doled out unprecedented privileges to his oligarchic allies (Puglisi 2003b).

By the turn of the century, Kuchma's Ukraine slipped back into semi-authoritarian governance. According to numerous accounts, his power rested on blackmail, suppression of the independent press and judiciary, nepotistic links with financial-industrial clans, and intimidation of adversaries (Kuzio 2005; Way 2005b). Darden called corruption "a technique of [Kuchma's] presidential control" (Darden 2001: 67), while others accused Kuchma of building an "oligarch country" (Puglisi 2003a, 2003b; Way 2005b). Ukraine's second president was also implicated in the murder of oppositional journalist Georgi

Gongadze and the sale of the Kolchuga Radar system to Iraq during the U.S.–Iraq conflict (Osborn 2011).

In 2004, at the end of Kuchma's second term, the two contenders for his position, Viktor Yuschenko and Viktor Yanukovich, ran their campaigns to capitalize on the growing divide between the two visions for the country's future. Yuschenko's pro-Western message represented a shift away from oligarchic policies in the shadow of Russia. For Western analysts and many Ukrainians, Yuschenko and his running mate, Yulia Timoshenko, embodied the promise of a Western-style democracy with a distinct national and cultural identity (Åslund and McFaul 2006; Kuzio 2007; Wilson 2005a). Yuschenko's opponent, Viktor Yanukovich, came from the Eastern industrial region of Donbass and served as Kuchma's prime minister (Osipian and Osipian 2006). His campaign favored closer economic ties to Russia and emphasized the rights of the Russian minority.

The run-up to the elections was marred by two alleged attempts on the life of the pro-Western candidate Viktor Yuschenko, including the infamous dioxin poisoning that left him temporarily disfigured. After the pro-Russian candidate's victory in the second round of elections on November 22, 2004, thousands of Ukrainians took to the streets to protest the reported voter fraud and intimidation. In response to these mass uprisings, the Supreme Court ordered a rerun of the elections, in which Yuschenko carried 52 percent of the vote. The mass protests, repeated elections, shift in leadership, and ensuing reform of the election machinery came to be known as the Orange Revolution (Kuzio 2006a; Lane 2008). According to Paul D'Anieri,

> The events of late 2004 caused a fundamental re-evaluation of Ukraine by key actors, including the European Union, the United States, and Russia. Better relationships with the West, and membership in NATO and the World Trade Organization (WTO) became real possibilities with the fall of Kuchma. At the same time, Russia's efforts to control Ukraine seemed to have been decisively rejected. (2005: 83)

Only three years later, however, the talk of the revolution's failure started to appear in academic, policy, and popular discourses (Tudoroiu 2007). Despite Yuschenko's ambitious campaign promises, which included everything from a war on corruption to the restitution of wage arrears and the creation of five million new jobs, his administration initiated the lowest number of draft laws in a single legislative session since the early 1990s (Arel 2005; Copsey 2005). Moreover,

Yuschenko's government engaged in repressive policies against its former political adversaries, while the judicial system remained heavily influenced by political interests (Arel 2005; Tudoroiu 2007). White and McAllister (2009) found that three years after the Orange Revolution, ordinary citizens experienced more economic troubles than they had prior to 2004, while ongoing power struggles between the new president and his prime minister, Yuliya Timoshenko, fueled the popular frustration with the regime's ineffectiveness (Haran 2011: 95).

Disappointed with the lack of tangible improvement, empty promises to curb corruption, and endless tensions within Yuschenko's team, Ukrainians withdrew their support for his coalition in 2010, voting, once again, for the pro-Russian presidential candidate and Yuschenko's opponent during the Orange Revolution, Viktor Yanukovych. Once in power, Yanukovych restored the pre-Orange constitutional order, consolidating presidential controls over the parliament, cabinet, and the judiciary. His policies favored the pro-Moscow branch of the Ukrainian Orthodox Church and upgraded the status of the Russian language (Haran 2011). During his three-year rule, Western monitors issued repeated warnings that Ukraine was "backsliding into soft authoritarianism" (Haran 2011) because of continued use of torture, police brutality, jailing of Yuliya Timoshenko, restrictions of citizens' expression and assembly, and other human rights abuses (Amnesty International 2010; Human Rights House Foundation 2014).

When Viktor Yanukovych, pressured by the Russian leader Vladimir Putin via impending restrictions on trade, backed out of the Association Agreement with the European Union in November 2013, thousands of Ukrainians took to the streets for a lengthy bout of protests known as Euromaidan. Within weeks, Euromaidan turned violent as protesters clashed with police in their demands for Yanukovich's resignation and accelerated European integration (Diuk 2014). According to David Marples, in the later stages of protests, "more attention was paid to the innate and grotesque corruption of the ruling regime, of the prevalence of oligarchs who had enriched themselves at the expense of the state, of the lack of legal reforms" (Marples and Mills 2014: 10–11). After months of encampment in Kiev's Independence Square, EU and U.S. sanctions against official Kiev, and hundreds of casualties, the protests ended on February 22 when Yanukovich fled to Russia and his government capitulated (Onuch 2014).

In the aftermath of Euromaidan, Ukraine faced a number of grave political and economic challenges. Following the deposition of Yanukovich's regime, the temporary government and the new president, Pavlo Poroshenko, were confronted with Russia's annexation of Crimea, a prolonged conflict with Russia-backed separatists in Ukraine's southeastern regions, and a de facto collapse of the country's economy under heavy debts to Russia and the IMF (Fishwick 2014; Myers and Barry 2014).

Such volatile political trajectory of the independent Ukraine contributed to the emergence of a two-tiered higher educational market in two distinct ways. First, it gave rise to a fragmented cultural landscape that accommodates both corruption-favorable and corruption-unfavorable institutional logics. As a result of ongoing oscillation between the pro-Russian and pro-Western governance models, Ukraine's normative landscape absorbed different ways of thinking and acting in regard to corruption. Second, this nonlinear political development created opportunities and generated pressures for individual organizations to adopt institutional logics that are either conducive or adverse to bureaucratic corruption. Specifically, contradictory legislative developments and flawed policy implementation in post-Soviet Ukraine created openings for the strategic alignment of some HEEs and the locking of others in either corrupt or non-corrupt educational markets.

CULTURAL MULTIPLICITY IN PRESENT-DAY UKRAINE

As a particularly volatile hybrid regime with high leadership turnover and a nonlinear developmental trajectory, Ukraine combines institutional and cultural characteristics that are usually associated with different governance systems. The country's political inconsistency over the past two decades gave rise to a normative landscape that accommodates democratic mores alongside ways of thinking that are common in authoritarian societies. Scholars describe this normative landscape as "ambivalent" (Riabchuk 2007: 70–89) and characterized by a "divided mentality".[6]

[6] Some scholars attribute the multiplicity of popular views on politics and economics to ethnic differences among Ukrainians. For instance, Dowlety and Silver (2002) argue that the Russian minority exhibits weaker support for democratic values than ethnic Ukrainians, while Khmelko and Wilson (1998) maintain that the latter are more supportive of economic liberalization than

For instance, the 2011 World Values Survey reveals that 71.3 percent of Ukrainians believe that "*having a strong leader who does not have to bother with parliament and elections*" is either a "*very good way*" or a "*fairly good way*" of governing the country. At the same time, 85.3 percent of respondents indicate that "*having a democratic political system*" is either "*very good*" or "*fairly good*" for the country (World Values Survey 2014). In the words of James Gibson, the prodemocratic beliefs of ordinary Ukrainians are "a mile wide but an inch deep" because they coexist with diametrically opposed convictions (1996).

The coexistence of favorable and unfavorable opinions about corruption among ordinary Ukrainians is one manifestation of this cultural multiplicity. According to research by Kiev International Institute of Sociology (2011), 59 percent of Ukrainians consider corruption justifiable if it helps them resolve personal problems, while 41 percent see it as unacceptable. Miller and his colleagues found that Ukrainians' views regarding the effects of corruption on the well-being of their country were almost equally split: 58 percent of their respondents considered corruption unequivocally bad, while 48 percent indicated that they preferred a system in which officials "sometimes accepted presents and in return did favors for people" (2001: 138–39). This nearly equal divide between proponents and opponents of corruption holds in local universities. According to the Democratic Initiatives Fund 2011 survey of university students, only a third of respondents considered such corruption a crime, while another third saw it as an effective way of solving problems and one fifth simply viewed it as "an integral part of modern life" (Onischenko 2012).

Such ambivalence about corruption is not typical for mature democracies. Instead, their citizens exhibit a strong dominant way of thinking about informal economic relations as unacceptable (Lipset and Lenz 2000: 119–20). According to the World Values Survey, 92.1 percent of U.S. citizens and 93.3 percent of citizens of the Netherlands gave a negative answer to the question of whether it is ever justifiable to accept a bribe in the course of one's professional duties (World Values Survey 2014).

The proliferation of different ways of thinking about corruption in present-day Ukraine is both a consequence and a manifestation of its

the former. Yet, empirical evidence on this issue is mixed. Other studies reveal that both Eastern and Western Ukrainians combine pro- and anti-democratic, as well as neoliberal and socialist cultural schemas to similar degrees (Miller and Listhaug 1999).

volatile and disjointed polity (Barrington and Herron 2004; Kulyk 2011). Aside from Kuchma's two-term presidency, every presidential turnover since Ukraine's independence has reversed the country's political course. From nationalistically inclined Kravchuk to pro-Russian Kuchma to pro-Western Yuschenko and back to pro-Russian Yanukovich, every Ukrainian president altered the legislative framework in ways that were antithetical to the work of his predecessor. At the same time, none has stayed in office long enough or had sufficient resources and political authority to oversee a consistent implementation and stabilization of the new course. Erratic reforms, partial changes in laws, and selective reversals of previous legislative initiatives resulted in the incomplete transformation of the local institutional landscape. As a result, the old ways of thinking endured alongside new mores and partially altered cultural schemas.

One way to think about this cultural multiplicity is in terms that Ann Swidler put forth in her canonical 1986 piece. In Swidler's theoretical framework, culture is a toolkit of "habits, skills, and styles" from which "people can construct diverse lines of action" (Swidler 1986: 273). Swidler writes that this model of culture is particularly salient for "unsettled lives," in which "competing ways of organizing are developing and contending for dominance" (Swidler 1986: 278). Contemporary Ukraine offers a clear instance of an unsettled context. In such systems, individuals adopt different and sometimes contradictory cultural schema to create context-appropriate strategies of action. Consistent with Swidler's predictions, my interviewees exhibited varying ways of thinking about corruption, influenced by their immediate circles of interaction and the incentive structures within specific bureaucracies.

Swidler's framework focuses on individual action and does not address the fate of organizations in unsettled cultural systems. According to a consensus in the literature, however, organizations can adopt varied institutional logics in ways that resemble individuals' adoption of cultural schema. Defined as "macro-level belief systems that shape cognitions and influence decision-making processes in organizational fields" (McPherson and Sauder 2013: 167; Friedland and Alford 1991; Thornton and Ocasio 1999), institutional logics link cultural mores to concrete tasks and processes in bureaucratic contexts. My data reveal that local universities function according to either corruption-favorable or corruption-unfavorable institutional logics. Chapter 2, for instance, discussed various facilitative bribery mechanisms that emerge in corruption-favorable HEEs. Such bureaucracies also implement selection mechanisms that favor actors predisposed to corruption and institutionalize organizational roles in which members take on corruption-related duties alongside their other professional responsibilities. Low-corruption universities, by contrast, develop organizational cultures and structures that impede informal exchanges.

Could organizations, then, maneuver between different institutional logics in the course of their everyday operation just as individuals navigate the fragmented normative landscape? There are theoretical reasons to suspect that such fluctuation is impossible. In contrast to individuals, organizations are subject to constraints that inhibit quick shifts from one institutional logic to another. Most importantly, structural dimensions of such logics (i.e., tasks and processes) require time to develop and take root within the organizations (Hannan and Freeman 1984). Once they develop, however, they tend toward continuity: organizational scholars contend that informal institutions embedded in organizations exhibit high resistance to change and "tenacious survivability" (Lauth 2000: 731). As the livelihoods of university employees become dependent on supplemental income from bribery and new instructors are recruited through nepotistic channels, universities develop reputations for being corrupt, bribery-facilitative mechanisms become non-reliant on specific individuals for survival, and university communities get "locked into" corruption-favorable institutional logics.

In other words, as a result of pressures for continuity in organizations, the heterogeneity of Ukraine's cultural landscape plays out differently for individuals than it does for organizations. While individuals appropriate dissimilar and often contradictory schemas in the course of their everyday lives, organizations tend to align with one specific kind of corruption logic. As a result, the field of higher education in present-day Ukraine is effectively split into bureaucracies with corruption-favorable and corruption-unfavorable organizational cultures. Each of these largely noncompetitive educational markets, then, hosts organizations of different levels of prestige.

OPPORTUNITIES AND PRESSURES FOR ORGANIZATIONAL ALIGNMENT

In addition to giving rise to a motley cultural landscape, Ukraine's high political turnover generated structural pressures and opportunities for organizational alignment with either high-corruption or low-corruption educational markets. Directly, each new presidential administration has legislated (and, more rarely, implemented) changes in postsecondary curricula, instructional processes, and accreditation requirements. Indirectly, constant shifts in political leadership affected the labor market prospects of university alumni, the spread of new instructional models, the economic well-being of instructors, and a gamut of other contextual factors. As organizational scholars would predict, universities adjusted to these transformations in different ways, depending on their organizational strategy, institutional history, isomorphic pressures, and resource availability (DiMaggio and Powell 2012; Oliver 1991; Peng 2003). In the following sections, I discuss several mechanisms whereby high turnover of political leadership in post-Soviet Ukraine affected HEEs' alignment with one of the two educational markets.

Inconsistent and Poorly Executed Reforms

Most directly, high turnover of political leadership impacted the institutional logics of local HEEs through disruptions and inconsistencies in educational reforms. Katherine Wanner (2010), Olena Fimyar (2010), and other students of independent Ukraine argue that its policy landscape fully reflects the ambivalence and inherent contradictions of post-socialism. Fimyar writes, "Ukrainian political and policy discourses present a bricolage of ideas, concepts, and strategies that draw on opposing sets of values (traditional and postmodern) and contrasting approaches to government (communist and neoliberal)" (2010: 65). Sundakov (2001) adds that local reform efforts suffer from the lack of coordination between different branches of the government, duplication of responsibilities, and insufficient feedback mechanisms. According to Fimyar, in post-Soviet Ukraine, "educational policy-making, as well as political decision-making in general, has been marked to date by persistent legacies of the previous regime, on the one hand, and extensive external advice, on the other" (2010: 67).

The state's oscillation between different courses of political development greatly undermined the consistency and effectiveness of its educational policies. Lacking resources and political will, government-mandated changes in higher education have been non-systematic, poorly orchestrated, and often inappropriate for local contexts. Most are neither pilot-tested prior to the implementation nor systematically evaluated after (Fimyar 2010; Krawchenko 1997). In their ambiguity, partiality, and oversight deficiency, such reforms create multiple opportunities for economic activity in the shadow of law and administrative regulations (Pavlenko 2012).

Ukraine's ratification of the Bologna Accords (popularly known as Bolognazation) in 2005 offers a telling illustration of how nonsystematic reforms amid the general institutional disintegration may create opportunities for bureaucratic corruption. The goal of the Bologna agreements is to uphold a set of shared standards and encourage educational exchanges in the European Higher Educational Area (EHEA). Bolognazation entails the adoption of standard temporal and topical modules in higher educational curricula, the implementation of common evaluation procedures, and a transition to a two-stage accreditation system consisting of bachelor's and master's degrees (instead of five-year specialist degrees) (Kovtun and Stick 2009).

One of my interviewees suggested that the Bologna reforms are emblematic of institutional change in post-Soviet Ukraine in general: "Bolognazation is an all-too-familiar process of destroying old principles, in the course of which those who are particularly 'flexible' will procure some bounty for themselves . . ., while the waters are murky" [UPr15]. Enthusiastically initiated in the late nineties, Bolognazation decreased in priority as Ukraine plunged into a period of unrest and instability under President Kuchma. Predictably, the Orange Revolution and the economic recession that followed were not conducive to the revival of government's focus (and ability to spend money) on education. Without institutional capacity and political will, Bolognazation has suffered from inconsistency, resource deficiency, and poor oversight (Shaw 2013).

Thus, at the time of my fieldwork, many Ukrainian HEEs continued to issue Soviet-style specialist diplomas either instead of or alongside the Bologna-mandated bachelor's and master's degrees (Kremen, Nikolajenko, and Stepko 2006: 29, Parusinski 2010: 5). My interviews also revealed that the lack of clear, systematic, and realistic guidelines led to the uneven incorporation of Bologna modules across different institutions. While some instructors did invest time and effort in figuring out how modules are meant to function [i.e., UPr7, UPr13, and UPr20], most adhered to the module system to the best of their understanding, often modifying and combining it with previous grading systems. Fearful of losing their authority, others purposefully subverted the Bologna reforms, running the old curricula and assessment practices parallel to the ones mandated by the agreement. One of my respondents noted that the resulting instructional system had "at least three parts to it. Part one is inherited from Soviet times and has remained unchanged; part two is whatever each VUZ [HEE, in English] took from Bologna . . .; and part three is total randomness" [UPr4]. This potpourri of institutional practices, varying within and across organizations, further complicated oversight and decreased the risks of detection for different parties to informal transactions.

I had a chance to observe exactly how Bolognazation created opportunities for bribery and nepotism at one prestigious Kiev institute. My fieldwork coincided with the first year that specialist degrees were officially abolished and BA recipients had to enroll into the master's program on a competitive basis. The guidelines from the Ministry of Education stated that enrollment decisions should reflect students' past academic and extracurricular performance as well as their admission exam scores. However, the ministry issued no specific instructions on how to compile these past performance rankings or how to combine them with students' exam scores. In the absence of guidance from the state, the dean devised an evaluation strategy that involved a series of one-on-one interviews with students, on the basis of which he personally ranked students' academic and extracurricular records. Department chairs then combined the dean's rankings with exam scores in ways that they considered appropriate for their specific disciplines. One instructor, concerned with the transparency of the dean's solution, confided in me, "Nobody knew where he [the dean] got this or that number to evaluate a student . . . it's not clear whether he used a mean grade for everything or whether it was weighted based on the importance of a subject for the focus of the student's planned master's studies, or whether last years' grades were more important" [UPr1].

Many respondents suspected that the institute's administration benefited significantly from this poorly coordinated transition to the two-stage accreditation model. Some, for instance, suggested that their department chairs picked grading schemes that favored less-qualified students (e.g., by lowering the weight of exam grades vis-à-vis the dean's rankings), whereas others insinuated that the dean reaped the biggest informal rewards by accepting "gratitude" payments from multiple students. Whether or not such accusations were accurate, the institute's employees had abundant opportunities to accept bribes and favors in exchange for unauthorized assistance with enrollment into the MA program. At the same time, students had plenty of reasons to offer informal incentives, since their ability to receive a postgraduate education hinged on the arbitrary choices of few university employees. Thus, the lack of clarity and transparency in the implementation of the Bologna regulations gave rise to ample opportunities and incentives for horizontal corruption in local universities.

Additionally, because of the changes in the national government, many educational reforms underwent either partial or complete reversal. Language politics in higher education offers an illustrative example of how a "turnaround" in the official position of the government gave rise to opportunities for corruption. In Ukraine, a linguistic divide is one of the few tangible distinctions between pro-Russian citizens in southern and eastern regions and pro-European citizens in the west (Bever 2010; Fournier 2002; Kulyk 2011). As a result, the nation's politicians have bitterly contested the status of the Russian and Ukrainian languages since Ukraine gained independence in 1991. As the country's leadership changed every several years, so did the language policy of the official Kiev.

Ukrainiazation was a top priority for Leonid Kravchuk, who identified the educational sector as "the key domain to reinvigorate the Ukrainian language and culture" (Kuzio 2002: 533). For Ukraine's first president, the tasks of nation building and reforming education went hand in hand. His "State National Programme 'Education'" required all HEEs to transition to instruction and record keeping in Ukrainian (Janmaat 2000). However, the brevity of Kravchuk's presidency and the dismal economic situation in the country made any systematic effort at enforcing this provision impossible. For the next decade, the policy endured on the books but had only a faint impact on the ground.

Even though Kravchuk's successor, Leonid Kuchma, was a staunch Russophile, he was apprehensive of instigating secessionist tendencies in the regions by repealing the so-called Ukrainiazation clause. At the same time, his administration informally undermined Kravchuk's language mandate as the Ministry of Education dedicated no resources to the replacement of Russian textbooks and offered no guidance to university staff on how to manage the transition (Bilaniuk and Melnyk 2008). As a result, both languages continued to be used in local HEEs throughout the nineties.[7]

[7] In 1997–1998, only 57 percent of students in state universities, 38.6 percent of students in polytechnic universities, 24.9 percent in mining-metallurgical institutes, and 61.9 percent of those in economic-commercial institutes received instruction in Ukrainian (Janmaat and Piattoeva 2007).

Kuchma's second term in office marked the rise of yet another educational policy objective: internationalization, spurred by the ratification of the European Convention on Human Rights, the Council of Europe's Framework Convention for the Protection of National Minorities, the European Charter for Regional and Minority Languages, and other international agreements protecting the linguistic rights of national minorities (Varfolomeyev 2003). While Ukrainian remained the sole official language, as specified by the Constitution, these treaties opened an avenue for legal contestations of minority language use in education, which have since happened in Donetsk, Luhansk, Kharkiv, and other Ukrainian cities (Besters-Dilger 2009; Bilaniuk and Melnyk 2008). Even though Yanukovich did not make good on his campaign promise to grant Russian official status, the use of Ukrainian in education further declined during his presidency (Moser 2013).

Like the partial and uncoordinated Bologniazation efforts, Ukraine's inconsistent language policy in higher education generated ambiguity and, consequently, abundant opportunities for informal economic activity in local universities. For instance, the lack of clarity on whether exclusive use of Ukrainian was a legal requirement allowed university employees to maximize their discretion and reap significant informal rewards. For instance, some interviewees suggested that their superiors had selectively used job candidates' ability to teach in Ukrainian to weed out qualified job candidates in favor of their protégés. Other HEE administrators were able to strategically maintain and nurture ambiguity stemming from an unstable policy landscape to maximize corruption opportunities. Legal vagueness allowed them to apply different standards to different students and employees and selectively invoke policy provisions to collect bribes and promote their nepotistic interests.

Persistent Centralization of Higher Education

Since Ukraine's higher educational reforms have been spotty and incomplete, many structural characteristics of local universities endured in their Soviet form. One of the major signs of the tertiary system's incomplete break from the past is its persistent centralization (Sundakov 2001). Although progressive reformers have long emphasized the importance of guaranteeing academic freedoms through university autonomy (Altbach 2001; Osipian 2008a), Ukraine's system of university governance remains thoroughly and rigidly centralized.

In the early years of independence, Kravchuk's administration emphasized decentralization as an important policy objective. His State National Programme 'Education' "called for . . . a radical restructuring of [educational] administration . . . through democratization, decentralization, and the institution of a regional system of educational authorities" (Janmaat and Piattoeva 2007: 7). Yet, few changes were actually implemented during his short presidency. As Kravhcuk's successor, Leonid Kuchma, struggled with the growing separatist sentiment in the regions, he sought to reconsolidate power in the hands of the central government. To that end, the temporarily weakened authority of the Ministry of Education was restored in the late nineties (Kremen, Nikolajenko, and Stepko 2006: 17). Janmaat writes that "recentralization . . . manifested itself in the 1996 Education Act. This law established the State Standards of Education, requirements as to the content, level and volume of education that were mandatory for both state and private schools " (Janmaat 2000: 535).

According to Ukraine's 1996 Education Act, the Ministry of Education and Science of Ukraine "approves the statutory documents of all higher education institutions, appoints rectors of State-owned higher education institutions subordinated directly to the Ministry and approves the appointment of rectors of other HEEs" (Kremen, Nikolajenko, and Stepko 2006: 38–39). The Ministry's approval is also required to change the curriculum, adopt operating budgets, and even use new classroom materials (Fond Effectivnoe Upravlenie 2015). In cooperation with the cabinet, the ministry also appoints each university's supervisory board, which "oversees the future development of [the] institution, assists the administration in implementing State policy, controls the institutional administration, and ensures efficient interaction with State governance bodies, the academic community, public, political, and commercial stakeholders" (Kremen, Nikolajenko, and Stepko 2006: 38–39).

The Ministry of Education's monopolistic authority creates both opportunities and incentives for educational institutions to preserve or adopt corruption-favorable institutional logics (Sovsun 2013). Persistent centralization allows the old guard of bureaucrats, accustomed to receiving informal payments, to continue abusing their professional privileges. As documented by Soviet historians (and discussed in previous chapters), most bureaucratic corruption under socialism entailed in-kind, delayed reciprocity exchanges, commonly known as *blat* (Grossman 1977; Lonkila 1997). *Blat* thrived on bureaucratic centralization, which created multiple points of contact between organizational gatekeepers and their clients and, therefore, many opportunities for bureaucrats to accept under-the-table compensation for their services. At the same time, the diffusion of responsibility and structural secrecy that characterize extensive chains of command made bureaucratic wrongdoings difficult to detect and punish (Ledeneva 1998; Vaughan 1998). Finally, the lack of market pressures and absence of political will to enforce transparency contributed to the spread of informal economic relations throughout centralized Soviet bureaucracies (Ledeneva 1998, 2008; Rehn and Taalas 2004).

Enduring centralization of higher education resulted in the retention of organizational structures that have long facilitated corruption. In the absence of cohesive reforms, many instructors and administrators, accustomed to *blat* under Soviet rule, were able to continue their informal economic activity after the fall of socialism. As the country's formal economy liberalized, the primary change in the corruption economies of HEEs related not to the amount or frequency of informal exchanges but to their medium. Since goods and services were no longer scarce, immediate monetary transactions, or bribes, replaced the in-kind and delayed reciprocity of *blat* (Humphrey 2000; Lonkila 1997).

Furthermore, in the context of political and economic instability, excessive centralization allowed some formerly non-corrupt HEEs to adopt corruption-favorable institutional logics. Over the past twenty-five years, Ukraine's educational sector has suffered from dire underfunding. According to Pleskovic, in the early 2000s, governmental spending on education amounted to "about one-third of its real level" a decade prior (Pleskovic 2002: 19). Such substantial deficit "has brought educational establishments a considerable number of students, pedagogical, and research staff to the brink of impoverishment" (Fimyar 2010: 89). Since Ukraine's government places heavy demands on local HEEs but does not provide the means to meet these demands, corruption emerges as a justified necessity for many Ukrainian administrators, instructors, and students. Some professors, such as Vera Nikolaevna, argue that informal payments actually help teaching personnel do their job right: "We are required to spend so much time in the classroom, but what we get for it is laughable. Maybe for somebody, a bribe makes a difference between really giving students an education and hurrying off to another job to make ends meet" [UPr18]. Another instructor, Grigoriy Yurievich, who teaches Russian literature, told me,

"I know that in some ВУЗ [VUZ], they are in a very bad situation, particularly in the regions, where they have to use students' money to finance not only textbooks [as required by the Ministry] but also things like heat and electricity in their buildings" [UPr19]. Such accounts suggest that some institutions of higher learning adopt corruption-favorable logics simply to stay afloat, maintain willing staff, and comply with governmental requirements.

Growth of Unregulated Private Markets

In Ukraine, high political turnover generated a pernicious combination of rapid institutional change and insufficient capacity for oversight and regulation in higher education. Arguably the most fundamental transformation of the sector – denationalization – happened in what largely amounted to a regulatory vacuum. An outcome of such chaotic institutional change was the rise of an entire subset of higher education institutions dedicated primarily to generating either formal, informal, or both types of profits.

The late Soviet-era and the early years of independence saw the emergence of new markets in multiple social spheres that had previously been fully controlled by the government. As the state regulation of social life weakened and the economy liberalized, private enterprises began capitalizing on the existing gaps in the supply of consumer goods and services. The field of higher education was quick to commercialize. The demand for postsecondary degrees, which had always been strong in the western parts of the Soviet Union, skyrocketed as former republics gained independence. For many Ukrainians, university diplomas offered an important marker of status in addition to and often regardless of their economic value. In the context of political instability and economic free-for-all, they also gave citizens some control over their rapidly changing circumstances (Astakhova 1997; Roberts et al. 2000).

The rollback of the state, along with the growing demand for postsecondary diplomas, created a fertile ground for the expansion of the educational sector. The number of Ukrainian HEEs steeply increased in the span of only two decades. Alongside old public institutes and universities, new private and semipublic academies, regional branches of large universities, technical colleges, and other higher educational institutions of all levels of accreditation opened their doors to students throughout the country. By the end of the nineties, the number of private, non-state-owned institutions at the highest accreditation level serving Ukraine's population of 46 million exceeded 150 (Gleason 2001). This number more than doubled over the following several years, rising to 351 by 2008. Compared to other European countries (such as Spain, which has 30 HEEs for a population of 47 million, and France, which has 78 HEEs serving a population of 49 million), Ukraine's higher education market is oversaturated with providers. In fact, Ministry of Education statistics show that in 2009 the number of positions opened for first-year admission actually exceeded the number of high school graduates (Yavorskaya 2009).[8]

In his analysis of Ukraine's denationalization reforms, Robert Reisz contends that "no coherent policies for private education existed ... and when these policies were designed, they had to regulate a sector that was largely unknown" (2013: 17). As a result of high political turnover, the Ukrainian state has struggled with oversight, regulation, and quality assessment in the rapidly expanding education market (Fimyar 2010: 78). Ukraine does not take part in international educational monitoring initiatives; local HEEs are evaluated on quantity rather than quality of their output; and incentives for improving instruction are largely nonexistent (Fond Effectivnoe Upravlenie 2015).

The chaotic changes in the ownership structures of higher education allowed for the institutionalization of corruption-favorable logics in many new HEEs. According to local experts and media reports, in many cases, the founders and investors strategically set out to make short-term profits by selling diplomas in trendy subjects, such as economics, law, psychology, and international relations (interview with Natalia Shulga [Nov. 11, 2009]; Reisz 2013; Segodnya.ua 2015). Many private HEEs have few admissions requirements and enroll most applicants willing to pay for their studies. Many of these institutions meet accreditation standards by hiring only a few professors with postgraduate degrees (while staffing most classrooms with lower-cost and underqualified instructors) and providing their students with the minimal resources required to maintain Ministry accreditation (Chekina 2012; Vgorodc.ua 2013).

8 Moreover, between 1995 and 2000, admissions to full-time postsecondary programs also grew by 46 percent, while the number of graduate students more than doubled from 13,374 in 1990 to 33,344 in 2008 (Kremen, Nikolajenko, and Stepko 2006: 40). As a result, by 2011, about 6.6 million employed Ukrainians (approximately one-third of the entire labor force) were overqualified for their positions (Tkachenko 2012).

One of the Ministry officials I interviewed did not conceal his indignation at the low quality of these institution: "There is just a bunch of so-called institutes out there ... They buy out a school building, move into one of the floors or, better, half a floor, and then get some students, who, by the way, pay insane money to study there, buy a license ... and call themselves an institute or, even better, a university!" [Feb. 5, 2010]. Although many interviewed instructors and administrators shared this sentiment, student respondents were often content to attend institutions that posed few hurdles on their way to a degree. Many of these students were working, taking care of family, or otherwise unable to dedicate time and effort to studying.

The stories of new private HEEs attest to another major way that political oscillation allowed some local bureaucracies in post-Soviet Ukraine to adopt corruption-favorable logics. In a 2010 meeting with leaders of private HEEs, then–Minister of Education Dmitriy Tabachnyk expressed concern that the primary purpose of these institutions was to "make money and print diplomas" (Petrosyan 2010). The normalization of what one of my respondents called the "money-for-grades culture" in these new HEEs served to accommodate corruption-favorable institutional logics on their premises [UPr1; UPr11; UPr16].

Moreover, studies show that such HEEs are often "resistant to even a hint of transparency and have little concern for academic integrity" (Stetar, Panych, and Cheng 2015: 14–15). Preoccupied primarily with maintaining enrollments, their administrations rarely control or regulate corruption. Consider the following account by a low-level administrator at a public institute:

> In the small town of Cherkassi they now have three departments preparing graphic designers! ... From what I gathered, these departments exist and prosper because the specialty is prestigious and students are ready to pay ... This is business, pure business! Everything goes there. They never expel anyone. If a student is failing then they simply pay a little more under the table. This is just how these institutions operate. No one cracks down on bribes. They are just regular payments there. [UPr21]

Another respondent, Nikita Evegnievich, who teaches English and French, corroborated:

> They [private HEEs] are a joke. Something that anyone with a little bit of money and enough connections in the Ministry of Education can set

up overnight. Hire a couple professors for one-tenth or one-sixteenth of their time and fill other teaching positions with starving graduate students, get some ads going, and voila, you got yourself a university! Some of them reach unbelievable levels of absurdity ... Like, I hear that in X [the name of a popular private institute], the admissions committee functions at all hours of the day. So you can go and enroll any time you want – for instance, on the way home from a bar on Saturday night. Pure business and ingenuity!" [UPr1]

Yet, not all private HEEs adopted corruption-favorable institutional logics. The openings in the regulatory landscape also allowed for a different type of new entrants: those whose very mission was to steer clear of university corruption. Kyiv-Mohyla Academy, located in Kiev's trendy Podol area, is an example of an institution that has taken advantage of relaxed ownership regulations to capitalize on the emergent demand from select employers (primarily international, but also some local) for qualified young specialists. The recent history of this notoriously non-corrupt and highly prestigious university illustrates the role of organizational strategy in navigating the fragmented cultural landscape of a hybrid political regime.

The academy revives the legacy of Ukraine's oldest university, which closed under political pressure from Russia in the early eighteenth century. It reopened in 1991 with support from local intellectuals and liberal activists, Ukrainian diaspora abroad, and foreign donors. Its original mission was to combine teaching and research and participate in international scientific and educational initiatives. All students and instructors from Kyiv-Mohyla Academy that I encountered during my research emphasized that it stood out among other local HEEs because of its strong anti-corruption culture. According to Sergey Kvit, the academy's president at the time of my research, its administration made a concerted effort to prioritize transparency (Ibnlive 2015; Politica-ua. 2014).

My respondents also suggested that for those who work and study at the academy, institutional incentives discourage corruption: instructors are well paid and respected, while students aspire for jobs in which bribes and connections are not critical. Thus, one of the academy's professors told me in an interview: "Even our part-timers who might be involved in some shady things wherever else they work wouldn't do it here. It's just not that kind of atmosphere ... it is a nice job, it would not make sense for them to risk it" [UPr23]. Maksim, a sophomore in software engineering at the academy, provided a student's perspective:

"It would be stupid for me to give bribes. It was difficult to get in, and . . . I want to benefit from what the place has to offer. If I try my best, I know I'll do pretty well in terms of a job" [USt1].

Kyiv School of Economics (KSE) is another HEE that has, through strategic choices of donors, administration, and faculty, adopted non-corrupt institutional logics. According to its official mission statement, KSE prepares students for foreign PhD programs and employment in international financial companies. With the sponsorship of Global Development Network and the government of Sweden, KSE pursues the broad goal of fostering the economic development of Ukraine and the entire region. The school is in partnership with the University of Texas and several European educational institutions, and all of its instructors hold Western PhDs (Kiev School of Economics 2015). By creating instrumental incentives that reward rule following and an organizational culture that discourages corruption, its leaders have situated KSE squarely within the non-corrupt higher educational sub-field. Leonid, an associate professor of economics at KSE, elaborated:

> We're very much into promoting academic honesty here . . . cheating and corruption are so pervasive, it is more of a default . . . People are proud to cheat the system. It's a skill that is worked on, that is developed. Ingenuity in it is endless too. People really perfect themselves in fraud against the system – the academic system included. And part of making a Western-style university is trying to prevent it. That's why we put real effort into this here – that's part of our educational mission. [UPr24]

BARRIERS TO ALIGNMENT WITH (NON) CORRUPT INSTITUTIONAL LOGICS

While previous discussion focused on structural openings for the organizational adoption of either corruption-favorable or corruption-unfavorable institutional logics, not all Ukrainian higher education establishments have an opportunity to align with either one or the other. Instead, institutional history, specialization, and organizational resources limit some HEEs' ability to adopt different corruption-related logics.

Hofstede writes, "as soon as an organization has a history, the options for organizational behavior thereafter are constrained by it" (Hofstede 1980: 27). As a result of their organizational pasts and current structural characteristics, some educational establishments encountered obstacles to moving out of or into the corrupt subsector of higher education, even when opportunities arose during the post-Soviet era. Presence of these constraints is another reason why some institutions have high levels of corruption, while others are relatively transparent.

Since informal transmission of untested assumptions plays an important role in perpetuating educational corruption, many constraints on organizational change are cultural. Among these, particularly apparent are the lingering effects of organizational reputations. Since universities' reputations carry corruption-related assumptions beyond organizational boundaries to the general public, they create continuity in local informal economies. Thus, Chapter 2 revealed that if students and parents believe that informal compensations are common in a particular department, they seek admissions only if they are able and willing to partake in corruption.

An important feature of organizational reputations is their longevity. As stories get passed from actor to actor, organizational reputations acquire a life of their own and lose strong connection to organizational realities. As a result, when organizations evolve, their reputations do not immediately reflect structural changes. When it comes to corruption, such inertia of organizational reputations has a strong independent effect on organizations. Universities that try to eradicate corruption are often set back by their reputations. Because of persistent "corrupt" reputations of some HEEs, their students continue to assume that without informal compensations they will fail classes or not earn the grades they want. With a continuous inflow of informal offers, instructors and administrators of such HEEs may be unable to resist informal economic activity. Organizational reputations, therefore, are potent agents of path dependence in regard to corruption.

Telling examples of these dynamics come from the international relations, law, and political science departments at large state universities. Under the Soviet Union, these specialties were highly coveted because of their political cache and exclusivity: they provided access to alternative markets for consumer goods and unique travel opportunities. As a result, *blat* was the only feasible way to enter institutions that offered degrees in these specialties in major Soviet cities (Ledeneva 1998; Osipian 2008b). According to my respondents and media reports, several decades later, such departments and HEEs remain the most prestigious and the most corrupt in the country (Korrepondent.net 2015b). Although the rewards they provide to their graduates no longer carry the same instrumental value as they did under socialism, their organizational reputations impede the eradication of corruption-favorable institutional logics. In these HEEs, low turnover of cadres and institutionalization of corruption mechanisms reinforce the effects of reputational continuity.

The constraints that prevent HEEs from aligning with non-corrupt institutional logics may also be structural. The stories of Kyiv-Mohyla Academy and Kiev School of Economics are in many ways atypical because both institutions enjoy significant resources and support from high-status donors and political actors. In contrast, many progressive educators who would like to establish non-corrupt HEEs, as well as the administrators of many existing universities who want to shed their corrupt past, simply do not have the necessary political clout to overcome the pressures for corruption emanating from other institutional players, such as the Ministry of Education or the National Tax Administration. Many university administrators I interviewed insisted that it was practically impossible to obtain first-time accreditation from the Ministry without any under-the-table offerings. This initial corrupt transaction is, in all likelihood, followed by a number of others that are inevitable (or perceived as such) for the creation of a functional institution. From the very outset, therefore, new institutions without sufficient social capital are likely to compromise their alignment with non-corrupt institutional logics.

At the same time, some structural constraints may also prevent non-corrupt institutions from embracing informal economies even if their administrations and instructors are eager to engage in corruption. The first barrier to entering the corrupt subsector is related to low demand for diplomas in select majors and specializations. For instance, while Kiev State University's Faculty of International Relations has a competitive admissions process with five or more contenders for every student spot, its Faculty of Ukrainian Language and Literature only receives one application per position (Goncharuk 2013; Kadrovik.ua 2015). To maintain enrollments, organizations with noncompetitive admissions are often also reluctant to expel underperforming students. As a result, their employees have little leverage to demand bribes, and their students have few incentives to pay for services they can easily get for free.

Survey data on educational corruption attest to these dynamics. According to the study by the Democratic Initiatives Fund, humanities and social science students are significantly less likely to be involved in university bribery and nepotism (25.4 percent of respondents reported having personal experience with corruption) than future lawyers, for instance (39 percent of whom were personally involved in university bribery or nepotism) (Onischenko 2012). Local experts also argue that "the level of corruption and price of a diploma depend on professional specialization – its popularity among the youth and the job market demand," suggesting that degrees in economics and law rank among the most desirable and corrupt, while degrees in the humanities and natural sciences rank significantly lower on both counts (Chuhlib 2011; Euroua.com 2014; Goncharuk 2013). Oleg Sergeevich, an instructor in a department of geo-construction and mining technologies that has been struggling to maintain enrollments, explained why there is no corruption in his HEE: "We can hardly get enough students to stay in business. Do you really think people are standing outside our doors, begging to be let in? Every year the faculty numbers are reduced because the demand is going down. In this situation, how can we think about demanding extra payments? That would be the end of us" [UPr17].

In addition, some HEEs face a different barrier to adopting corruption-favorable institutional logics: the easy testability of their graduates' skills. Kiev Academy of Fine Arts is a telling example. Ukraine's most prestigious HEE for aspiring architects, painters, and designers, the academy is virtually free of bribery between students and their instructors. Although other types of informal transactions, such as private tutoring, nepotistic string pulling, and hereditary admissions do reportedly happen on a regular basis, their scale and impact are significantly lower than at many equally prestigious institutions. One of the primary reasons for this academy's institutional transparency is the visibility of deviations in the quality of students' work. Sonya, a third-year painting student, makes this argument: "You cannot pretend that you are a good artist if you are not. Our work here is very public. We paint in the same workshop, and we have exhibits. We spend nights and weekends at the Academy, working together ... There is no way someone who's not good could pass" [USt29].

Throughout my fieldwork in Ukraine, I heard similar explanations from students and instructors across different HEEs and departments, including those specializing in information technology, physics, engineering, dance, genetics, architecture, surgery, construction, and stomatology. For some, the skill-visibility constraint combined with low demand, while for others it decreased opportunities for corruption generated by high popularity among applicants.

CONCLUSION

Diane Vaughan writes that the roots of organizational deviance lie in the "nested and dynamic interrelationship between environment, organizational characteristics, cognition, and choice" (Vaughan 1999: 283). While earlier parts of this book focused on how micro-level cultural processes in organizations shape ordinary Ukrainians' involvement in university corruption, this chapter links such micro-processes to their organizational contexts and macro-level determinants. Ukraine is a hybrid regime, characterized by lower levels of state capture and higher turnover of political leadership than in many of its post-Soviet neighbors. In this chapter, I argue that such political inconsistency resulted in some universities developing corruption-conducive cultures while others adopted institutional logics that discourage corruption. First, Ukraine's cultural multiplicity allows for the coexistence of corruption-favorable and corruption-unfavorable ways of thinking, acting, and organizing. Second, high political turnover leads to inconsistent, partial, and poorly implemented reforms in higher education, which, in turn, create opportunities and barriers for organizational alignment with different institutional logics.

What about other organizational fields? Has high political turnover in post-transitional Ukraine also generated cross-organizational variation in bureaucratic sectors other than higher education? My data provide some preliminary answers to this question. During my interviews with university-affiliated Ukrainians, I also asked about their experiences with corruption in local hospitals and clinics. Respondents' stories, in fact, suggest that universities are not unique in their alignment with two distinct bureaucratic subfields: similar fragmentation also occurs in Ukrainian health care. Based on responses that I collected from thirty-seven adults (instructors and parents), I identified types of Kiev hospitals and clinics that have dissimilar corruption levels. Like higher education institutions, both high- and low-corruption hospitals include organizations of different prestige levels.

According to my data, in present-day Ukraine, there exist completely non-corrupt private medical practices that have fixed, nonnegotiable fees and accept medical insurance. These clinics are reputed to provide excellent care but are often too expensive for an average *киевлянин* (resident of Kiev, in English). Respondents often referenced Boris Medical Center, ISIDA, and American Medical Centers as examples of these high-quality, high-cost providers. The second set of non-corrupt health care institutions consists of public hospitals and clinics in rural regions or non-central parts of urban areas (*районные больницы*, in Russian). These institutions suffer from dire underfunding: their staff is overworked and underpaid, and the conditions of care that they provide are dismal. They primarily serve elderly and low-income Ukrainians, while well-to-do citizens usually turn to other providers.

Alongside the free, low-quality health care options are hospitals and clinics that have rampant corruption but generally do not offer more effective services. What their patients pay for under the table is comfort. While such organizations might provide results that are similar to those of non-corrupt free clinics, their patients' overall experience is significantly more pleasant because of their clean and updated facilities and attentive staff. Thirty-eight-year-old Nataliya explains:

> Actually, I don't know if they [these hospitals] are better . . . but at least you don't have to wait in line for hours or lie on dirty sheets. But from what I understand, it's the same doctors and nurses who work here. I guess they do have better equipment, so that's an improvement. Now, if it's worth the cognacs and whatever else people bring, I can't really tell you. [UPa5]

Finally, the organizational landscape of Ukrainian health care also includes corrupt high-quality providers – specialized clinics staffed with doctors who are acclaimed for their expertise in specific medical fields. Nikita Evgenievich, a forty-three-year-old language instructor, told me about the logistics of informal transactions in such institutions:

> Usually, when you have an issue that's more serious . . . you ask around . . . look for advice, and someone recommends a doctor to you. To get in to see him, you usually need more help . . . because of course they tell you they don't have any openings for months. And then, when you get to see them, you offer money. I guess as much as you think, and . . . it really depends on how serious your problem is and how much they are helping you. You also need to thank the person who helped you get in, but that depends on if they are a friend or relative, and it's more complicated. Money is generally not requested explicitly, but you still need to give it. It's like a tip in America. [UPr1]

Since hospitals were not the primary focus of my study, I did not collect other data to corroborate these interview accounts. In general, more research is needed to verify that cross-organizational variation in corruption also characterizes other bureaucratic fields in contemporary Ukraine. However, there are good reasons to hypothesize that it does. Given the heterogeneity of the Ukrainian cultural landscape, the absence of political pressures to adopt specific institutional logics, and the internal organizational drive for continuity, individual bureaucracies, likely, align with either corruption-favorable or corruption-unfavorable subsectors. Another reason for fragmentation of other organizational sectors has to do with the informal socialization of ordinary Ukrainians. What citizens learn about corruption in higher education, where many engage in their first-ever illicit exchanges, influences their behavior in other bureaucracies. Thus, a graduate of a corrupt university might be more likely to patronize corrupt hospitals and vice versa. In other words, informal socialization in local HEEs, likely, contributes to fragmentation of other organizational fields.

CHAPTER FIVE

LOW POLITICAL TURNOVER AND CROSS-SECTORAL VARIATION IN CORRUPTION IN POST-SOVIET BELARUS

As a nation, Belarusians do three things best: fear, tolerate, and adjust.
[BPr13]

My arrival in Minsk marked an unexpected shift in the trajectory of my research. Based on everything I had read and heard about bureaucratic corruption in former Soviet republics, I expected to find vibrant informal economies in Belarusian universities. After all, Transparency International rankings and dominant corruptological theories suggest that, just like Ukraine, Belarus has a "transitional political system" that generates pervasive corruption throughout its street-level bureaucracies (Abed and Davoodi 2000; Hellman 2000; Wallace and Latcheva 2006).

Yet, in contrast to my expectations, I discovered a transparent, rule-based, and relatively meritocratic system of higher education in present-day Belarus. Despite ubiquitous informal exchanges in Belarusian hospitals, passport tables, and secondary schools, Minsk universities are conspicuously free of petty bribery, exchanges of favors, unsanctioned gifts, and other horizontal transactions between students, professors, and administrators. Based on the different types of data I collected, vertical corruption – illicit favors performed by lower-level university officials at the request of their superiors – is the only type of bureaucratic corruption in Belarusian HEEs.

My early discovery of the horizontal transparency of local higher education set an intellectual agenda for my fieldwork in Minsk. I was determined to understand from a sociological perspective why ordinary Belarusians, who are accustomed to using connections, paying bribes, and giving presents in most bureaucratic organizations, set their corruption habits aside in colleges and universities. I began unraveling the puzzle of the uneven distribution of bureaucratic corruption across Belarusian organizational sectors with a clue from Aleksandr, a sixty-one-year-old professor of history at a large state university. Like other instructors I had interviewed, Aleksandr complained about lack of resources and stalled modernization in higher education, along with students' lack of interest in subjects that have low commercial value. But when we started talking about bribery, Aleksandr's comments revealed something I had not heard before: "It's not common at all – what you see is what you get . . . The time of cognacs, envelopes, and golden chains hidden in flowers is over. But I remember when students were buying TVs and vacuum cleaners for professors, when bouquets of flowers were . . . a way to give professors jewelry. It was not that long ago" [BPr7].

Aleksandr's suggestion that the lack of corruption in Belarusian universities was a relatively recent phenomenon surprised me. By then, I had spoken to multiple students and instructors who took higher educational transparency for granted. As I probed further, Aleksandr suggested that the transition to corruption-free higher education happened in the early 2000s in response to the changing patterns of governance over local universities:

> If I were to tell you a date . . . I would say probably sometime after the year 2000. There were several years there, around that time, when many changes were happening in education. Mostly stricter regulations and new protocols that changed . . . the ways instructors did their jobs. All of a sudden, multiple controls appeared . . . and you had to get permissions and explain yourself, even . . . umm . . . if you are just lecturing or doing what you'd always been doing. I would say all the presents and bribes started disappearing around that time too . . . But of course, this is simply my approximate . . . my impression. I am not really involved with the administration. [BPr7]

Many respondents I interviewed later corroborated Aleksandr's testimony. Nine professors, each of whom had been affiliated with universities for more than ten years, as well as seven parents who had encounters with the higher education sector during the nineties, either as students or as parents of students, all agreed that current absence of university corruption was a new development that dated back just over a decade. A number of online publications I discovered during my analysis of local press coverage also framed university corruption as a problem of the past that had been mostly conquered in recent years (e.g., Belta.by 2013; Ej.by: Ezhednevnik 2013). These articles discussed singular instances of corrupt exchanges and framed them as exceptions to the general rule of transparency and meritocracy in higher education. Many news stories adopted a tone of accomplishment, claiming that university corruption had been "eradicated" or "decreased substantially" (Belaruspartisan.org 2015a; Rogov 2012).

These data suggest that in the early 2000s, Belarusian universities underwent a series of major changes that resulted in the withering of their informal economies while other bureaucratic sectors continued to maintain high levels of horizontal corruption. To understand the nature and roots of this transformation, I traced the institutional history of Belarusian HEEs over the past several decades. My goal was to find out what happened in the early years of the new millennium that altered the way that students and professors related to one another, perceived the goals of the educational process, and interpreted the meaning of under-the-table transactions.

My investigation relied on interviews with Belarusians who had been affiliated with universities in the 1990s and early 2000s, as well as conversations with a number of political analysts and oppositional activists. I also examined governmental reports on higher education reforms carried out prior to 2005, which are publicly available online or in organizational archives. Based on these data, I identified three time periods characterized by changes in the formal and informal makeup of Belarusian universities: the period immediately following the breakdown of the Soviet Union (which I call the "Wild Nineties"); the period of change and transformation that lasted from the early to the mid-2000s; and the period of transparency, dating from around 2005 to 2010. During these three periods, Belarusian higher education was subject to different styles of governance by the state, which generated different preconditions for corruption in local universities.

POLITICIZATION OF BELARUSIAN UNIVERSITIES

Period I: The "Wild Nineties"

In contrast to neighboring Ukraine, the Republic of Belarus did not have an organized dissident movement or *nomenklatura* elites vying for liberalization in the later years of the Soviet era. In fact, most

Belarusians felt at best ambivalent about national independence after the failed August putsch of 1991. Some scholars argue that this absence of a strong pro-independence movement and weak popular support for national statehood during *perestroika* portended Aleksandr Lukashenka's ascent to an unchallenged, decades-long reign over post-Soviet Belarus (Eke and Kuzio 2000; Lenzi 2002).

The country's early movement toward a more liberal and open system of governance in the wake of the Soviet demise (i.e. surrender of nuclear weapons, joining in the Partnership for Peace, and cooperation with the European Union) came to a halt after the first presidential elections in 1994 (Allison, White, and Light 2005). President Lukashenka, a self-proclaimed "ordinary man," rose to power with the overwhelming support of the country's rural and aging population. A charismatic leader with "simple answers to complicated questions" (Davidonis 2001: 9), Lukashenka openly and unapologetically pursued authoritarian-style governance, relegating the prodemocratic oppositional forces to the ranks of "domestic enemies" (Manaev 1997: 270).

During his first term as Belarusian president, Lukahsenka paid surprisingly little attention to the country's higher education. Some analysts suggest that political importance of universities eluded the new president, who came from a farming background and underestimated the potential of intellectual elites to threaten his power (Feduta 2005).[1] Instead, during his early years in office, the new president focused on establishing a basic institutional framework for his dictatorship, implementing personal controls over the government, and suppressing political opposition via symbolic and institutional channels. In 1996, he dissolved the Parliament and amended the constitution, limiting parliamentary prerogatives, strengthening presidential grip on the judiciary, and extending his own first term in office. By 1997, all of Belarus's major political institutions, including a bicameral legislature, the Constitutional Court, and the Cabinet of Ministers, were staffed with officials whom the president had either directly chosen or indirectly approved (Eke and Kuzio 2000: 523–24). At this time, Lukashenka also began reversing economic denationalization and rekindling a close relationship with neighboring Russia (Marples 1999).

[1] Although Lukashenka holds two bachelor's degrees from Mogilev Pedagogical Institute and Belarusian Agricultural Academy, he spent his formative years in the military and in the administration of various collective farms. Reflecting his training and experience, the president's policies have consistently prioritized technical and agricultural know-how over liberal education in humanities and social sciences (Feduta 2005).

In his early days in office, the president embarked on a campaign to align the national identity of independent Belarus with his vision of the country's economic and political future. Lukashenka held an all-country referendum to legitimize a set of changes in Belarusian national symbols that reflected his plan for a renewed political alliance with Russia. Based on the results of this referendum, the president reestablished the national status of the Russian language, which had been briefly abolished in the aftermath of Belarusian independence (Feduta 2005). During this time, the central government also limited popular venues for free expression and instituted a number of mechanisms to discourage political dissent. For instance, the late nineties saw the closing of multiple independent news outlets and TV channels under increasing pressure from the authorities (including "Svaboda," "Naviny," "Day," "Pahohya," "Rabochy," and many others), while new registration and oversight requirements effectively eliminated Belarusians' ability to organize outside of the purview of the state (Sannikov 2003).

While the president focused on consolidating controls over core political institutions, he largely overlooked organizations that he believed played a secondary role in helping him retain his dictatorial power. Since, in Lukashenka's eyes, higher education establishments were a low priority, the government left Belarusian colleges and universities to their own devices. As a result of relaxed institutional oversight and fiscal neglect of the country's HEEs during the nineties, their administrations exercised substantial freedoms in hiring, budgetary allocations, curriculum development, and teaching methods (Ministry of Education of the Republic of Belarus 2015, interview with Vladimir Dunaev). Free from political pressure, Belarusian intellectual elites shed Soviet-era controls over the curriculum, teaching methods, and funding structures. Uninhibited by excessive regulation, universities grew; changed; and, most importantly, liberalized.

One of the major institutional changes in higher education had to do with the ownership and funding structures of organizational providers. During this period, new private colleges and institutes opened their doors to students in Minsk, Mahilyow, Brest, Vitebsk, and other Belarusian cities. By 1999, more than a dozen private higher education institutions in the capital alone enrolled their first cohorts of students (Belarus Miscellany 2014). In contrast to old public HEEs, these institutions operated on a tuition basis and appealed to students by offering new majors that better fit the demands of the changing economy. Their slogans promised an easy, if expensive, way to join the emergent class of middle managers through degrees in business administration, law, marketing, communications, and other subjects.

At this time, many public universities also introduced new courses in basic social sciences, such as sociology, economics, and political science, to replace the outdated and unpopular course offerings in the history of the Communist Party and Marxist-Leninist teachings. Despite the lack of resources, scarcity of qualified teaching personnel, and dearth of appropriate textbooks and other materials, the new social sciences curriculum marked a significant departure from Soviet-style instruction in nontechnical disciplines, which had been reduced, for all intents and purposes, to political propaganda, fear mongering, and promotion of Soviet ideology. Besides the introduction of new courses, instructional practices in established disciplines also modernized. The softening of restrictions on information flows, development of the Internet, and relaxed regulations on foreign travel facilitated the introduction of innovative teaching methods and educational materials across local universities (Graham 1993; Mitter 1992).

At this time, activist lawmakers also introduced a number of consequential legislative innovations. Most importantly, the Ministry of Education and the National Institute for Higher Education collaborated with the Council of Europe to update Belarus's "Law on Higher Education" with the goal of institutionalizing core academic freedoms. Under the Soviet model, the state mandated the form and content of university instruction and assessment. This new law, however, granted Belarusian HEEs the discretion to determine enrollment thresholds, define the curriculum, and set tuition schedules largely without governmental intervention (Kopissky 1996: 99–104). For the first time in history, Belarusian university administrators and faculty members could exercise substantial control over the educational process.

During this period, important legislative and executive steps were also made toward joining the Bologna Agreement, discussed in previous chapters. This pan-European educational standardization accord mandates the adoption of module-based instructional systems and two-level degree programs granting bachelor's and master's diplomas (European Commission 2015). In the late nineties, many Belarusian universities lay concrete groundwork for the transition to educational and accreditation practices prescribed by Bologna (Belarus Digest 2013; Belarus Project 2012). According to my interviews, some HEEs began experimenting with the module system, initiated research and training sessions to prepare staff, and started developing curricula for the two-level degree system.

During this period of change and innovation came significant growth in university corruption. Although there is practically no documentary or statistical evidence of HEEs' informal economies (particularly in the tumultuous years following independence, when the Internet was in its early stages of development), many interview accounts suggest that educational liberalization also triggered the transformation of university corruption systems. Specifically, in the context of little regulation, openness to new models of funding, and rapid changes in university governance, informal transactions between university employees and their clients monetized and spread through various levels of the education process. Bribery, unsanctioned favors, informal arrangements, and reliance on connections permeated admissions, evaluation, and credentialing processes throughout the country's HEEs. In their vibrancy, complexity, and dynamism, the informal economies of Belarusian universities in the nineties resembled the motley horizontal exchange systems currently flourishing in higher education in Kiev and other Ukrainian cities. Like contemporary Ukrainian universities, Belarusian HEEs were filled with bribery between students and instructors, nepotistic admission and retention practices, purchase of grades and diplomas, embezzlement of university funds and resources, bribery in organizational accreditation, and various other unsanctioned transactions.

Irina, a fifty-six-year-old doctor whose daughter attended one of Minsk HEEs between 1995 and 2000, described her experience:

> This time was . . . interesting [chuckles] . . . and it was very tough for us! The only way to get Vika [her daughter] in was through acquaintances . . . And then I would buy presents for her professors to help push her through. It is such a relief that it is different with Seryosha [her younger son, who was attending a university at the time of my fieldwork]. Now it's hard to even remember what a mess it was, but we lived it. And survived it. What I remember most . . . is that we could not count on anything and that everything was so confusing and unclear. We just had to pay and pull strings and hope that everything would work out. It was just that kind of time. [BPa1]

Rhaisa, a mother of two university alumnae, corroborated Irina's perceptions of unbridled gift giving and nepotism in universities during this time: "We just did all we possibly could, because we weren't able to count on our kids getting in and studying on their own. Every day there were some new rules, some new requirements. You never quite knew if your child was going to manage . . . but kids . . . they had to get a higher education somehow!" [BPa18].

From the perspective of university employees, rampant corruption in Belarusian universities resulted from meager funding, hasty and inconsistent reforms, and insufficient regulation and oversight. Dmitriy, a forty-eight-year-old chemistry instructor, explained: "In the nineties the salaries of my colleagues were dismal, but at least they were complementing them under the table. [These] 'bonuses' . . . kept their families from starvation. Now we just work for the straight salary, that's it" [BPr16].

Other faculty were not as understanding of their colleagues who benefited from corruption during this time. For instance, Faina Lvovna attributed high levels of informal economic activity to lowly profiteering by bureaucrats, eager to take advantage of this vulnerable period in the history of universities:

> Back then HEEs were in the period of transformation into more modern organizations, so we tried a lot of new things . . . and maybe sometimes we didn't quite get it right on the fist try, so there was, if I am completely honest, very little order. But overall it was a very positive time for our higher education, very positive . . . but of course, humans are like that . . . there always will be people who will take advantage of any situation, and this one was particularly easy to . . . use for own enrichment. And some people did, and got rich off common folk just trying to educate their children. [BPr15]

Period II: Lukashenka Discovers the Threat

The period of openness and experimentation in Belarusian higher education ended in the early 2000s when President Lukashenka first realized that his laissez-faire attitude to universities could be risky for the stability of his regime. Several events contributed to the president's growing awareness of political dangers emanating from university students and instructors.

By the end of the decade, Lukashenka's administration began to experience forceful electoral resistance from local university students. During the 2001 presidential elections, the number of Lukashenka supporters among young educated Belarusians was at an all-time low. While the official statement of the Belarusian Central Elections

Committee claimed that the president had received 40 percent of university students' votes, independent monitors estimate their real support level to have been as low as 5 percent (Barber 2013). Even though all presidential elections in Belarus since Lukashenka's ascent to power have been recognized by the international community as rigged, in few instances has the inflation of their results been as sizable as in the case of student voters (Marples 2006). In fact, the president openly lamented his loss of ground with young voters in his infamous inauguration speech in 2001. With obvious chagrin and thinly veiled menace, Lukashenka declared that despite support from many Belarusians, university students had not been loyal (Cole 2013).

Declining rates of electoral support for the autocratic president were indicative of the growing liberal sentiment among the country's youth. With new opportunities for foreign travel, an influx of information, and unprecedented academic freedom, more and more young Belarusians became aware of the dangers associated with Lukashenka's capture of power and grew attracted to the progressive alternatives to his isolationist and backward-looking regime. A major manifestation of their brewing disgruntlement were several grassroots groups that mobilized oppositional forces and raised awareness about the president's abuses of Belarusians' civil and human rights. Inspired by Ukraine's *Pora*, Georgia's *Kmara*, and the former Yugoslavia's *Otpor*!, these student-led movements grew and developed complex organizational structures throughout late 1990s and early 2000s.

One of the most active student groups in Belarus, ZUBR ("Bison" in English), relied on an extensive network of volunteers and skillful use of cyberspace to disseminate prodemocracy messages and educate ordinary Belarusians about the dangers of Lukashenka's regime. In the words of one ZUBR member, twenty-seven-year-old Grisha, the group pursued its mission though "social campaigns, street actions, graffiti, leaflet distribution, demonstrations, and marches" [BSt28]. By 2006, despite its illegal status and the growing risks associated with membership, ZUBR attracted five thousand activists and more than a thousand volunteers across 152 Belarusian cities and towns (Donnari 2006; Viasna 2005). As a result of arrests, university expulsions, and other forms of persecution against ZUBR, some of its members had to flee Belarus and continue their oppositional activity from abroad. For instance, Antos Cialezhnikau escaped the growing pressure from Lukashenka's administration by moving in 2002 to Poland, where he continued the work of ZUBR on social media (*The Economist* 2011).

Another example is Aleksei Shydlovski, a former political prisoner and ZUBR member, who was expelled from the university and "encouraged" to move abroad. Aleksei relocated to Prague, where he led the local anti-Lukashenka movement (Shydlovski 2013).

Another political youth organization, Malady Front ("The Young Front," in English), became famous in Belarus and abroad for organizing the annual "I Love Belarus" anti-government protest, held in Minsk on Valentine's Day for several years in a row (Bekus 2010). Among the most effective early campaigns of the Front was an agreement of support with the oppositional presidential candidate Siamion Domash during the 2001 election. Despite the expected failure of Domash's presidential bid, this initiative attracted the attention of oppositional youth throughout the country and generated a major membership drive for the organization. By October 2002, the Young Front had enlisted more than 14 percent of Belarusians between the ages of eighteen and thirty (Malady Front 2015). Despite relentless persecution by the government and the imprisonment of dozens of its student members, Malady Front continues to organize anti-government campaigns, support a number of outreach and educational initiatives, call for economic and diplomatic sanctions against Lukashenka, and even formally recognize and reward oppositional activism. In recent years, the organization moved its headquarters to the Ukrainian capital city of Kiev in an attempt to avoid interruptions in activity and escape the increasingly adverse environment at home (Charter 97 2015h, 2015i; Naviny.by 2015).

The political threat emanating from young and educated Belarusians consolidated when several neighboring countries experienced popular prodemocratic uprisings. Georgia's 2003 Rose Revolution, Ukraine's 2004 Orange Revolution, and the 2005 Tulip Revolution in Kyrgyzstan shook up the region and signaled to the remaining dictators, including Lukashenka, the dangers of gradual liberalization (Berg-Schlosser 2008; Wilson 2010). In the words of Silitski, "*as many surviving autocratic leaders saw it, the great mistake of their fallen colleagues was to tolerate social and even political pluralism*" (2005: 84). Intellectual elites in general and university students in particular were among the most active progressive forces in every prodemocratic movement in the region (Finkel and Brudny 2012; Kuzio 2006b). In the mid-2000s, Lukashenka publicly declared that in Belarus "there will be no pink or orange, not even a banana revolution" and set out on a political crusade to make sure that Belarusian opposition was not as successful as its counterparts in neighboring countries (Schipani-Aduriz 2005). Intellectual elites, young educated Belarusians, and the universities that have for centuries served as platforms for their mobilization all became important targets of Lukashenka's repression.

Period III: Repression against Universities

Lukashenka's growing awareness of the risks that his government faced from a group that he had largely ignored for the first ten years of his presidency brought about a wave of repression against university members (Schipani-Aduriz 2005). Since the mid-2000s, Human Rights Watch, Amnesty International, and local independent and oppositional news sources have reported frequent incidents in which university members were fired, expelled, and imprisoned for participating in NGOs, attending international conferences, or simply traveling abroad. Many faced hefty fines, community service, and even exile for engaging in these alleged anti-government activities (Petra 2007).

Members and leaders of unregistered youth organizations have constituted special targets of government repression. Several Malady Front activists have been investigated and imprisoned, including the organization's founder Pavel Severinets, one of its leaders Dmitriy Dashkevich, and at least six other active members (Panchenko 2007). Other high-profile cases include the detention of Denis Denisov for nationalist propaganda, the two-year imprisonment of Artur Finkevich for political drawings, and the incarceration of Katsyaryna Manchuk for participating in a history club (Kamitet Salidarnist' 2007; Nielsen 2012). In 2010, twenty-seven students from Minsk State University spent a night in jail for posting anti-government statuses on Facebook and its local equivalent, *V Kontakte* (Newsland 2015). By 2011, the number of criminally and administratively sanctioned students and instructors exceeded three hundred (European Forum for Democracy and Solidarity 2013; RT 2013; UN News Center 2011).

However, according to Inna Kuley, the head of Solidarity, the Committee for the Defense of Repressed Citizens, direct punishment has not been the most common way of pressuring university students into political compliance. Instead, the more widespread and certainly more insidious mechanism of ideological coercion involves covert attacks on the academic status of oppositional youth, whereby their grades are artificially lowered, their admission applications are denied, their exams are marked below the passing level, and their disciplinary records are tainted with fabricated offenses. As a result of such practices, Kuley says that final exam sessions in mid-winter and early summer have effectively turned into periods of repression against university students. Between final exams, politically disobedient students are falsely charged with rowdy behavior in dormitories, absences from extracurricular events, and other nonacademic matters (Kraini 2011). The goal of this pressure is to either strong-arm young activists into conformity or remove them from centers of oppositional activity through expulsion. According to some sources, more than seven hundred students were expelled or pressured to leave their HEEs for political reasons between 2006 and 2012 (e.g., Nielsen 2012).

In addition to prosecuting individual activists, Lukashenka also embarked on a crusade to limit institutional freedoms in higher education and tighten the ideological grip over HEEs that had, up to that point, provided organizational platforms for the mobilization of oppositional youth. The year 2001, in the words of the prominent Belarusian educational and political activist Vladimir Dunaev, was when Soviet totalitarianism returned to Belarusian universities [Interview with author, May 15, 2010].

As a first order of business, Lukashenka closed down a number of new private institutions in Minsk and other Belarusian cities. Besides their openness to new trends in pedagogy and Western educational models, these HEEs exercised relative independence from the Ministry of Education because of their self-reliant funding structures and were, therefore, particularly threatening to the regime. According to the official statistics of the Belarusian Ministry of Education and the European Commission's Report on Higher Education in Belarus, the number of private HEEs operating in the country declined from more than twenty-five in 2001 to ten in 2005, remaining more or less stable since (European Commission 2015; Ministry of Education of the Republic of Belarus 2015). Independent journalistic accounts suggest that only private colleges and universities amenable to governmental influence were allowed to remain in operation (Maksimiyuk 2004).

Arguably the most infamous case of governmental crackdown on an independent educational institution was the closing of the hugely popular European Humanities University (EHU), which was supported by the European Commission and several Western European governments. A not-for-profit institution with its own endowment, EHU was modeled after liberal arts institutions in Norway and Sweden. It pursued an explicit mission to offer instruction in humanities and social sciences that foster critical thinking. Founded in 1992, EHU quickly gained recognition from liberal and educated Belarusians (European Humanities University 2014; Friends of European Humanities University 2014). According to its cofounder Vladimir Dunaev, the university's leaders did not share any explicit political goals. Rather, their "only goal was to ... teach [students] to ask questions about what is going on around them" [Interview with author, May 15, 2010]. Yet, this educational mission did not sit well with Lukashenka and his cronies.

In an interview with BBC's *Crossing Continents*, Anatoli Mikhailov, one of the university's founders, claimed that repressions against EHU started in the early 2000s, when the minister of education requested that Mikhailov resign from his position as the university's president (Barber 2013). After Mikhailov's refusal, pressure from the government continued to mount. In a booklet published by the university, Mikhailov describes this period in EHU history:

> Checks and "signals" from above came constantly ... We were slowly being deprived of all the privileges of an experimental university ... Little by little, the requirements ... became tougher and tougher. In 2003, when another wave of Belarusian ideology appeared, the situation became absolutely bad. Throughout the whole summer and autumn of 2003, supervising commissions kept coming, one after another. They went on checking everything ... We were required to not only follow all normative documents and ministerial formalities, but also perform ideological rituals ... (introducing special courses on ideology, issuing political briefings explaining the key role of the president in the country's life, making students join the "correct" youth organizations, restricting contact with foreigners, and so on). (2015: 29–32)

Unwilling to meet the demands of the government, EHU's founders closed the university in August 2004. After a period of online instruction that followed the closure, EHU reopened its doors in Vilnius, the capital of Lithuania, located 170 kilometers from Minsk. To this day, the university continues to operate in exile and attract freethinking young Belarusians interested in Western-style education (European Humanities University 2014; Reisz 2013).

In addition to targeting new private HEEs, Lukashenka's repressive policies extended to large classical universities. In Belarus, as in many other post-Soviet countries, these HEEs enjoy high prestige and sizable resources, often attracting prominent intellectuals and progressive, well-traveled students from all around the country. As a part of his intimidation campaign, Lukashenka orchestrated an overhaul of several university administrations, replacing the leadership of large state HEEs with handpicked regime loyalists. For instance, Aleksandr Kozulin, the president of Belarusian State University from 1996 to 2003, was forced to resign as a result of the anti-government tendencies of his students. After his banishment from the university, Kozulin became heavily involved with political opposition, assuming the leadership of the Social Democratic Party *Hramada*. He subsequently ran as a candidate in the presidential election of 2006 and endured significant pressure during his election campaign. In the aftermath of Lukashenka's reelection, Kozulin was beaten and imprisoned for two years, allegedly for his involvement in anti-government protests (International League for Human Rights 2013).

Lukashenka handpicked new university administrators with an explicit goal of eradicating the subversive political element from local universities. *Belarusian Review* reported that "[Lukashenka] advised rectors of both state-run and private universities to get rid of professors and lecturers who oppose government policies or are 'wavering' in their opinions regarding the government's course. 'If you do not accept the ideas declared by the government and the president, do not apply to a state university for a job,' Lukashenka said explicitly" (Maksimiyuk 2004). Lacking the independent judiciary, faculty and administrative staff who did not exhibit appropriate loyalty could be charged with corruption, hooliganism, or other minor offenses and removed from the public sphere through criminal justice channels (Marples 2006; Silitski 2005).

Additionally, a rigid code of conduct regulated the mobility of university members (particularly foreign travel), collaboration with Western colleagues, professionalization initiatives, and participation in nongovernmental organizations, protests, and even select cultural celebrations (Korosteleva 2012; Silitski 2005: 92). Lukashenka's appointees were tasked with ensuring that all the country's HEEs observed this code. Another tool that Lukashenka's men used to pursue the absolute political loyalty of intellectual elites was the strict censorship of academic research. Since the mid-2000s, special committees of vetted "ideology specialists" have closely monitored the selection of dissertation topics and the publication of results of scientific studies (Silitski 2005).

During this period, Belarusian universities also underwent a series of structural reforms aimed at quelling the oppositional element on their premises. All liberal and experimental initiatives, including new degree programs and Bologna-mandated modules, were abruptly discontinued. New textbooks were replaced with old Soviet manuals, the pre-independence curricula were partially or fully reinstated, and many social science courses were canceled altogether (Rich 2003). The instructional process, reinstituted throughout the country's HEEs, followed the familiar Soviet model that prioritized deductive instruction, memorization, and recital at the expense of critical and analytical skills, public speaking, and creative writing (*The Higher Education* 2011; Shraibman 2013).

Development and dissemination of state ideology has been Aleksandr Lukashenka's priority since the early days of his presidency. In his articulation, the main pillars of such belief system, strongly reminiscent of its Soviet predecessor, include strong presidential power, a socially oriented economy, and Orthodox Christian values. It was not till 2003, however, that the president made concrete steps toward mandating that university students were directly exposed to the ideological precepts that underpinned his regime. At a March 2003 seminar entitled "On Measures to Improve Ideological Work," the president laid out a plan for ideological indoctrination in different social spheres, including higher education. Central to this plan were the introduction of "state ideology" as a mandatory subject in the university curriculum and the publication of state-approved textbooks for this course. Both initiatives were promptly instituted the following year (Bekus 2010; Klyuchnikova 2003; Telegraf.by 2011).

The university course on Belarusian state ideology consists of twenty-four academic hours and includes sixteen lectures and eight seminar-style meetings. Ideology instructors go through rigorous training at the Academy of Administration of the President of Belarus and in the Republican Institute of Higher School (Charter97.com 2015b). According to Lidia, a thirty-two-year-old instructor of "The Basics of Ideology" whom I interviewed during my time in Minsk, the goal of the course is "to explain the choices made by the president and convey how his vision of the country's future is the correct path" [BPr13].

Another instrument of governmental control in local universities, activated during this time, is the Belarusian Republican Youth Movement (BRYM, or *BRSM*, in Russian). The objective of BRSM is to counterbalance youth opposition movements by mobilizing students loyal to the incumbent regime (Stushinskaya 2005). Its official goal is to "instill patriotism and moral values in Belarusian youth," and its repertoire of activities includes celebrations of national holidays, voter mobilization, patriotic demonstrations, camping, concerts, and sports competitions (BRSM 2012). BRSM is highly reminiscent of Soviet-era Komsomol and, like its predecessor, is widely recognized as an instrument of political propaganda. More than half of the Belarusian students I interviewed for this project (twenty-three out of thirty-seven) reported pressure to join BRSM.

Coercion toward membership in BRSM takes a variety of forms. Some news outlets, for instance, report economic pressures. For instance, Lukashenka's allies in the municipal government of Mahilyow, the third-largest city in the country, proposed legislation that would fine Belarusians of eligible age who were not enrolled in BRSM and direct the collected funds toward municipal needs (Laptsevich 2013). In other instances, the government instituted economic incentives for joining BRSM. Some local newspapers report that its members receive substantial discounts at beauty salons, fitness clubs, bowling and pool halls, and even nightclubs. Such enticements are particularly attractive to poorer students from the provinces, whose parents struggle with financing expensive entertainment and beauty treatments in the capital (Inanets 2012; Nyegosh 2001). Several of the parents I interviewed described the pressure that tax administration and various government inspectors put on businesses to offer such discounts to BRSM members [e.g., BPa11; BPa19]. Many instructors referred to the recruitment of BRSM members as one of their professional obligations. Most believed that supervisors considered their effectiveness at increasing BRSM enrollments during promotion and contract renewal decisions [i.e., BPr8; BPr12; Bpr19].

Coercion toward membership in the Belarusian Republican Youth Movement is palpable for most Belarusian students. Local newspapers report that those who refuse to join are often framed as disloyal (and, in many cases, amoral) citizens (Euroline.by 2015; Nn.by 2015a). The majority of my interviewees reported fearing that not becoming a BRSM member would disadvantage them in their job search, change their professors' attitude toward them, or otherwise negatively impact their academic and professional outcomes. Online student forums abound with discussions of pressure to join, illustrated by the following entries: "Today our староста ["starosta," or student leader of a class, in English] met with the dean, who warned her that this Sunday BRSM is having some event and that if none of our students show up, she will personally expel her" [Unofficial forum of Belarusian National Technical University 2012]. And: "Our dean actually told us pretty straightforwardly that her plan is to have 65–70 percent of each class in BRSM. And then she said that whoever is interested in going to grad school won't get in unless they join" [Para.by 2012].

Another control mechanism instituted in Belarusian universities during this time is the Soviet practice of распределение ("raspredelenie," or redistribution, in English), whereby university graduates are assigned to their first jobs for a period of two to five years. Распределение offers a convenient way to track and manipulate the physical location of young professionals. Originally developed to ensure that the industrializing Soviet periphery received its fair share of young specialists, распределение allows the government to direct the flow of highly educated cadres to the regions with specific needs and, coincidentally, provides a façade of legitimacy for keeping new graduates away from Minsk during their most troublesome years. Most распределение jobs are in small towns and villages far from major urban centers and, consequently, from most organized opposition activity. Young specialists are enticed to stay in these remote locations beyond the required term through a variety of economic incentives, such as subsidized housing and promotion opportunities (Branstein 2001; Martynovich 2013).

According to the Decree of the Soviet of Ministers of Belarus #1702, state enterprises can submit employment requests for the alumni of specific departments, while special committees, appointed by university presidents, match the graduates with such requests on the basis of their "academic performance, participation in research initiatives, involvement in social and extracurricular activity, health and disability status, marital situation, family location, and location of any internships, as well as the recommendations of instructors and students' own preferences" (Pravo.by 2015). Although the law specifies exactly how students' disability status or marital situation should affect their job assignment, social and extracurricular activities and their effects on students' professional futures are left purposefully undefined.

According to my interviews, this legislative ambiguity allows authorities to manipulate the распределение assignments to minimize the threat emanating from oppositional youth. Although it is hard to document systematically, many respondents and independent news sources hypothesize that an inverse relationship exists between students' political engagement and the desirability of their job assignment (e.g., Gurinovich 2010; Viasna 2013). In fact, the manipulation of распределение outcomes is so blatant that many social analysts argue that it constitutes an abuse of Belarusian students' civil rights (Viasna 2010, 2012).

The majority of my student interviewees (twenty-six out of thirty-seven) had a negative view of распределение. Many believed that they could find better employment options on their own and resented the prospect of leaving Minsk for underdeveloped rural areas. Several respondents also opposed распределение on economic grounds. While the law frames the obligation to work according to the assignment as repaying the state for tuition-free education, these students argued that they had already made their payments via taxes. Most students in this group (sixteen out of twenty-six) also acknowledged the political significance of распределение. Although few were eager to discuss this issue at length, some interviewees hinted that authorities use this program to punish and discipline noncompliant youth. A quote from an interview with Slava, an older student of engineering at Belarusian State Technical University, reveals this recognition:

> A lot of people try to avoid being sent away [on распределение] ... There are a few ways ... Sometimes people can arrange with a company, for instance where your parents work or where you yourself used to work, to send a request for you as you are finishing your last year. And these can be granted, but they aren't always. For some students, they will never be granted ... Some students are just in bad standing with the government – you know what I mean. For them, распределение assignment is like Siberia, a kind of exile. [BSt37]

At the same time, a substantial minority of student interviewees (eleven out of thirty-seven), mostly from outside Minsk, had a positive view of распределение. Mainly, these students were content not to worry about the job search after the graduation. Except for one respondent, they were not aware of the program's political implications.

THE EFFECT OF LUKASHENKA'S RETALIATION ON UNIVERSITIES

While the lack of cohesive government control and oversight in the early years of Lukashenka's presidency created spaces for vibrant informal economies to flourish in Belarusian universities, the situation changed drastically as Lukashenka and his team became aware of potential political dangers associated with universities' liberalization outside of governmental purview. My interviews reveal that Lukashenka's retaliation against freethinking students and noncompliant intellectual elites took a number of forms, ranging from the expulsion of politically active students and faculty to the adoption of curricular changes and oversight programs. These measures significantly decreased oppositional activity in and around Belarusian HEEs, undermined the mobilization of politically active youth, and created a climate of fear in university classrooms. In addition to these anticipated outcomes, the president's reactive policies also produced a series of largely unintended side effects on the informal economies in higher education.

Decrease in Opportunities for Horizontal Corruption

The consolidation of state control over Belarusian universities shrank the spaces of bureaucratic discretion available to their employees, eradicating opportunities to carry out unsanctioned exchanges with their students. Specifically, my data reveal that discretion of university officials decreased drastically in response to the tightening of employee hierarchies and the rise in mandatory accountability procedures in local HEEs.

In contrast to Ukrainian universities, which grant their faculty a fair amount of freedom both inside and outside the classroom, their Belarusian counterparts are controlled through tightly integrated chains of command over all educational, disciplinary, and administrative affairs. Most of my Minsk respondents reported strong vertical connections in the employee hierarchies of their HEEs, which significantly limited professors' ability to control the instructional process. For instance, Oksana, a twenty-six-year-old who teaches English, complained about the pressure from her superiors:

> It's like there's always someone behind your back, watching your every step. That's because I have to report on everything I do . . . there are all these rules that the department chair makes sure we never forget. If you step out of line, even just a little bit, and do something different, even if it is for the good of students . . . then it's all questions: Why did you do this? Why did you do that? And what did you mean by that? Along with hints that you might have trouble when you try to renew your

> contract ... We need to feed our families today and tomorrow and the day after tomorrow. No matter how important my job and my students are to me, my family is still more important. So I behave. [BPr11]

Oksana explained her supervisors' rigidness with reference to the pressure that their own supervisors place on them: "Our chair is dependent on the dean because he signs her contract every year ... Everything has to be perfect so the dean can't say anything. And since she signs our contracts ... we have to do exactly what she says" [BPr11].

During several months at Oksana's department, I observed a number of instances when faculty members were tacitly threatened with forgone promotions and employment termination. The first instance involved an unsanctioned use of a foreign textbook by an instructor of English whom I will call Alesya. Alesya was invited into the chair's office for a brief meeting, which left her visibly distraught. She later told me that she had gotten in trouble for using handouts photocopied from an English-language textbook, *Headway* by Oxford University Press, popular among English teachers in post-Soviet countries. Some days later, I got a chance to ask the department chair why Alesya's behavior warranted a reprimand. The chair explained that she sought to avoid any potential missteps that could provoke dissatisfaction of university administrators:

> I have to demand some basic compliance with formalities ... It is so easy to pick on something to bring a person down! It's just better ... to be impeccable ... No one said anything specifically about *Headway* but it is not one of the textbooks listed in our methodological materials. Again, why do it if there is a chance of ... chance of making someone upset. I don't know what they [pointing her figure upward] will decide is not acceptable. We have rules that tell us what to do – why experiment? And my boss makes sure we follow them – and so do I, when it comes to my instructors. [BPr14]

Faculty from other departments and HEEs told me similar stories about strict hierarchical controls and pressures in their organizations. By planting regime loyalists on top of university hierarchies and by making the professional success of their every layer a function of the docility of the one below, Lukashenka's reforms effectively eradicated academic autonomy and discouraged creativity. Alexei, a forty-two-year-old instructor of law, offered the following compelling description of the military-style discipline in his department: "It's like an army over here. Precise execution of your superiors' commands is your best quality as a worker. You should never try to think too much ... that's not what you are paid for here" [BPr19].

My faculty respondents insisted that oversight and regulation of their professional conduct were highly systematic. To ensure that no questionable activity goes unnoticed, university administrators require that instructors leave an extensive paper trail describing their instructional, research, and administrative duties. Most interviewees, in fact, complained about the copious amounts of paperwork that they had to fill out on a regular basis. Some claimed that they had to provide explanations for just about everything they did, from the grades they issued to the materials and equipment they used in their classrooms. For example, Ljubov, an instructor of musicology, said, "It feels like I am ... not able to do anything without having to explain ... why. Why is this student nominated to go to this competition? Why have I included this topic in this lesson? Why am I using the projector more than other instructors? I feel like I write these papers [explanations] more than I write lesson plans" [BPr17].

Regina, who teaches Spanish at a large Minsk university, elaborated:

> It's strange how little trust I receive from my colleagues and superiors. I used to work as a translator, and I felt so much more respected than I do now, despite my job here being maybe more worthy of respect. I just try not to think about it too much and pay attention to the positive things instead. Well, for example, that I don't need to try too much. All these papers, they're burdensome, but they're not difficult. I'm told, in detail, what I need to do, so I do it and save my intellectual energy for other things. I'm now working on translating some poetry, for example ... Why would I try to argue with the administration? They have their reasons, I am sure. And why do I need trouble? I have a family, after all. [BPr2]

Pressured by incessant demands for accountability and intimidated by repression against their colleagues and students who "stepped out of line," Belarusian instructors work in a climate of fear and intellectual suppression. In fact, my interviews reveal that the desire to avoid trouble is the driving force behind much of instructors' and administrators' behavior on the job. Amorphous yet strong, this fear permeates the professional lives of university bureaucrats, limiting their intellectual exploration and discouraging independent initiative. Galina, a chemistry instructor who claimed to be very diligent in "filling out the papers," put it succinctly: "All this bureaucracy is out of fear. They tell us there are new laws that we have to observe ... Nobody wants trouble" [BPr6].

At the same time, the sudden halt put on the Bologna process and other innovations in higher education created an artificial stasis, reducing the "gray spaces" in which informality had previously existed (Mundell 2012; Preiherman 2011). As higher education establishments went back to operating in familiar Soviet ways, the exercise of discretion and experimentation with alternative models of funding was no longer feasible (Gorbachev, Malchenko, and Zenchanka 2006; Shaton 2009).

Several of the instructors I interviewed told me that their respective departments functioned just like they used to during the Soviet era. Consider, for instance, my conversation with a professor of architecture, Arkadiy Andreevich:

I: *Tell me a little bit about your experience here ... How have things changed during your time in this department?*

R: *I started working at* [the name of the department and university] *in the eighties. It was my first and maybe my last job* [laughs] ... *what can I tell you? Not much has changed really ...*

I: *So there was never a time ... of ... trying out new things, maybe experimenting with new materials, subjects, and pedagogical approaches?*

R: *Well, I don't even know ... For a while, in my opinion, we did try a lot of new things ... after independence, when people were still hopeful that things would be different, fifteen years ago or so, but then we went back to Soviet mores.*

I: *So what does this stability mean for you and your colleagues on an everyday basis?*

R: *I don't know. Probably, it means that things are predictable around here. Everything is rolling down a well-oiled track.* [BPr1]

As Arkadiy's testimony suggests, the return to the Soviet educational model implied stability, standardization, and easy control of university actors. Return to clear and familiar expectations made any deviations immediately obvious and easily sanctionable by peers and supervisors. In combination with the dramatically increased bureaucratic oversight, this move back to the deeply entrenched protocols of organizational activity has significantly reduced opportunities for bureaucratic corruption.

At the same time, Lukashenka's new approach to university governance also decreased Belarusian students' perceived need to bring bribes, offer presents, or pull strings to get ahead academically. My observations and interviews reveal that in contrast to their Ukrainian counterparts, Minsk students were convinced that they could gain university admission, pass exams, and receive good grades without unsanctioned offerings to instructors and administrators. The stories that students told me during interviews revealed that tacit pressures for corruption, ever-present in Ukrainian HEEs, were practically absent in Belarusian higher education. Almost all students concurred that university instructors and administrators expected nothing beyond academic effort, discipline, and abstinence from political engagement. Neither did our conversations reveal any traces of informal socialization into corruption cultures, akin to those in many Ukrainian HEEs. While Kiev students could easily describe a typical bribery exchange in local universities (regardless of their personal involvement), Belarusian interviewees could not name an average bribe amount or describe a hypothetical bribery transaction.

Instead, as mentioned earlier, local students insisted that diligence (or, more precisely, an appearance of diligence), semi-regular attendance, some effort, and a low political profile were the only de facto requirements for graduation. Consider, for instance, the following quotes from Sergei, a third-year student of geography, and Yana, a fourth-year student of philology, who claim that for Belarusian students, offering bribes is not only unnecessary but outright foolish:

> Sometimes I wonder if it is actually possible to flunk out [of university] ... short of not showing up for exams ... So I don't really understand why anyone would pay. All you need to do is attend, listen, and put in minimal effort. No one is asking you for your money. Honestly, I don't believe anyone who says that money was demanded of them. All the demands we get are normal demands for any students – for example, know the material and don't miss too many lectures. On the contrary, I can't even imagine how someone could give a bribe to a professor. Like, how do you do that without getting yourself in trouble? Also, to tell you the truth, our department is just not that demanding. Idiots pass and graduate all the time, left and right. I guess you need to be totally dumb to throw your money away on bribes. [BSt9]

And:

> I don't really feel a need to pay. Simply throwing my money away is not something I can afford. I am confident that everything will be OK if I put effort into my studies. That's why I'm here – why would I be trying to

> pay? Maybe … the only reason that I can imagine would be if my teachers were demanding … even then, maybe … but it's not like that. Extortion is absent. [BSt13]

These testimonies suggest that an important reason behind the decrease in university corruption was the decline in the pressure that students felt from their instructors. Studies show that clients of street-level bureaucracies who have heard about previous instances of corruption in their organizations are more likely to perceive extortion from officials than are clients who have not been exposed to such rumors (Čábelková and Hanousek 2004; Miller, Grødeland, and Koshechkina 2001; Zaloznaya 2012). In other words, when ordinary people hear stories of coercion in the organizations they frequent, they tend to also feel pressure "to give." Conversely, in the contexts where bureaucratic discretion is virtually absent and informal interactions about corruption are infrequent, students do not experience pressure to provide their instructors with under-the-table compensation for their services. The following quote from Katya, a first-year journalism student at Minsk State University, illustrates this point: "Have I considered bribery? No. Why? … If you are a good student, you will do well" [BSt21]. Similarly, Yana, mentioned earlier, concluded, "I can get what I need without paying. Nobody tells me or hints that I should pay" [BSt13].

Decreased Need to Engage in University Corruption

The second way that repressions decreased students' perceived need for corruption had to do with **распределение**. This mandatory job placement had a strong effect on students' attitude toward their studies. According to raspredelenie rules, every student on the tuition-free track gets assigned to her first job, and the quality of this placement does not directly depend on the student's academic performance (but rather on students' political engagement and the needs of the industry). As a result, **распределение** has effectively decreased the competition for grades among Belarusian students. For some, the diminished importance of grades had positive motivational outcomes. For example, a few of my interviewees, such as Kolya, a third-year student of computer science at Minsk State University, cherished their ability to focus on learning instead of looking for employment:

R: *I don't really understand why anyone would actually buy a grade. Really, who cares about grades? My studies will be over really soon, and then for the rest of my life I will be programming . . . and if I don't really know how to program, then you know who's really going to suffer?* Me.

I: *So, do you think that you feel the way you feel about your future work because of the prospect of undergoing распределение at the end of your studies?*

R: *Of course. If there was no распределение, I could go into any branch of industry, not just something related to computer programming. Then, maybe, I would not want to learn programming and would just want to get the document* [the diploma]. *So, for example, if I decided halfway through my time at the university that I instead wanted to become a . . . a . . . I don't know, a hairdresser, I would probably still want to have a higher education, so I'd finish . . . but maybe try to do as little as possible to just get by. But распределение limits us in what we can do, so you have to concentrate on your subject.* [BSt36]

In most cases, however, распределение decreased students' motivation to do anything – study or buy grades. For instance, Misha, a junior at Belarusian State Agrarian University, stated unequivocally, "I wouldn't waste my money on bribes. I know they will send me to some village anyway . . . so what's the point?" [BSt15].

In summary, whether распределение had a negative or positive effect on students' work ethic and motivation, there is little doubt that this mandatory job assignment program significantly reduced Belarusian youths' need to resort to corruption.

Cultural Reasons for the Decrease in Corruption

My discussion of students' changing attitudes toward university corruption would not be complete without a description of the informal climate that has developed in Belarusian universities since the beginning of governmental retaliation against higher education. The introduction of ideology classes, the activation of BRSM, the tightening of university hierarchies, and occasional acts of repression have created a climate that discourages all informal activity in Belarus's universities. The unspoken yet acutely felt consensus among Belarusian students and instructors is that any conduct that challenges formal rules should be avoided for the sake of one's safety and economic security. According to Vasiliy, a professor of political science, "People are afraid . . . and if you take each individual instance, their fears may be ungrounded, but if you look at them as a collective, then it makes a lot of sense . . . And because from time to time they get confirmation of their fears, they keep on believing" [BPr3].

The fear that Vasiliy describes was apparent in the behavior and testimonies of Belarusian students and instructors I encountered during my fieldwork in Minsk. A number of students attributed their fear of "being noticed" to copious accountability requirements, such as mandatory attendance at cultural and sporting events, early voting, and membership in BRSM. Some instructors even suggested that there were undercover KGB (state security) agents positioned at universities to oversee students' and instructors' conduct. Whether grounded or not, the collective fear, palpable among Belarusian university members, considerably diminishes their likelihood of corrupt engagement.

Overall, my analysis of the institutional history of Belarusian universities suggests that the eradication of horizontal corruption in local HEEs at the turn of the century was associated with President Lukashenka's growing awareness of oppositional tendencies in university communities. The political threat emanating from the country's higher education institutions led him to eliminate academic freedoms that had previously existed in local HEEs. Central government's new policies tightened organizational hierarchies and instituted strict accountability requirements, reducing spaces of bureaucratic discretion and, consequently, opportunities for horizontal corruption in Belarusian universities. By increasing control over the alumni through mandatory job assignments, Lukashenka's government decreased students' need to resort to corruption, while ideological pressures through BRSM, a politically charged curriculum, and selective persecutions generated a culture of fear and diminished popular propensity toward rule breaking.

At the same time, these very changes in the governance of local universities created a favorable environment for politically vetted, higher-standing officials to engage in vertical corruption by manipulating the admissions and hiring decisions.

CONCLUSION

The Belarusian case reveals that hybrid regimes may generate uneven preconditions for corruption across different organizational sectors. Specifically, if hybrid regime leaders successfully prevent the turnover of political power through nondemocratic means, the type of governance they exercise over any given bureaucratic sector may depend on the perceived political loyalty of its members. Organizational sectors whose members do not show any tendencies toward dissent and are therefore not threatening to the regime may experience lenient governance that offers multiple opportunities for bureaucratic corruption, generates the need for such transactions, and gives rise to local cultures that normalize them. Such governance entails relaxed accountability requirements, misaligned incentive structures whereby rule breaking is more lucrative than rule following, and the decoupling of formal regulations and laws from on-the-ground organizational processes. Moreover, since in many nondemocratic regimes public salaries are unresponsive to the quality of bureaucrats' performance, the latter have few instrumental incentives to abstain from corruption.

My data show that in the 1990s, Belarusian universities, as well as Belarusian hospitals, secondary schools, and many other bureaucracies, experienced lenient governance under Lukashenka's regime. Within these bureaucracies, street-level officials enjoyed significant discretion because of relaxed accountability mechanisms and procedural ambiguity. Horizontal corruption proliferated in such institutional contexts.

In contrast, bureaucracies that autocratic political leadership sees as threatening experience consolidated – and sometimes despotic – governance in low-turnover hybrid regimes. This type of governance encourages social control and diffuses the responsibility of ensuring political loyalty down the organizational hierarchy.

Under consolidated autocratic governance, bureaucracies are closely controlled through tightened organizational hierarchies and stringent accountability requirements that decrease opportunities and the perceived need for bureaucratic corruption. Such governance builds on administrative centralization, whereby higher-standing officials subject lower ranks of the government to rigid controls. While political elites enjoy significant freedoms, their subordinates face heavy accountability pressures. Under such governance, the hierarchies of organizational employees are tightly integrated so that bureaucrats' status and income depend directly on the political loyalty and complicity of their subordinates.

Among street-level bureaucrats and their direct supervisors, rewards for lawful behavior and political compliance, as well as punishment for noncompliance, are primarily economic. Bureaucrats who observe formal rules and have well-behaved subordinates receive more promotions and higher pay than their colleagues. The consolidation of governance over select bureaucratic sectors also happens through symbolic rewards and punishments. Nonmaterial reinforcement for political loyalty and compliance may range from group membership (e.g., in state-run organizations like BRSM) to symbolic recognition through professional titles, awards, and other status symbols.

Hierarchical integration, characteristic of consolidated governance, is therefore not conducive to proliferation of petty illicit exchanges between bureaucrats and their clients. Vertical corruption, in which higher-level officials make illicit requests of their subordinates, is the only type of bureaucratic corruption feasible in organizations subjected to such governance.

In our second conversation, Aleksandr, whose suggestion had led me to explore the institutional changes that transformed the corruption landscape in local universities, found apt words to describe what life in a country with different types of bureaucratic governance feels like to ordinary citizens:

> When I think about our country, it seems to me that in some ways we have changed, but in other cases this change was either stopped or reversed. Today, Belarus is really a mixed country in which some things function exactly as they did forty years ago but others have changed significantly. Some people say it is a complete Совок ["Sovok," derogative way to say "Soviet"] but I disagree. Well, partially disagree, at least. Universities might be like that, but other places are far from being the same. Like, we got new technology, more things in general, and money matters so much more than it used to. But I guess it is this weird combination of old and new that makes us different [chuckles]. I am not saying this is good – on the contrary, I think it is unnatural to be both Soviet and post-Soviet at the same time. Other countries, I think, have moved on, but we are stuck in some sort of neither-here-nor-there place. I am just saying that's what most people, particularly abroad, don't understand about Belarus. [BPr7]

The Belarusian case, therefore, exemplifies the second pathway of hybrid political development in the wake of the Soviet collapse – a pathway that has a distinct impact on local informal economies. Like Ukraine and other hybrid regimes, Belarus has a variegated cultural landscape that accommodates corruption-favorable as well as corruption-unfavorable institutional logics. In Chapter 3, I show that ordinary Belarusians hold cultural schemas and definitions that justify under-the-table exchanges with bureaucrats as well as schemas that are unfavorable to bureaucratic corruption. Like their Ukrainian counterparts, ordinary Belarusians draw on their assorted cultural repertoires, invoking different definitions in different interactional contexts in accordance with their changing incentive structures. For instance, my interviews reveal that the same Belarusians who consider bribes and presents normal in hospitals do not construe corruption as feasible, necessary, or acceptable in local universities.

As argued previously, in contrast to individual actors, bureaucracies cannot maneuver between different institutional logics because of structural inertia, the longevity of organizational cultures, reputational effects, and other organizational pressures for continuity. Instead, the way that organizational landscapes respond to cultural multiplicity largely depends on the political governance. The Ukrainian case suggests that in the absence of any governmental coercion – characteristic of regimes with high political turnover – organizations adopt either corruption-favorable or corruption-unfavorable institutional logics by responding to the specific constraints and opportunities they encounter. The outcome is the cross-organizational variation in corruption levels.

The Belarusian case, in contrast, exemplifies the impact of an alternative hybrid political trajectory in which low political turnover and the capture of power by a nondemocratic leader have put uneven pressures on the bureaucratic sectors. Preoccupied with preserving his power, Lukashenka's administration decreased freedoms and solidified government controls in the organizational sectors that the leadership saw as threatening, thereby creating unfavorable preconditions for horizontal corruption and interfering with the processes of organizational alignment with different institutional logics that coexist in the motley cultural repertoire of post-Soviet Belarus. The resulting cross-sectoral variation in informal economic activity across Belarusian organizational fields is, therefore, a result of strategic political governance and a correlate of the low turnover of power in a hybrid political regime.

CONCLUSION

Only by understanding the baseline – how much corruption, in what areas, with what consequences – can we begin to formulate the necessary policy responses to it.

Robin Hodess, Director of Policy and Research, Transparency International (Sampford et al. 2006: xiii)

Today, the movement against corruption spans all continents, uniting ordinary people in the Global North and the Global South (Bukovansky 2002; Hindess 2005; Sampson 2005; Zaloznaya 2013). The fight against corruption is also a flagship issue on the foreign policy dockets of most Western governments, the agendas of global governance organizations, and the mission statements of many transnational NGOs. Every year, the international community spends millions of dollars to fuel anti-corruption campaigns carried out by local grassroots groups and national governments and coordinated by intragovernmental organizations such as the World Bank, the International Monetary Fund (IMD), the Organization for Economic Cooperation and Development (OECD), and the United Nations (Blake 2009; Kennedy 1999; Rose-Sender et al. 2010; Sampson 2010; Stapenhurst and Kpundeh 1999). Through conditional loans, policy development, and research, these organizations generate funding, political support, data, and the ideological grounding for global anti-corruptionism.

Anti-corruption activists worldwide pursue a monumental political objective: establishment and maintenance of democratic governments. For ordinary people, democratization brings a promise that political leaders will hear their voices and address their needs through policy.

Increased integrity in political office brings with it a meaningful consideration of constituents' interests and, consequently, a fair distribution of resources (Bowser 2001; Gray 1998; Gupta and Abed 2002; Morris and Klesner 2010; Rothstein 2011; Uslaner 2008). While ordinary people denounce corruption as an obstacle to equality and fairness, the IMF, the World Bank, and other financial organizations are also concerned with its negative implications for global markets (Brown and Cloke 2004; Hankivsky 2006; Sampson 2005). By diverting resources from the most competitive market actors, corruption undermines the laws of supply and demand, decreases the predictability of economic transactions, and diminishes profits from foreign investment (Hopkin 2002; Javorcik and Wei 2009; Ng 2006). For the IMF, the World Bank, and the OECD, democratic governance is an important guarantor of desired economic outcomes. Authoritarian regimes are generally antithetical to a neoliberal agenda: they hamper free markets with excessive regulation, politicized resource distribution mechanisms, and sprawling governmental bureaucracies. The lack of independent media and judiciaries, along with popular distrust toward formal institutions, undermines Western countries' ability to conduct business with such regimes (Feng 1997; Linz 2000; Mobarak 2005; Wright 2008).

Even though corruption is at the forefront of international politics, sociologists have not yet pursued the study of corruption in a systematic fashion. Because of the well-documented negative effects of corruption on democratic governance and free markets, its academic study is concentrated in the disciplines of political science and economics. Thus, a brief survey of the past sixteen years of publications in three flagships journals of sociology, *American Sociological Review*, *American Journal of Sociology*, and *Social Forces*, yields only two articles whose main subject is corruption: a 2005 article by Jong-Sung and Khagram and a 2010 piece by Margit Tavits. By comparison, in the same time period, the *American Journal of Political Science* alone published five articles that explicitly reference corruption in the title and at least ten more that address corruption more generally.

The absence of sociological voices in the existing research on corruption is surprising in light of the discipline's preoccupation with issues of power and social justice (Khondker 2006; Kurczewski 2004). It is also consequential. This noninvolvement of sociologists resulted in the lack of systematic attention to how macro-social contexts shape informal economic behavior of individual actors. The essence of the sociological imagination, after all, lies in uncovering systematic social forces that mold seemingly random micro-level processes. *The Politics of Bureaucratic Corruption* takes an important step toward the development of a sociological alternative to the dominant way of thinking about corruption in the hybrid governance systems of post-transitional regimes.

In his manifesto on the sociological study of the economy, Mark Granovetter emphasized the importance of treating purposive economic action as "embedded in concrete, ongoing systems of social relations" (1985: 487). Granovetter's approach stresses "concrete personal relations and structures" and embraces the fact that any behavior, including explicitly economic behavior, aims not only at "economic goals, but also at sociability, approval, status, and power" (Granovetter 1985: 490, 506). The sociological perspective on corruption, laid out in this book, appreciates its embeddedness in concrete social relations, from the micro level of interactions among ordinary people to the meso level of organizations and the macro level of political processes. Such approach generates a number of theoretical and policy-relevant insights about corruption that previous accounts simply could not offer. In this conclusion, I briefly discuss some implications of this sociological analysis and identify the ways that it can help policy makers and anti-corruption activists create more equitable systems of economic distribution and more transparent regimes of political governance.

COUNTRYWIDE CULTURES OF CORRUPTION DO NOT EXIST

First and foremost, a sociological approach embraces the complexity of informal economic action. Through stories of ordinary Ukrainians and Belarusians and descriptions of the formal and informal lives of the institutions that bring them together, this book reveals a wealth of meanings behind bureaucratic corruption, the wide range of behaviors that it entails, and a gamut of functions that it serves for local citizens. By emphasizing the heterogeneity and systematic variation within informal economies, *The Politics of Bureaucratic Corruption* dispels the dangerous and empirically inaccurate myth of nationwide cultures of corruption in post-Soviet societies.

Popular in mass media and policy circles, this myth implies that citizens of transitioning and underdeveloped societies have lower ethical impediments against breaking the law than their counterparts in mature Western democracies. Consider, for instance, the following headlines from major international news outlets that put forth the idea that a culture of corruption prevails in Ukraine: "Breaking the Bribe Culture is Still a Challenge for Ukraine" (Prentice and Polityuk 2016), "Ukraine's Unyielding Corruption" (*New York Times* 2016), "Ukraine's Culture of Corruption" (*KyivPost* 2016). Similar claims are also made about other post-Soviet countries, including Russia ("The Culture of Corruption: Russians Pay but They Don't Like It" (Frye 2014), "Russia's Culture of Corruption: Easier to Accept than Fight" (Kabanov 2011)), as well as the region in general ("From Bolshevism to Backhanders: Corruption Has Replaced Communism as the Scourge of Eastern Europe" (*The Economist* 2016)). A number of social scientists also invoke the myth of nationwide corruption cultures to explain the wide spread of informal economic activity in some regions. In reference to Eastern Europe, Bova and Valliere (1999) refer to the allegedly ubiquitous embrace of corruption economies as the "infralaw of corruption and bribonomy," while Frederico Varese (2000) labels it "pervasive corruption."

The culture of the corruption myth has deep roots in moralistic thinking about corruption. In the context of the worldwide anticorruption movement, social scientists have approached corruption from the vantage point of its negative consequences for economic development and democratization. The patterns of variation, cultural meanings, and noneconomic implications of informal exchanges have therefore never emerged as focal points for academic corruptology. In this book, I argued that this oversight distorts our understanding of the political determinants of bureaucratic corruption.

The Politics of Bureaucratic Corruption dispels the myth of countrywide corruption cultures in Ukraine and Belarus. It reveals that while many local citizens engage in bureaucratic illegality, many also avoid it, despite high potential rewards and low risks of punishment. Furthermore, those who do participate in corruption choose from a variety of possible methods of engagement, ranging from the use of connections to the invocation of bribery mechanisms to direct, unmediated money-for-service transactions. Most importantly, my data suggest that citizens' cultural propensity for corruption is neither universal nor evenly distributed within countries. Rather, it is highly variable across local organizations: while many Ukrainian HEEs have organizational cultures that encourage horizontal corruption, others develop corruption-unfavorable local environments. Through exposure to these organizational cultures, Ukrainian students and instructors evaluate the appropriateness and inevitability of corruption. They then translate such organizationally acquired beliefs into different corruption behaviors. In Belarus, citizens' propensity for corruption is also a function of exposure to organizational cultures. While certain Belarusian bureaucracies are highly conducive to informal economic exchanges, others provide neither structural opportunities nor favorable cultural environments for horizontal transactions. As a result, both countries exhibit systematic subnational variation in people's beliefs about bureaucratic corruption that undermines the myth of national corruption cultures.

In contrast to this nuanced portrayal of the variegated economies of exchange in local organizations, the culture of corruption myth reflects a highly reductionist understanding of corruption in the Global South. This myth offers a digestible heuristic for Western policy makers and academics that is as erroneous as it is dangerous: it implicitly builds a hierarchy of cultures in which non-Western societies emerge as inferior.

Sensitivity to the variation in on-the-ground informal economies of hybrid regimes is crucial for a culturally conscious and nonpoliticized study of corruption. Only by appreciating the complexity of local exchange systems can Western scholars build critical and socially embedded accounts of corruption in nondemocratic societies.

INVERSE RELATIONSHIP BETWEEN POLITICAL AND BUREAUCRATIC CORRUPTION

A sociological effort to embed bureaucratic corruption in its macrosocial context also reveals an important relationship among its different types that nonsociological accounts often obscure. In contrast to corruption indicators, the data analyzed in this book distinguish between bureaucratic and political corruption. Sociological process tracing, then, reveals an inverse relationship between these two types of corruption under hybrid political governance.

Thus, large pockets of transparency in select organizational fields in Belarus are an outcome of repressive governance over these bureaucratic sectors and consequently of state capture by a nondemocratic leader. In institutional contexts subjected to strict governmental controls and oversight, such as Belarusian universities, legality stems from fear of repression or desire for greater political power. When the law is oppressive and subservient to the power-preservation interests of a nondemocratic leader, corruption – or the violation of law for personal benefit – represents ordinary people's struggle to maintain their voice and resist political oppression (Ginsburg and Moustafa 2008; Hendley 1999; Yang 1994). In contrast, horizontal corruption in all bureaucratic sectors of post-Soviet Ukraine is a correlate of the country's political freedoms and the ensuing high rates of leadership turnover. Together, the Belarusian and the Ukrainian cases demonstrate that the less political choice the citizens of a hybrid regime have (and, consequently, the higher the level of political corruption), the less economic corruption may occur in its street-level bureaucracies. In other words, in hybrid political systems, bureaucratic corruption emerges as an indication of ordinary citizens' political agency and, therefore, an avenue for popular resistance against nondemocratic governance.

The inverse relationship between political and bureaucratic corruption in hybrid regimes also has important theoretical implications for future academic and policy work on the topic. It suggests that the analytic category of corruption entails a variety of practices with dissimilar local meanings, power dynamics, and relationships to one another. It also implies that critical studies of the political roots of corruption should not fall into the dominant moralistic trap of assuming that corruption is always bad while the absence of corruption is always good. As this book shows, organizational transparency may be a sign of oppression and slippage into authoritarian governance that undermines citizens' human rights and deprives them of freedom of speech, mobility, and political choice. The meaning of corruption in non-Western settings, therefore, should not to be presumed by Western scholars. Rather, the functions and power implications of corruption should be considered in relation to the social value of legality within the local political system, and assessed vis-à-vis the effectiveness of the formal law in providing basic protections, guaranteeing rights, and ensuring citizens' representation in the political process.

ORGANIZATIONS AS TARGETS FOR ANTI-CORRUPTION POLICY

In addition to its theoretical contributions, a comparative sociology of corruption offers ways to further policy-relevant knowledge about informal economies of exchange that are inaccessible to dominant corruptology. Specifically, it can help evaluate the on-the-ground implications of different anti-corruption initiatives, separate negative and positive effects of illicit economies, and reveal the importance of different political and economic determinants of rule breaking vis-à-vis one another.

For instance, the arguments of this book imply that current anti-corruption policy in the region is, in some ways, misguided. As a rule, such policy prescribes a mixture of educational and punitive measures. On one hand, it includes countrywide outreach programs to eradicate the alleged national culture of corruption. On the other, it entails the tightening of legal and administrative accountability mechanisms and harsh treatment of apprehended offenders (Osyka 2003; Rousso and Steves 2007; Steves and Rousso 2003). The evidence presented in *The Politics of Bureaucratic Corruption* suggests that the basal premises of many such initiatives are as empirically unsupported as they are mutually contradictory (the first one assumes that corruption is a norm, and the rest treat corruption as a deviation from a norm).

As I argued earlier in this Conclusion, nationwide cultures of corruption simply do not exist. There is no uniform, decontextualized popular acceptance of corruption as a normal and appropriate thing to do. Instead, hybrid post-Soviet regimes host numerous organizational domains with more and less corruption-favorable climates, and ordinary citizens make decisions about corrupt engagement based on their experiences within these specific organizational environments. Focusing anti-corruption efforts on the eradication of national corruption cultures, therefore, is unlikely to have much effect on behaviors that are actually encouraged by subnational cultural systems.

This book also shows that most local citizens perpetrate corruption not because they tend toward deviance but rather because they comply with the informal rules of different organizations. The conceptualization of corrupt behavior as a deviation from the norm, the treatment of offenders as criminals, and the reliance on the principles of general deterrence, common in anti-corruption policy, are therefore unlikely to be effective.

The Politics of Bureaucratic Corruption suggests that eradicating bureaucratic corruption in hybrid regimes will require changing local organizational norms instead of eliminating the alleged national culture of corruption or severely punishing individual perpetrators. As sites for anti-corruption policy, organizations have a lot to offer. They represent self-contained cultural domains with built-in reproduction and enforcement mechanisms that can instill either corruption-favorable or corruption-unfavorable ways of thinking and encourage corresponding behaviors from their members. In contrast to country-wide cultures, they also offer reachable policy targets.

Policies tailored specifically to eliminate organizationally embedded bribery mechanisms in Ukrainian bureaucracies are likely to alter their corruption-conducive cultures. In local universities, such policies may include identifying intermediaries and preventing them from facilitating illicit transactions, eradicating price lists, regulating tutoring practices and capping tutoring fees, abolishing exam celebrations, and so on. Although the structural changes mandated by these policies would be relatively small, the organizational cultures of transparency that they would foster could have far-reaching effects on the behavior of organizational members. Comparable small changes in Belarusian hospitals and schools could also produce a major decline in corrupt engagement by their employees and clients.

More broadly, the findings of *The Politics of Bureaucratic Corruption* prove that academic corruptology would be most useful for policy makers if it were not rooted in data generated by the global anti-corruption movement. Paradoxically, an increased distance between academic and policy worlds could bring about a more fruitful cooperation between them. Nuanced sociological studies that appreciate the complexity of local informal economies and embed them into their real-life social contexts could offer highly effective policy recommendations. By unveiling the meanings and functions of informal economies in non-Western societies, such studies could help refocus policy efforts away from attacking the alleged criminality of non-Western populations and toward fostering the sociopolitical conditions that minimize adverse economic and human rights outcomes for ordinary citizens.

APPENDIX I

TABLE 4 TICPI, Ukraine and Belarus 2005–2011

	2005	2006	2007	2008	2009	2010	2011
UKRAINE	2.6	2.8	2.7	2.5	2.2	2.4	2.3
BELARUS	2.6	2.1	2.1	2.0	2.4	2.5	2.4

Note: TICPI ranges from 0 (highly corrupt) to 10 (very clean)
Source: Transparency International (2015)

TABLE 5 Descriptive statistics for corruption variable

	Descriptive Statistics					
	N	Range	Minimum	Maximum	Mean	Std. Deviation
HEE 1 Corruption	193	4	1	5	1.93	.836
HEE 2 Corruption	193	4	1	5	4.07	1.018
HEE 3 Corruption	193	4	1	5	2.48	.963
HEE 4 Corruption	193	4	1	5	4.34	.887
HEE 5 Corruption	193	4	1	5	3.52	.890
HEE 6 Corruption	193	4	1	5	2.37	.788
HEE 7 Corruption	193	3	1	4	1.74	.711
HEE 8 Corruption	192	4	1	5	3.33	.951
Valid *N* (listwise)	192					

TABLE 6 Descriptive statistics for quality variable

	Descriptive Statistics					
	N	Range	Minimum	Maximum	Mean	Std. Deviation
HEE 1 Quality	193	3	2	5	4.20	.766
HEE 2 Quality	193	4	1	5	3.90	.960
HEE 3 Quality	193	4	1	5	3.17	.937
HEE 4 Quality	193	4	1	5	2.10	1.015
HEE 5 Quality	192	5	1	6	2.70	.927
HEE 6 Quality	193	4	1	5	3.50	.931
HEE 7 Quality	193	4	1	5	4.18	.837
HEE 8 Quality	192	4	1	5	2.62	1.016
Valid *N* (listwise)	191					

TABLE 7 Descriptive statistics for prestige variable

	Descriptive Statistics					
	N	Range	Minimum	Maximum	Mean	Std. Deviation
HEE 1 Prestige	193	3	2	5	4.28	.813
HEE 2 Prestige	193	3	2	5	4.75	.523
HEE 3 Prestige	193	4	1	5	2.33	1.002
HEE 4 Prestige	193	4	1	5	2.36	1.077
HEE 5 Prestige	193	4	1	5	2.83	1.024
HEE 6 Prestige	193	4	1	5	2.78	.950
HEE 7 Prestige	193	4	1	5	3.54	1.099
HEE 8 Prestige	192	4	1	5	2.55	1.022
Valid *N* (listwise)	192					

TABLE 8 Pearson correlation between corruption and prestige

HEE #	Correlation	Sig. (2-tailed)
HEE 1	−.072	.321
HEE 2	.113	.118
HEE 3	.192*	.008
HEE 4	−.058	.426
HEE 5	.104	.149
HEE 6	.063	.385
HEE 7	−.039	.594
HEE 8	.068	.347

* Correlation is significant at the .01 level (2-tailed).

APPENDIX II

List of Respondents

UKRAINE

I Professors

[UPr1]: 43-year-old male instructor of foreign languages and a department chair at a large specialized public institute

[UPr2]: 35-year-old female instructor of art history at a large specialized public institute

[UPr3]: 45-year-old female professor of economics

[UPr4]: 41-year-old female professor at the Department of Marketing and Business Administration in a large private HEE

[UPr5]: 43-year-old female instructor of a foreign language at a large public specialized HEE

[UPr6]: 27-year-old female instructor of languages in a large public HEE

[UPr7]: 55-year-old female professor and chair of a language department in a large Kiev HEE

[UPr8]: 35-year-old male instructor of engineering at a large specialized institute

[UPr9]: 42-year-old male professor of applied mathematics

[UPr10]: 36-year-old female instructor at a psychology department of a large public HEE

[UPr11]: 28-year-old male instructor of journalism at a private institute

[UPr12]: 34-year-old female instructor of political science

[UPr13]: 37-year-old male instructor of social science at a middle-sized specialized institute in Kiev

[UPr14]: 66-year-old male professor of chemistry in a medium-size public HEE

[UPr15]: 50-year-old male instructor at a private mid-size institute that specializes in social sciences

[UPr16]: 39-year-old female instructor of sociology, at a small private specialized HEE and a large state university
[UPr17]: 37-year-old male instructor in the department of geoconstruction and mining technologies at a large specialized state institute
[UPr18]: 58-year-old female professor of Russian philology at a large prestigious public university
[UPr19]: 67-year-old male professor of Russian literature
[UPr20]: 68-year-old male professor of applied mathematics at a large specialized institute in Kiev
[UPr21]: 59-year-old male chair of graphic design department at an old public specialized institute
[UPr22]: 55-year-old female professor of English and English literature
[UPr23]: female professor of social science at Kyiv-Mohyla Academy
[UPr24]: male associate professor of economics at Kyiv School of Economics
[UPr25]: female associate professor of economics at Kyiv School of Economics
[UPr26]: 42-year-old male instructor in a theater department of a large specialized institute
[UPr27]: 66-year-old female professor of law at a large state university

II Students

[USt1]: 20-year-old second-year male student at a software engineering department, originally from Kiev
[USt2] 23-year-old female alumna of a Romance philology department, originally from L'viv
[USt3]: 28-year-old alumna of a language department and of an art history department, originally from Kiev
[Ust4]: 20-year-old second-year male student of engineering, originally from Kharkov
[USt5]: 18-year-old first-year female student of linguistics, originally from Kiev
[USt6]: 23-year-old female advanced student of social work, originally from Myrhorod
[USt7]: 21-year-old male student of an electronics department, originally from Odessa

[USt8]: 21-year-old male student of advertising and public relations, originally from Dniepropetrovsk
[USt9]: 18-year-old male second-year student at a journalism department, originally from Cherkassi
[USt10]: 20-year-old male third-year student of economics, originally from Kiev
[USt11]: 22-year-old female master's student of foreign languages, originally from Kerch
[USt12]: 24-year-old male advanced student of a chemical engineering, originally from Poltava
[USt13]: 21-year-old male student at the Department of Management of Informational Security, originally from Kiev
[USt14]: 21-year-old second-year male student of aviation technology, originally from Kerch
[USt15]: 18-year-male first-year student at a computer science department, originally from Kerch
[USt16]: 19-year-old first-year female student at the department of translation, originally from Kerch
[USt17]: 23-year-old male medical radio-physics student, originally from Kremenchuk region
[USt18]: 20-year-old second-year female student of graphic design, originally from Yevpatoria
[USt19]: 19-year-old second-year female student of geography of recreation and tourism department, originally from Donetsk
[USt20]: 24-year-old alumna of an architecture department, originally from Kharkiv
[USt21]: 21-year-old student of management, originally from Kiev
[USt22]: 21-year-old female student of management of foreign economic activity, originally from Zaporozhie
[USt23]: 21-year-old third-year female student of management, originally from Melitopol
[USt24]: 19-year-old first-year male student of veterinary medicine, originally from Rivne
[USt25]: 24-year-old male advanced student of International Relations, originally from Kiev
[USt26]: 27-year-old male alumnus of a marine navigation department, originally from Kerch
[USt27]: 23-year-old female senior in a political science department, originally from Kiev

[USt28] 22-year-old fourth-year male student of accounting, originally from Dniepropetrovsk

[USt29]: 26-year-old female third-year student of painting, originally from Uzhgorod

[USt30]: 34-year-old female student of graphic design, originally from Kiev

[USt31]: 21-year-old male third-year student of law, originally from Kiev

[USt32]: 20-year-old female student of management and marketing, originally from Kiev

[USt33]: 19-year-old first-year student of editing and journalism, originally from Kiev

[US34]: 21-year-old female student of a humanities department, originally from Bila Tserkva

[USt35]: 26-year-old female alumna of Middle Eastern languages department, originally from Brovary

[USt36]: 22-year-old third-year male student of microbiology and biosafety, originally from Lutsk

[USt37]: 20-year-old second-year female student of French department, originally from Kiev

[USt38]: 20-year-old third-year male student at the finances department, originally from Kiev

[USt39]: 21-year-old third-year female student of a land management faculty, originally from Ternopil region

[USt40]: 26-year-old fourth-year male student of civil engineering, originally from Ivano-Frankivs'k

III Parents

[UPa1]: 44-year-old mother of a second-year student of humanities, an artist

[UPa2]: 60-year-old father of two university alumni (of philology and of psychology departments), a medical doctor

[UPa3]: 46-year-old father of a second-year student of computer science, a manager

[UPa4]: 55-year-old mother of two children, one alumna of an education department and one current student of tourism, a housewife

[UPa5]: 38-year-old mother of a first-year student of an accounting department, a beautician and a psychologist

[UPa6]: 47-year-old father of a third-year student of economics, an engineer
[UPa7]: 59-year-old mother of two university alumni in social sciences, a veterinarian
[UPa8]: 41-year-old mother of a first-year student in a psychology department, high school teacher
[UPa9]: 45-year-old mother of a first-year student of applied mathematics, a government worker
[UPa10]: 43-year-old mother of a student of translation, administrative assistant
[UPa11]: 47-year-old father of a student of computer science, a notary
[UPa12]: 39-year-old mother of a first-year student of international relations, a housewife
[UPa13]: 53-year-old mother of an alumna of an education-related department, a government clerk
[UPa14]: 41-year-old father of a first-year student of history, an accountant
[UPa15]: 54-year-old father of a 21-year-old student of management, IT specialist
[UPa16]: 48-year-old father of a recent alumnus of an international relations department, a businessman
[UPa17]: 51-year-old father of a last-year student at a transportation faculty, a former pilot, retired
[UPa18]: 47-year-old mother of a third-year student at the finances department, a pediatrician
[UPa19]: 49-year-old father of an alumna of a sociology faculty, a businessman
[UPa20]: 43-year-old mother of a sophomore at a city development department, a musician
[UPa21]: 50-year-old mother of two former university students, a real estate agent

BELARUS

I Professors

[BPr1]: 65-year-old male professor of architecture at a large university
[BPr2]: 31-year-old female instructor of Spanish at a large university
[BPr3]: 59-year-old male professor of political science at a large university

[BPr4]: 50-year-old female instructor of humanities at a medium-sized university
[BPr5]: 67-year-old female chair of a language department at a large specialized institute
[BPr6]: 44-year-old female instructor of natural sciences at a large university
[BPr7]: 61-year-old male professor of history in a large university
[BPr8]: 41-year-old female former instructor of English at a large university
[BPr9]: 64-year-old female language instructor at a specialized institute
[BPr10]: 30-year-old male instructor of economics in a small institute
[BPr11]: 26-year-old female language instructor at a large specialized institute
[BPr12]: 34-year-old male instructor of a social science at a medium-sized university
[BPr13]: 32-year-old female instructor of ideology at a large university
[BPr14]: 67-year-old female chair of a language department at a large specialized institute
[BPr15]: 58-year-old female professor of humanities at a large university
[BPr16]: 48-year-old male instructor of chemistry in a small institute
[BPr17]: 43-year-old female instructor of musicology at a small specialized institute
[BPr18]: 50-year-old male instructor of mathematics in a small institute
[BPr19]: 42-year-old male instructor of environmental law in a large university
[BPr20]: 51-year-old senior female instructor of graphics in a large specialized institute

II Students

[BSt1]: 28-year-old alumnus of Minsk Institute of Management
[BSt2]: 19-year-old female sophomore at Minsk State University
[BSt3]: 25-year-old alumnus of the State Academy of Arts
[BSt4]: 20-year-old third-year female student at Belarusian State University
[BSt5]: 27-year-old alumnus of the Belarusian State Agrarian Technical University

[BSt6]: 20-year-old third-year female student at a small Minsk institute
[BSt7]: 21-year-old fourth-year female student at Belarusian National Technical University
[BSt8]: 19-year-old male student at Belarusian National Technical University
[BSt9]: 21-year-old third-year male student at a small institute
[BSt10]: 18-year-old second-year female student at large Minsk University
[BSt11]: 27-year-old alumna of Belarusian State University of Culture and Arts
[BSt12]: 24-year-old fifth-year male student at Belarusian National Technological University
[BSt13]: 22-year-old fourth-year female student at Belarusian State University
[BSt14]: 18-year-old second-year male student at Belarusian State Agrarian Technical University
[BSt15]: 20-year-old third-year male student at Belarusian State Agrarian Technical University
[BSt16]: 24-year-old fifth-year male student at Belarusian State Medical University
[BSt17]: 26-year-old alumna of Belarusian State Medical University
[BSt18]: 19-year-old second-year female student at Belarusian State Medical University
[BSt19]: 18-year-old second-year male student at Belarusian State University
[BSt20]: 20-year-old second-year male student at Belarusian State University
[BSt21]: 18-year-old first-year female student at Belarusian State University
[BSt22]: 23-year-old fourth-year female student at Belarusian State Technical University
[BSt23]: 20-year-old second-year male student at Belarusian State Technical University
[BSt24]: 22-year-old fourth-year female student at a major Minsk university
[BSt25]: 19-year-old male student at Belarusian State Economic University

[BSt26]: 22-year-old fourth-year student at Belarusian State Economic University
[BSt27]: 26-year-old graduate student at a large Minsk HEE
[BSt28]: 27-year-old alumnus of Minsk State Linguistic University
[BSt29]: 21-year-old third-year male student at Minsk State Linguistic University
[BSt30]: 20-year-old third-year female student at Minsk Pedagogical University
[BSt31]: 19-year-old female student at Minsk Pedagogical University
[BSt32]: 22-year-old male student at a small specialized institute
[BSt33]: 29-year-old alumnus of Belarusian State University of Informatics and Radioelectronics
[BSt34]: 18-year-old first-year male student at Belarusian State Economic University
[BSt35]: 18-year-old first-year female student of the Institute of Modern Knowledge
[BSt36]: 20-year-old third-year male student at Minsk State University
[BSt37]: 25-year-old fifth-year male student at Belarusian State Technical University

III Parents

[BPa1]: 56-year-old mother of a former student of the Belarusian Institute of Culture and Arts and a current student at the Belarusian State Economic University, a doctor
[BPa2]: 49-year-old father of a second-year student at Belarusian State University, a pilot
[BPa3] 41-year-old mother of a second-year student at Belarusian State Pedagogic (Maxim Tank) University, a housewife
[BPa4]: 56-year-old mother of an alumna of Belarusian State Physical Culture University and a current student of Minsk State Linguistic University, an engineer
[BPa5]: 39-year-old father of a first-year student at Belarusian State University, a business owner
[BPa6]: 40-year-old father of a first-year student at Belarusian State University of Transport, temporarily unemployed accountant
[BPa7]: 47-year-old mother of a fourth-year student at Belarusian Agricultural Technical University, tourist agency employee

[BPa8]: 60-year-old mother of two alumni Belarusian State University, a real estate broker
[BPa9]: 55-year-old mother of a recent graduate of Belarusian State Medical University, retail worker
[BPa10]: 38-year-old mother of a first-year student of the Institute of Modern Knowledge, housewife
[BPa11]: 39-year-old father of a first-year student at the International Sakharov Environmental University, a banker

APPENDIX III

1 LIST OF FORUMS

Ukraine

1. "The Forum of Students of Kyiv National Economic University." Available online at http://forum.kneu.net.ua/
2. "Forum Fakul'teta Sotciologii Kievskogo Natsional'nogo Universiteta Imeni Tarasa Shevchenko." Available online at http://forum.sociology.org.ua/
3. "StudZona." Available online at www.studzona.com/univer
4. "Mogilyanskiy Forum." Available online at http://bo.net.ua/lo-.version/index.php/
5. "TNU. Uchimsya i Otdyhaem Vmeste." Available online at http://bo.net.ua/lo.version/index.php/
6. "Studencheskiy Forum ONUA." Available online at http://student.onua.edu.ua/forum/
7. "Studencheskiy Portal." Available online at http://studportal.net.ua/forums.php
8. "Students Talk." Available online at http://students-talk.com/index.php?name=Forums
9. "Forum HNEU." Available online at www.hneu.org.ua/forum/
10. "Obschestvo Studentov-Medikov Ukraini." Available online at www.medin.org.ua/index.php?option=com_-.reboard&Itemid=64&func=listcat
11. "Sait Studentov NMU im. Bogomol'tsa." Available online at http://bogomolca.com/
12. "Neofitsial'niy Forum Studentov Vinnitskogo Politeha." Available online at http://bogomolca.com/
13. "Forum Studentvo KISI." Available online at http://kisi.com.ua/
14. "Visshee Obrazovanie VUZ, VNZ." Available online at http://forumkiev.com/f10/
15. "Sayt I Forum Studentov Knuba." Available online at http://top.a.ua/options.php?action=more&id=1736

Belarus

1. "Unofficial Forum of Belarusian State University of Informatics and Radiolectronics." Available online at http://bsuir.info/forum
2. "Unofficial forum of Belarusian National Technical University." Available online at http://www.bntu.su/
3. "Obrazovanie.by." Available online at www.obrazovanie.by/forum/
4. "Univer.by." Available online at www.univer.by/forum
5. "Para.by." Available online at http://para.by/forum
6. "Mass.by." Available online at http://forum.mass.by/index.php?s=a619466841b8daf4ebbbb855c2b56ac7&showforum=4
7. "Tut.by." Available online at http://forums.tut.by/forumdisplay.php?f=4
8. "EduBelarus.info." Available at http://forum.edubelarus.info/

2 EXPERT RESPONDENTS

Belarus

- A co-founder of European Humanities University, Vladimir Dunaev
- One former instructor at European Humanities University
- One current instructor at European Humanities University
- Two Ministry of Education officials
- One journalist and an active member of Young Front
- Three members of a student opposition group who asked to remain unidentified
- Two active members of Belarusian Youth Republican Front
- One editor of an oppositional online edition
- Two managers of anti-trafficking NGOs
- A project manager at the Belarusian branch of a human rights NGO

Ukraine

- Natalia Shulga, Associate Professor, Department of Environmental Studies, Kyiv-Mohyla Academy, a regular contributor to "Dzerkalo Tyzhdnya" newspaper
- Tom Coupe, Kyiv School of Economics, Director and Associate Professor and European Economic Research Council President
- Three Ministry of Education officials
- Sergiy Kurbatov, a research fellow at Institute of Higher Education, National Academy of Pedagogical Sciences of Ukraine
- A member of DAK (State Accreditation Committee)

- A former secretary of VAK (Higher Accreditation Committee)
- Three journalists from two online editions that have published articles about university corruption in the past five years
- Two employees of the USAID Ukraine
- Two fellows of Kiev International Institute of Sociology

3 PRIMARY SOURCES: LOCAL MEDIA PUBLICATIONS, NGO REPORTS, AND GOVERNMENTAL DOCUMENTS

Abitutient.in.ua. "Рейтинг "Компас." Accessed December 11, 2014. www.abiturient.in.ua/ru/rating/rating_kompas

Amnesty International. "Ukraine Needs Accountability for Human Rights Violations." April 14, 2010. Accessed December 17, 2014. www.amnesty.org/en/news-and-updates/report/ukraine-needs-accountability-human-rights-violations-2010-04-14

Amnesty International. "Belarus." Accessed June 4, 2015. www.amnesty.org/en/countries/europe-and-central-asia/belarus/

Ampby.org. "Академические Свободы в Беларуси Тоже в Дефиците." Accessed June 14, 2015. http://ampby.org/2011/07/31/9418/

Amzoomby.org. "Белорусское Образование – Нежизнеспособный Гибрид Советской Системы: Мнение Бывшего Проректора ЕГУ." Accessed June 14, 2015. http://am.zoomby.org/node/658

Antikorruptsionniy Portal. "Академия Коррупционных Наук." Accessed January 12, 2014. http://job-sbu.org/akademiya-korruptsionnyih-nauk.html

Antipenko, Olga. "Минобразования Хочет Проверять Документы об Образовании на Подлинность." *Kraina.by*. June 8, 2006. Accessed June 14, 2015. www.kraina.by/newspaper/education/education_1978.html

Antonovich, Miroslava and Aleksandr Merezhko. "Как Преодолеть Коррупцию." *Куда Пойти Учиться*. Accessed January 3, 2014. http://gotostudy.com.ua/articles/79.html

Argumentua.com. "Почти Половина Преподавателей Украинских ВУЗов Получают Зарплату Ниже Средней в Украине." Accessed January 12, 2014. http://argumentua.com/novosti/pochti-polovina-prepodavatelei-ukrainskikh-vuzov-poluchayut-zarplatu-nizhe-srednei-v-ukraine

Bekus, Nelly. "Belarus: The National Vice." *Open Democracy*, October 21, 2010. Accessed January 2, 2015. www.opendemocracy.net/nelly-bekus/belarus-national-vice

Belarus Digest. "Bologna Process." Accessed April 30, 2013. http://belarusdigest.com/category/free-tags/bologna-process

Belarus Miscellany. "Private and/or For-Profit, Post-Secondary Education." Accessed January 23, 2014. www.belarus-misc.org/bel-pped.html

Belarus Project. "Bologna Process: Last Outsider in Europe." Accessed January 2, 2012. http://belarus-project.eu/2012/11/bologna-process-outsider/

Belaruspartisan.org. "Лукашенко: В Белорусских Вузах Невозможны Скандалы и Коррупция." Accessed June 26, 2015a. www.belaruspartisan.org/politic/241651/

Belaruspartisan.org. "Продолжаются Политические Репрессии в Гродненском Университете." Accessed June 21, 2015b. www.belaruspartisan.org/politic/253825/

Belta.by. "При Проведении Вступительной Компании в ВУЗах и ССУЗах Беларуси Практически Исчезла Коррупция." Accessed online April 10, 2013. www.belta.by/ru/all_news/society/Pri-provedenii-vstupitelnoj-kampanii-v-vuzax-i-ssuzax-Belarusi-prakticheski-ischezla-korruptsija–Rubinov_i_569432.html

Bogomolca.com. "Взятки в Медунивере." Accessed January 12, 2014. http://bogomolca.com/blog_entry.php?user=murzik&blogentry_id=8

Branstein, Jeremy. "Belarus: Students Resist Lukashenka's Efforts to Turn the Clock Back." *Radio Free Europe/Radio Liberty*, June 6, 2001. Accessed January 2, 2015. www.rferl.org/content/article/1096615.html

BRSM. "Белорусский Республиканский Союз Молодёжи." Accessed May 16, 2012. http://brsm.by/ru/about

Charter97.com. "Международная Лига по Правам Человека Бьет Тревогу по Поводу Закрытия ЗБС." Accessed June 20, 2015a. www.charter97.org/rus/news/2001/12/03/20

Charter97.com. 'Basics of Ideology' Introduced in Belarusian Universities." Accessed January 2, 2015b. www.charter97.org/eng/news/2004/02/05/ideology

Charter97.com. "California Students Hike to Raise Funds for ZUBR." Accessed January 2, 2015c. www.charter97.org/eng/news/2005/05/05/zubr

Charter 97.com. "Repressions against the Youth Continued Buy 'Mopping Ups' in Universities." Accessed January 2, 2015d. www.charter97.eu/en/news/2008/7/2/7868/

Charter97.com. "'Крепостное Право' в Барановичском Университете." Accessed June 21, 2015e. http://obrazovanie.by/news/2009-02-11.html

Charter97.com. "Власти Пытаются «Замаскировать» Высшее Образование под Европейское." Accessed June 14, 2015f. www.charter97.org/ru/news/2010/3/16/27362/

Charter97.com. "В ИнЯзе Начались Политические Репрессии против Студентов." Accessed January 2, 2015g. www.charter97.org/bc/news/2011/12/12/45641/

Charter 97.com. "Malady Front Calls to Impose Economic Sanctions." Accessed online January 2, 2015h. www.charter97.org/en/news/2013/10/28/78582/

Charter 97.com. "Political Prisoner Lobaw Became a Co-chair of Malady Front." Accessed January 2, 2015i. www.charter97.org/en/news/2013/10/28/78583/

Charter97.com. "Беларусь в Списке Нарушителей Свободы Прессы." Accessed June 21, 2015j. www.charter97.org/ru/news/2012/1/5/46454/comments/

Chekina, Olga. "Опыт Англии Украине не Подходит – Зам Табачника Выступил против Частных ВУЗов." *Khadija.ru*, February 9, 2012. www.khadija.ru/Opit_Anglii_Ukraine_ne_podhodit.php

Chuhlib, Viktor. "Названы Самые "Коррумпированные" Специальности в Украинских Вузах."*Ukrinform.ua*, April 12, 2011. Accessed January 10, 2015. www.ukrinform.ua/rus/news/nazvani_samie_korrumpirovannie_spetsialnosti_v_ukrainskih_vuzah___issledovanie_1043521

CNN. "Court Convict's Ukraine's Former Prime Minister," October 11, 2011. Accessed April 16, 2016. www.cnn.com/2011/10/11/world/europe/ukraine-prime-minister-trial/

Cole, V. "Belarus Update." *International League for Human Rights* 4(8). Accessed June 8, 2013. www.ilhr.org/ilhr/regional/belarus/updates/2001/38.htm

Ctv.by. "Мингорисполком Объявил Войну Родительским Поборам в Школах." Accessed June 22, 2015a. www.ctv.by/mingorispolkom-obyavil-voynu-roditelskim-poboram-v-shkolah

Ctv.by. "Столичные Власти Предлагают Инициативным Студентам Сотрудничать со Структурами Горисполкома Уже с Первых Курсов." Accessed June 20, 2015b. www.ctv.by/novosti-minska-i-minskoy-oblasti/andrey-shorec-10-aprelya-vstretilsya-so-studentami-vedushchih-vuzov

Donnari, Elena. "Zubr Opposition Movement: Strong Like Bison." *Café Babel*, March 13, 2006. Accessed January 2, 2015. www.cafebabel.co.uk/article/zubr-opposition-movement-strong-like-bison.html

The Economist. "Belarus's Young Dissidents: Home and Away." July 13, 2011. Accessed January 19, 2015. www.economist.com/blogs/easternapproaches/2011/07/belaruss-young-dissidents

The Economist. "From Bolshevism to Backhanders: Corruption Has Replaced Communism as the Scourge of Eastern Europe." Accessed April 16, 2016. www.economist.com/node/18560605

EduBelarus.info. "Белорусское Образование: Взгляд со Стороны." Accessed June 14, 2015a. www.edubelarus.info/index.php?newsid=557

EduBelarus.info. "Выдача Фальшивых Дипломов Белорусского Вуза." Accessed June 21, 2015b. www.edubelarus.info/index.php?newsid=197

EduBelarus.info. "Крупное Хищение в Вузе." Accessed June 21, 2015c. www.edubelarus.info/index.php?newsid=197

EduBelarus.info. "Взяточничество в Высшем Образовании Искоренено?" Accessed June 21, 2015d. www.edubelarus.info/index.php?newsid=366

EduBelarus.info. "Взятка или Подарок?" Accessed June 21, 2015e. www.edubelarus.info/index.php?newsid=95&news_page=1

Ej.by: Ezhednevnik. "Коррупцией в Сфере Образования Занялась Генпрокуратура." Accessed April 10, 2013. www.ej.by/news/sociaty/2012/04/20/korruptsiey_v_sfere_obrazovaniya_zanyalas__genprokuratura.html

Ekzamen.Kiev.ua. "Дипломные Работы." Accessed January 7, 2014. http://ekzamen.kiev.ua

EtalonOnline. "КОДЕКС РЕСПУБЛИКИ БЕЛАРУСЬ ОБ ОБРАЗОВАНИИ 13 Января 2011 г. № 243-3." Accessed online June 14, 2015. http://etalonline.by/?type=text&regnum=hk1100243#load_text_none_1_

Euroline.by. "Школьник из Докшиц Пожаловался на Давление за Отказ Вступить в БРСМ." Accessed online January 5, 2015. www.euroline.by/belarus/606-shkolnik-iz-dokshic-pozhalovalsja-na-davlenie-za.html

European Commission. "Higher Education in Belarus." Accessed January 5, 2015. http://eacea.ec.europa.eu/tempus/participating_countries/overview/belarus_tempus_country_fiche_final.pdf

European Forum for Democracy and Solidarity. "Belarus." Accessed April 8, 2013. www.europeanforum.net/country/belarus

European Humanities University. "About." Accessed January 23, 2014. www.ehu.lt/en/aboutEuroua.com.

EuroUA.com. "Украинский Диплом Не Каждому по Карману – Эксперты." Accessed online January 12, 2014. http://euroua.com/ukraine/corruption/2093-ukrainskij-diplom-ne-kazhdomu-po-karmanu-eksperty

FindTheData. "Belarus." Accessed April 16, 2016. http://country-corruption.findthedata.com/l/123/Belarus

Fishwick, Carmen. "'We Are So Naïve and Optimistic': Ukraine Euromaidan Protesters Tell Us What Changed for Them." *The Guardian*, March 4, 2014. Accessed December 18, 2014. www.theguardian.com/world/2014/mar/04/ukraine-crisis-protesters-kiev-euromaidan-independence-square

Friends of European Humanities University. "EHU's Story: Promoting Intellectual Freedom." Accessed January 23, 2014. www.ehufriends.org/story.php

Fond Effectivnoe Upravlenie. "Система Высшего Образования в Украине: Количество, не Переходящее в Качество." Accessed online January 5, 2015. www.feg.org.ua/docs/sistema.pdf

Frye, Timothy. "The Culture of Corruption: Russians Pay but They Don't Like It." *Washington Post*, February 17, 2014. Accessed April 16, 2016. www.washingtonpost.com/news/monkey-cage/wp/2014/02/17/the-culture-of-corruption-russians-pay-but-they-dont-like-it-2/

Gadyatski, Vladimir. "Псевдоконкурси – Невигластво чи Корупція," *ZN.UA*. Accessed April 29, 2012. www.dt.ua/3000/3300/67617/

Gavrish, Kristina. "В УКРАЇНІ НАЙБІЛЬШЕ ХАБАРНИКІВ У МЕДИЦИНІ, ОСВІТІ ТА ЖКГ – ЕКСПЕРТ." *Ubr.ua*, May 17, 2013. Accessed January 12, 2014. http://ubr.ua/uk/ukraine-and-world/society/-kran-naiblshe-habarnikv-u-medicin-osvt-ta-ekspert-227598

Glavpost.com. "Коррупция в Госорганах в 2015 г. Осталась Неизменной – Опрос среди Украинского Бизнеса." Accessed June 20, 2015. http://glavpost.com/post/15apr2015/Society/25249-korrupciya-v-gosorganah-v-2015-g-ostalas-neizmennoy-opros-sredi-ukrainskogobiznesa.html?utm_source=glavpost&utm_medium=internal_linking&utm_campaign=last_news_under_post

Golos-ameriki.ru. "Беларусь и Узбекистан Вошли в Десятку Стран с Самой Жесткой Цензурой." Accessed June 21, 2015. www.golos-ameriki.ru/content/press-freedom-cpj-2012-05-02-149795895/664782.html

Goncharuk, Inna. "В Университете им. Шевченко Самые Дорогие Факультеты." *Golos.ua*, August 1, 2013. Accessed January 10, 2015. http://ru.golos.ua/social_problem/13_08_01_v_universitete_im_shevchenko_samyie_dorogie_fakultetyi__mejdunarodnyih_otno

Gurinovich, Tatiana. "Почему Беларусы Едут Учиться на Запад?" *Новая Европа*, September 14, 2010. Accessed online January 5, 2015. http://n-europe.eu/article/2010/09/14/pochemu_belarusy_edut_uchitsya_na_zapad

Hardtechno.ua. "Неофициальный Форум Студентов ВНТУ." Accessed January 7, 2014. http://hardtechno.at.ua/forum/14-1292-1

The Higher Education. "Presidential Duress: Fears for Belarusian Academic Freedom." February 10, 2011. Accessed January 2015. www.timeshighereducation.co.uk/415114.article

Hrabro.com. "Факты Коррупции в Национальной Академии Медицинских Наук Украины." Accessed January 12, 2014. http://hrabro.com/33731

Human Rights House Foundation. "Complete Restriction to Fundamental Rights in Ukraine." January 17, 2014. Accessed December 18, 2014. http://humanrightshouse.org/Articles/19918.html

Ibnlive.com. "Interview with Serhiy Kvit, National University of Kyiv-Mohyla Academy." Accessed January 10, 2015. http://topic.ibnlive.in.com/ajit-pawar/videos/interview-with-serhiy-kvit-national-university-of-kyiv-mohyla-academy-OlTmlMfHINo-1881933.html

Inanets, Snezhana. "Наращивание Ногтей и Солярий: на Что Еще Есть Скидки у Членов БРСМ?" *News.tut.by*, August 17, 2012. Accessed January 5, 2015. http://news.tut.by/society/305626.html

Informatsionniy Tsentr. "Коррупция в Высших Образовательных Учереждениях." May 27, 2013. Accessed online January 3, 2014. http://info-center.od.ua/statti/2826-korrupciya-v-vysshih-obrazovatelnyh-uchrezhdeniyah.html

International League for Human Rights. "Case of Aleksandr Kozulin." Accessed April 8, 2013. www.ilhr.org/ilhr/regional/belarus/cases/kozulin.htm

JAE. "Берегитесь ВУЗов-халтурщиков." Accessed April 27, 2012. http://jae.org.ua/article/note/47.html

Kabanov, Kirill. "Russia's Culture of Corruption: Easier to Accept than Fight." *Russia Beyond the Headlines*, May 11, 2011. Accessed April 16, 2016. http://rbth.com/articles/2011/05/11/russias_culture_of_corruption_easier_to_accept_than_fight_12858.html

Kachur, Inna. "Вже П'ятий Рік поспіль ЗНО Доводить Свою Дієвість і Об'єктивність при Оцінні Знань Випускників." *Ministry of Education and Science of Ukraine*. Accessed January 5, 2014. www.mon.gov.ua/ua/news/archive-news/91/230/ivan-kachur-vzhe-pyatij-rik-pospil-zno-dovodit-svoyu-dievist-ta-obektivnist-pri-otsintsi-znan-vipusknikiv/

Kadrovik.ua. "Зарплатный Рейтинг Вузов: Выпускникам Каких Учебных Заведений Платят Больше." Accessed January 10, 2015. www.kadrovik.ua/content/zarplatnyi-reiting-vuzov-vypusknikam-kakikh-uchebnykh-zavedenii-platyat-bolshe

Kamitet Salidarnist'. "No to Repressions against Belarusian Youth!" April 12, 2007. Accessed January 5, 2015. www.salidarnasc.org/en/content/no-repressions-against-belarusian-youth

KharkovForum.com. "Самый Коррумпированный ВУЗ в Харькове?" Accessed December 16, 2014. www.kharkovforum.com/showthread.php?t=3343547&page=5

Kiev International Institute of Sociology. "Коррупцией в Украине Больше Всего Поражены ГАИ, Суды и Медицина." *Censor.net*, September 21, 2011. Accessed January 5, 2015. http://censor.net.ua/n182319

Kiev International Institute of Sociology. "Press Releases and Reports." Accessed April 16, 2016. http://kiis.com.ua/?lang=eng&cat=reports&page=1

Kiev School of Economics. "KSE at a Glance." Accessed June 2015. www.kse.org.ua/en/about/kse-at-glance/

Kievskiy Natsionalniy Universitet im Tarasa Shevchenko. "Преподаватели – Наша Гордость." Accessed January 12, 2014a. http://knush.univerlife.com

Kievskiy Natsionalniy Universitet im Tarasa Shevchenko. "Андрейцев Владимир Иванович." Accessed January 12, 2014b. http://knush.univerlife.com/андрейцев-владимир-иванович/p12237/

Kievskiy Natsionalniy Universitet im Tarasa Shevchenko. "Балюк Галина Ивановна." Accessed January 12, 2014c. http://knush.univerlife.com/балюк-галина-ивановна/p12285/

Kievskiy Natsionalniy Universitet im Tarasa Shevchenko. "Pikus Ruslana Vladimirovna." Accessed January 12, 2014d. http://knush.univerlife.com/пикус-руслана-владимировна/p11985/

Klyuchnikova, Ljudmila. "Belarus Introduces Educational Program of State Ideology." *ITAR-TASS Daily*, September 23, 2003.

Kneu.ua. "KNEU Community." Accessed December 11, 2014a. http://kneu.in.ua

Kneu.ua. "Преподаватели КНЭУ." Accessed January 12, 2014b. http://kneu.in.ua/prepodu.html

KnubaHelp. "Преподаватели." Accessed January 12, 2014. http://knuba-help.kiev.ua/publ

Kontrol'naya Rabota. "Коррупция в Высшем Образовании." Accessed January 3, 2014. http://firstua.com/ru/video/program/kontrolna_robota/2013/07/12/6886

Korrespondent.net. "Корреспондент Составил Рейтинг Вузов Страны, Опросив Лучших Работодателей." Accessed January 10, 2015. news.bigmir.net/ukraine/551067-Korrespondent-sostavil-reiting-vyzov-strani-oprosiv-lychshih-rabotodatelei

Kulyagin, Sergey. "Центр по Изучению Китайского Языка и Культуры Планируют Создать в Могилевском Госуниверситете." *Tut.by*, May 11, 2015. Accessed June 14, 2015. http://news.tut.by/society/447408.html

Kursor: Obrazovatel'niy Portal. "Большинство Украинцев Поддерживает Внешнее Оценивание." Accessed January 5, 2014. http://kursor.org.ua/posts/662-bolshinstvo-ukraintsev-podderzhivaet-vneshnee-otsenivani

Kursovik.com.ua. "Дипломные и Курсовые Работы на Заказ." Accessed January 7, 2014. http://kursovik.com.ua

Kyiv Post. "Ukraine's Culture of Corruption." Accessed April 16, 2016. www.kyivpost.com/article/content/ukraine-abroad/foreign-policy-ukraines-culture-of-corruption-342276.html

Laptsevich, Vladimir. "В Могилеве Предложили Взимать Налог с Не Состоящих в БРСМ или "Белой Руси." *Tut.by*, November 18, 2013. Accessed January 8, 2015. http://news.tut.by/kaleidoscope/375187.html

LB.ua. "Киевская Консерватория Сокращает Зарплаты Проподавателей – Денег Нет." Accessed January 12, 2014. http://society.lb.ua/education/2013/02/05/188180_kievskaya_konservatoriya_sokrashchaet.html

Maina, Nadiya. "Відмова від ЗНО Поверне Хабарі та Перекриє Доступ у ВНЗ Талановитим Дітям." *Osvita.ua*, January 21, 2013. Accessed January 3, 2014. www.osvita.org.ua/articles/1356.html

Maksymiuk, Jan. "Returning to Good Old Ideology." *The Rational Argumentator* XXVIII, December 15, 2004. Accessed in April 8, 2013. http://rationalargumentator.com/issue28/Belarus_ideology.html

Malady Front. "Belarusian and World News." Accessed January 10, 2015. http://mfront.net/engl_index.html

Manaev, Oleg. "По тонкому льду," *Novosti NISEPI* 3(5), 1997. www.iiseps.org/?p=2322

Martynovich, Artyom. "Как Выпускники Откосили от Распределения." *Euroradio.fm*, September 2, 2013. Accessed January 10, 2015. http://euroradio.fm/ru/kak-vypuskniki-otkosili-ot-raspredeleniya

Mazurkevich, Marina. "Высшая Школа в Беларуси Переживает Кризис." *Dw.com*. Accessed June 14, 2015. www.dw.de/высшая-школа-в-беларуси-переживает-кризис/a-5356089

Mikhailov, Anatoly. "European Humanities University. 15 years: New History." Accessed January 10, 2015. www.ehu.lt/files/New_history_ehu_EN.pdf

Ministerstvo Osviti ta Nauky, Molodi ta Sportu Ukraini. "Освіта." Accessed January 7, 2014. www.mon.gov.ua/index.php/ua/diyalnist/zno

Ministry of Education of the Republic of Belarus. "Privately-Owned Institutions." Accessed January 10, 2015. http://edu.gov.by/en/main.aspx?guid=2391

Mozheyko, Vadim. "Академические Свободы в Беларуси: Что Это и Как Они Нарушаются." Accessed June 14, 2015. http://neurope.eu/article/2013/01/23/akademicheskie_svobody_v_belarusi_chto_eto_i_kak_oni_narushayutsya

Mundell, Ian. "No Bologna for Belarus." *EuropeanVoice.com*, April 4, 2012. Accessed June 8, 2013. www.europeanvoice.com/CWS/Index.aspx?PageID=178&articleID=74079

Myers, Steven, and Ellen Barry. "Putin Reclaims Crimea for Russia and Bitterly Denounces the West." *New York Times*, March 18, 2014. www.nytimes.com/2014/03/19/world/europe/ukraine.html?_r=0

Narbut, Inn. "Глаза Боятся, а Руки Берут: Сколько Стоит Высшее Образование в Запорожье." *Reportyor*, June 14, 2012. Accessed January 3, 2014. http://reporter-ua.com/2012/06/14/glaza-boyatsya-ruki-berut-skolko-stoit-vysshee-obrazovanie-v-zaporozhe

Naviny.by. "Malady Front Activists Set Up Belarusian Headquarter in Kyiv." Accessed January 10, 2015. http://naviny.by/rubrics/english/2013/12/09/ic_news_259_429365/

Newsland. "Репрессии Против Студентов в Белоруссии." Accessed January 10, 2015. http://newsland.com/news/detail/id/606213/

News.tut.by. "За Подстрекательство к Даче Взятки Задержана Член Приемной Комиссии БГУФК." Accessed June 22, 2015. http://news.tut.by/society/143804.html

New York Times. 2016. "Ukraine's Unyielding Corruption." Accessed online April 16, 2016. hwww.nytimes.com/2016/04/01/opinion/ukraines-unyielding-corruption.html?_r=0

Nielsen, Nikolay. "Белоруссия: Репрессии Против Молодежи и Студентов." *InoPressa*, April 9, 2012. Accessed January 10, 2015. www.inopressa.ru/article/09apr2012/lastampa/belorussia.html

Nn.by. "Не Уступіш у БРСМ – Будзеш Здраднікам." Accessed online January 10, 2015a. http://nn.by/?c=ar&i=49191

Nn.by. "В Гродно Продолжаются Репрессии против Преподавателей: из Университета Уволена Инна Соркина." Accessed June 21, 2015b. http://nn.by/?c=ar&i=120577&lang=ru

Numbeo.com. "Cost of Living Comparison between Chicago, IL and Kiev." Accessed January 12, 2014. www.numbeo.com/cost-of living/compare_cities.jsp?country1=United+States&city1=Chicago%2C+IL&country2=Ukraine&city2=Kiev

Nyegosh, D. "Belarusian Civil Society: Between Repression and Dialogue." *SEAL – Social Economy and Law*, 2001. Brussels, Belgium: European Foundation Centre.

Obozrevatel.com. "Студентов Валят на Сессии, чтобы не Платить Стипендии." Accessed April 28, 2012. http://obozrevatel.com/news/2010/1/27/346836.htm

Odarenko, Sergey and Kristina Abramovskaya. "Преступление и Образование. Коррупционные Скандалы Добывают Отечественные ВУЗы." *Tema*, August 21, 2013. Accessed January 3, 2014. http://tema.in.ua/article/7962.html

Onischenko, Oksana. "Коррупция – не Преступление?" *Zn.ua*, November 23, 2012. Accessed January 3, 2014. http://gazeta.zn.ua/EDUCATION/korruptsiya__ne_prestuplenie__o_hronicheskoy_bolezni_vysshego_obrazovaniya_i_o_tom,_kak_ee_lechit.html

Orlov, Ivan. "Баллы по Сходной Цене." Accessed June 21, 2014. www.edubelarus.info/index.php?newsid=265

Osborn, Andrew. "Former Ukraine President Leonid Kuchma Investigated over Journalist Murder." *The Telegraph*, March 22, 2011. Accessed December 17, 2014. www.telegraph.co.uk/news/worldnews/europe/ukraine/8398500/Former-Ukraine-President-Leonid-Kuchma-investigated-over-journalist-murder.html

Osvita.ua. "Азаров: Выпускные Экзамены Должны Пройти Организованно и без Коррупции." Accessed January 3, 2014a. http://ru.osvita.ua/school/news/7350/

Osvita.ua. "Коррупция в Высших Учебных Заведениях: Виновата Система и . . .Студент." Accessed January 3, 2014b. http://ru.osvita.ua/vnz/high_school/17152/

Osvita.ua. "Коррупция в Украинских Университетах: Преодолеть Нельзя Оставить." Accessed January 3, 2014c. http://ru.osvita.ua/vnz/high_school/17373/

Osvita.ua. "О Коррупции в ВУЗах Болтают Грантоеды, – Министр Образования." Accessed January 3, 2014d. http://ru.osvita.ua/vnz/news/27589/

Osvita.ua. "Семь Коррупционных Скандалов в Образовании." Accessed January 3, 2014e. http://ru.osvita.ua/vnz/36665/

Osvita.ua. "Вступительная Компания: Лазейки для Нарушений и Взяточничества." Accessed January 3, 2014f. http://ru.osvita.ua/vnz/consultations/36702/

Osvita. ua. "Возможностей для Взяток при Поступлении Нет – Табачник." Accessed January 3, 2014g. http://ru.osvita.ua/vnz/consultations/36661/

Osvita.ua. "Результати Пошуку: Корупція." Accessed January 3, 2014h. http://osvita.ua/google_search.html?cx=partner-pub-7936802855264727%3Ae0y7x37fbpn&cof=FORID%3A11&ie=utf-8&q=коррупция&siteurl=osvita.ua%2F&ref=&ss=&siteurl=osvita.ua%2 F

Panchenko, Sergey. "Молодой ф ронт» в Профиль и Анфас." *Dw.com*, April 12, 2007. Accessed January 15, 2015. www.dw.de/молодой-фронт-в-профиль-и-анфас/a-2440861-1

Pavlenko, Yuriy. "Министерство Образования Способствует Коррупции в Вузах." *Osvita.ua*, May 25, 2012. Accessed January 15, 2015. http://ru.osvita.ua/vnz/news/29629/

Pervynna Profspilkova Organizatsija. "Соціальні Умови Співробітників та Студентів КНУ Імені Тараса Шевченка." *Osvita.ua*, January 18, 2013. Accessed January 12, 2014. www.prof.univ.kiev.ua/prof/home/2010-12-22-00-05-45/2-events/265-2013-01-18-11-27-15.html

Petra, Aleksandr. "Прокурор Потребовал для Активистов «Молодого Фронта» Штрафа в 500 Базо." *3rdWay.org*, May 28, 2007. Accessed January 15, 2015. http://3dway.org/node/6892

Petrosyan, Arevik. "Частные Вузы: Рискованная Альтернатива?" *LB.ua*, June 7, 2010. Accessed January 15, 2015. http://society.lb.ua/education/2010/06/07/49113_chastnie_vuzi_riskovannaya_alter.html

Politica.ua. "Коррупции в Вузах: Живее Всех Живых." Accessed December 16, 2014. http://politica-ua.com/korrupcii-v-vuzax-zhivee-vsex-zhivyx/

Pravo.by. "ПОСТАНОВЛЕНИЕ СОВЕТА МИНИСТРОВ РЕСПУБЛИКИ БЕЛАРУСЬ, 10 декабря 2007 г. № 1702." Accessed January 15, 2015. www.pravo.by/main.aspx?guid=3871&p0=c20701702&p2=%7BNRPA%7D

Preiherman, Yauheni. "Three Reasons Why Belarus Should Be a Part of the Bologna Process." *Belarus Digest*, December 16, 2011. Accessed January 2, 2015. http://belarusdigest.com/story/three-reasons-why-belarus-should-be-part-bologna-process-6960

Prentice, Alessandra and Pavel Polityuk. "Breaking the Bribe Culture Is Still a Challenge for Ukraine." *Reuters*, January 26, 2016. Accessed April 16,

2016. www.reuters.com/article/us-ukraine-crisis-corruption-idUSKCN0V41CD

Rakova, Elena. "Двойственные Результаты Борьбы с Коррупцией." *Nashe Mnenie*, September 28, 2008. Accessed April 5, 2012. http://nmnby.eu/news/analytics/1524.html

Ranking Web of Universities. "Ukraine." Accessed January 15, 2015. www.webometrics.info/en/Europe/Ukraine%20

Ravchev, Alex. "Спасает ли ВНО от Коррупции при Поступлении?" *Durdom.ua*, May 17, 2013. Accessed January 5, 2014. http://durdom.in.ua/ru/main/article_print/article_id/18081.phtml

Reisz, Matthew. "Freedom for Belarusians at European Humanities University." *Times Higher Education*, February 7, 2013. Accessed April 7, 2013. www.timeshighereducation.co.uk/news/freedom-for-belarusians-at-european-humanities-university/2001291.article

Rich, V. "State Ideology on Belarus Syllabus." *Times Higher Education*, September 12, 2003. Accessed April 7, 2013. www.timeshighereducation.co.uk/story.asp?storyCode=179150&sectioncode=26

Rogov, Vasiliy. "Почему Преподаватели БГУ не Берут Взяток?" *Web Journalist*, July 30, 2012. Accessed June 25, 2015. www.websmi.by/2012/07/pochemu-prepodavateli-bgu-ne-berut-vzyatok/

RT. "Belorussian Students Expelled for Anti-Government Protests." Accessed online June 8, 2013. http://rt.com/politics/belarus-students-protests-expulsion/

Rubinov, Anatoliy. "Педагогический Зуд Реформаторства." *Belarus Segodnya*, March 6, 2008. Accessed June 14, 2015. www.sb.by/obshchestvo/article/pedagogicheskiy-zud-reformatorstva.html

Ryabchun, Yulia. "Есть с Кого Взять," *Kommersant Ukraina*, May 17, 2012. Accessed January 3, 2014. www.kommersant.ua/doc/1935646

Sandakov, Dmitriy. "Системный Кризис Высшего Образования в Беларуси. Попытка Осмысления и Анализа." *Obrazovanie.by*, February 22, 2010. Accessed June 14, 2015. http://obrazovanie.by/sandakov/krizis.html

Sannikov, A. "Belarusian Totalitarianism Is a Reality." *Charter97*, July 28, 2003. Accessed January 23, 2014. http://charter97.org/eng/news/2003/07/28/sannikov

SciVerse Scopus. "Рейтинг Вищих Навчальних Закладів України." Accessed December 11, 2014. www.jsi.net.ua/scopus/ratings_uni/index.html

Segodnya.ua. "В Украине Массово Закрывают Частные Вузы: в Минобразования Обещают Пристроить Всех Студентов." Accessed January 19, 2015. www.segodnya.ua/criminal/v-ukraine-maccovo-zakryvajut-chactnye-vuzy-v-minobrazovanija-obeshchajut-prictroit-vcekh-ctudentov.html

Shik, Konstantin. "Сущность П атриотического Воспитания учащейся Молодежи и Некоторые Способы Его Реализации в Республике Беларусь." 2012. Accessed June 21, 2015. www.moluch.ru/conf/ped/archive/58/2337/

Shkolota.net. "Как Сдать ЗНО?" Accessed January 5, 2014. http://shkolota.net/kak-sdat-zno/

Shraibman, Artyom. "Belarus Needs a Strategic Vision in Higher Education Management." *Belarus Digest*, March 12, 2013. Accessed January 19, 2015. http://belarusdigest.com/story/belarus-needs-strategic-vision-higher-education-management-13272

Shtrahova, Marina. "Нарушение Прав Студентов в 2014 Году: Картошка, Распределение, Вызовы 'на Ковер.'" *Tut.by*, April 16, 2016. Accessed June 21, 2015. http://news.tut.by/society/443970.html

Shulga, Olga. "Преподаватели, Которые Стали 'Лишними в Системе'." *Nashe Mnenie*, March 1, 2013. Accessed June 21, 2015. http://nmnby.eu/news/analytics/5102.html

Shydlovski, Aliaksandr. "Belarus from Abroad Is Perceived Differently, but the Attitude to the Political Opposition in the Country Is Unchanging." *Freedom for Political Prisoners*, August 28, 2013. Accessed August 8, 2015. http://palitviazni.info/%D0%BD%D0%B0%D0%B2%D1%96%D0%BD%D1%8B-en/2013/08/14685?lang=en

Sidorchenko, Viktor. "Проблема Коррупции в ВУЗах." *Propaganda*, January 18, 2011. Accessed January 12, 2014. http://propaganda-journal.net/3242.html

Sidorchik, Valeriy. "Гомельская Область и Китайская Провинция Сычуань Будут Сотрудничать." *Tut.by*, May 12, 2015. Accessed June 14, 2015. http://news.tut.by/society/447548.html

Sovadmin.gov.by. "Организация Идеологической и Воспитательной Работы среди Студентов и Преподавателей в УО «Гомельский Государственный Технический Университет им. П.О. Сухого»," 2013. Accessed June 21, 2015. www.sovadmin.gov.by/index.php?option=com_content&view=article&id=1224:organizatsiya-ideologicheskoj-raboty-v-uo-ggtu-im-p-o-sukhogo&catid=9:bez-kategorii

Sovsun, Inna. "Теорія і Практика Корупції в Освіті." *Tyzhden.ua*, September 6, 2013. Accessed May 20, 2016. http://tyzhden.ua/Society/88089

Spasjuk, Elena. "Эксперт: Включение Беларуси в Болонский Процесс Запустит Реформу Высшего Образования." *Belapan*, February 8, 2010. Accessed June 14, 2015. http://belapan.com/archive/2010/02/08/eu_eu1928/

Spasjuk, Elena. "Академические Свободы в Беларуси По-прежнему в Дефиците." *Naviny.by*, November 20, 2014. Accessed June 14, 2015. http://naviny.by/rubrics/society/2014/11/20/ic_articles_116_187583/

Spring96.org. "'Young Front' Activist Andrei Tsianiuta Secretly Expelled from Bryansk Agricultural Academy." August 11, 2009. Accessed June 20, 2015. http://spring96.org/en/news/29355

Spring96.org. "'Young Front' Activist Yuliya Mikhailava Expelled from College." February 11, 2010. Accessed June 20, 2015. http://spring96.org/en/news/31319/

Spring96.org. "Valiantsin Stefanovich: 'Ministry of Education Should Adequately React to Its Official's Actions.'" January 19, 2010. Accessed June 20, 2015. http://spring96.org/en/news/30862

Spring96.org. "Кухня TV: Беларусь, Болонский Процесс и Академические Свободы." May 12, 2015. Accessed June 14, 2015. http://spring96.org/ru/news/77212

StudPorta.net.ua. "Студенческий Форум/ Учёба/ Злобный Препод." Accessed January 12, 2014. http://studportal.net.ua/forums.php?m=topics&s=5

Stushinskaya, O. "Belarusian Youth: Europeanisation on the Agenda." Accessed January 19, 2005. http://link.springer.com/article/10.1007/s12290-013-0279-x/fulltext.html

Telegraf.by. "WikiLeaks: Официальная Идеология Беларуси – Это Самообман." August, 2011. Accessed January 19, 2015. http://telegraf.by/en/2011/08/wikileaks-oficialnaya-ideologiya-belarusi-eto-samoobman

Tkachenko, Lidiya. "Высшее Образование в Украине: Количество или Качество?" *Dovidkove Buro*, March 12, 2012. Accessed January 19, 2015. http://finforum.org/page/index.html/_/life/vysshee-obrazovanie-v-ukraine-kolichestvo-ili-ka-r47122?pg=2

Transparency International. "What Is the Corruption Perception Index?" Accessed December 28, 2011. www.transparency.org/cpi2011/in_detail#myAnchor1

Transparency International. "Corruption Perceptions Index: Overview." Accessed June 9, 2015. www.transparency.org/research/cpi/overview

Ukrainskiy Tsentr Otsinjuvannya Yakosti Osvity. "Оприлюднено Результати ЗНО з Трьох Предметів." Accessed January 5, 2014. http://testportal.gov.ua

Univer-sity.com. "Студентський Форум." Accessed January 12, 2014. www.univer-sity.com/index.php?showtopic=1737

UN News Center. "Belarus: UN Human Rights Council Condemns Election-Related Violence." June 17, 2011. Accessed June 8, 2013. www.un.org/apps/news/story.asp?Cr=belarus&NewsID=38764#.UbF9I0LdBUQ

VAK Belarusi. "Высшая Аттестационная Комиссия Республики Беларусь." Accessed June 20, 2015. www.vak.org.by

Varfolomeyev, Oleg. "The End of Unity." *Transitions Online* 10(7). 2003. Accessed August 8, 2015. www.tol.org/client/article/10753-the-end-of-unity.html?print

Vasilev, Yegor. "Ukraine and Belarus: The Dawn of Change." *ODR: Russia and Beyond*, October 16, 2012. Accessed June 24, 2015. www.opendemocracy.net/od-russia/yegor-vasylyev/ukraine-and-belarus-dawn-of-change

Vgorode.ua. "Рейтинг Симферопольских Вузов: Где Самые Большие Взятки, а Где Студентам Легко Учиться." November 27, 2011. Accessed December 11, 2014. http://crimea.vgorode.ua/news/sobytyia/86571/

Vgorode.ua. "Узнай, Какие ВУЗЫ Закроют в Запорожье и Области." December 1, 2013. Accessed January 19, 2015. http://zp.vgorode.ua/news/transport_y_ynfrastruktura/244024-v-ukrayne-sobyrauitsia-zakryt-53-vuza-uznai-koho-zakrouit-v-zaporozhe

Vgorodok. com. "Коррупция в Украине. Смертная Казнь для Коррупционера." Accessed June 20, 2015. http://vgorodok.com/agregator/1645-korrupciya-v-ukraine-smertnaya-kazn-dlya-korrupcionera.html

Viasna: Human Rights Center. "The Zubr Movement Activist Is Expelled from University for Taking Part in Protests." July 20, 2005. Accessed January 19, 2015. http://spring96.org/en/news/13786

Viasna: Human Rights Center. "Материалы Белорусских НПО, Подготовленные для Универсального Периодического Обзора по Беларуси в Совете по Правам Человека ООН." February 12, 2010. Accessed January 19, 2015. http://spring96.org/ru/news/31343

Viasna: Human Rights Center. "Хочешь в Университет – Отработай Распределение," June 13, 2012. Accessed January 19, 2015. http://spring96.org/ru/news/53208

Viasna: Human Rights Center. "Распределение: Что Нужно Знать Студенту?" April 10, 2013. Accessed January 19, 2015. http://spring96.org/ru/news/62514

VIPDiplom. "Заказать Диплом или Дипломы на Заказ, Заказ Дипломной Работы или Купить Дипломную Работу – Всё Это Можно Сделать у Нас!" 2012. Accessed January 7, 2014. http://vipdiplom.kharkov.ua

World Bank. "World Governance Indicators." Accessed June 9, 2015. http://info.worldbank.org/governance/wgi/index.aspx#home

World Values Survey. "Online Data Analysis." Accessed December 18, 2014. www.worldvaluessurvey.org/WVSOnline.jsp

Yavorskaya, Nataliya. "Зачистка ВУЗов Продолжается." *Segodnya.ua*, July 14, 2009. Accessed April 30, 2012. www.segodnya.ua/useful/education/14064818.html

Zan'ko, Nastasya. "Какие же это поборы в школе, если ты сам добровольно сдаешь деньги?" April 6, 2015. Accessed January 12, 2017. www.kp.by/daily/26363.5/3244764/

Zautra Tvoey Kraini. "Репрессии против Студентов Могут Продолжаться до 1 Сентября." February 1, 2011. Accessed January 19, 2015. http://www.zautra.by/art.php?sn_nid=7993&sn_cat=4

Zayats, Anatoliy. "Анатолий Михайлов: Был Наивно Уверен в том, что Созданием ЕГУ Делал Нужное для Беларуси Дело." Accessed June 14, 2015. http://obrazovanie.by/01_articles/a_08_056.html

Zhegulo, Petr. "Крупное Хищение в Вузе." Accessed June 14, 2015. www.edubelarus.info/index.php?newsid=245

Zn.sb.by. "Родительский Взнос или Школьный Оброк?" November 23, 2009. Accessed June 22, 2015. http://zn.sb.by/obrazovanie-i-nauka-2/article/roditelskiy-vznos-ili-shkolnyy-obrok.html

056.ua. "Выбираем Самый Коррумпированный ВУЗ Днепропетровска." 2013. Accessed December 16, 2014. www.056.ua/news/298790

3rdway.org. "СМИ в Беларуси. Цензура Информации." Accessed online June 21, 2015. http://3dway.org/publications/belarus/smi-v-belarusi-tsenzura-informatsii

BIBLIOGRAPHY

Abed, George T. and Hamid R. Davoodi. 2000. "Corruption, Structural Reforms, and Economic Performance in the Transition Economies." IMF Working Paper WP/00/132.

Ades, Alberto and Rafael Di Tella. 1997. "The New Economics of Corruption: A Survey and Some New Results." *Political Studies* 45(3): 496–515.

AFAF. 2016. "About Afaf." Retrieved: May 25, 2016 (http://afafreedom.tumblr.com/about).

Alderfer, Clayton P. and Ken K. Smith. 1982. "Studying Intergroup Relations Embedded in Organizations." *Administrative Science Quarterly* 27(1): 35–65.

Ali, Abdiweli M. and Hodan Said Isse. 2003. "Determinants of Economic Corruption: A Cross-Country Comparison." *Cato Journal* 22(3): 449–66.

Allina-Pisano, Jessica. 2010. "Social Contracts and Authoritarian Projects in Post-Soviet Space: The Use of Administrative Resource." *Communist and Post-Communist Studies* 43: 373–82. doi: http://dx.doi.org/10.1016/j.postcomstud.2010.10.001

Allison, Roy, Stephen White, and Margot Light. 2005. "Belarus between East and West." *Journal of Communist Studies and Transition Politics* 21(4): 487–511.

Altbach, Philip. 2001. "Academic Freedom: International Realities and Challenges." *Higher Education* 41(1): 205–19.

Amundsen, Inge. 1999. "Political Corruption: An Introduction to the Issues." *Working Papers*. Bergen: Chr. Michelsen Institute.

Arel, D. 2005. "The 'Orange Revolution': Analysis and Implications of the 2004 Presidential Election in Ukraine," in *Third Annual Stasiuk-Cambridge Lecture on Contemporary Ukraine*. Cambridge: Cambridge University Press.

Ash, Konstantin. 2015. "The Election Trap: The Cycle of Post-Electoral Repression and Opposition Fragmentation in Lukashenko's Belarus." *Democratization* 22(6): 1030 53.

Ashforth, Blake E. and Vikas Anand. 2003. "The Normalization of Corruption in Organizations." *Research in Organizational Behavior* 25: 1–52.

Åslund, Anders and Michael McFaul. 2006. *Revolution in Orange: The Origins of Ukraine's Democratic Breakthrough*. Washington, DC: Carnegie Endowment for International Peace.

Astakhova, V. I. 1997. "On the Development of Private Higher Education in Ukraine." *Russian Education & Society* 39(5): 73–83.

Barber, Jack. 2013. "The Country That Never Came in from the Cold." *The Oxonian Globalist*. Retrieved: May 25, 2016 (http://toglobalist.org/2013/05/the-country-that-never-came-in-from-the-cold/).

Bardhan, Pranab. 1997. "Corruption and Development: A Review of Issues." *Journal of Economic Literature* 35(3): 1230–346.

Barrington, Lowell W. and Erik S. Herron. 2004. "One Ukraine or Many? Regionalism in Ukraine and Its Political Consequences." *Nationalities Papers* 32(1): 53–86.

Bendix, Reinhard. 1998. *Max Weber: An Intellectual Portrait*, Vol. 2. New York: Psychology Press.

Bennett, Brian M. 2011. *The Last Dictatorship in Europe: Belarus under Lukashenko*. New York: Columbia University Press.

Berg-Schlosser, Dirk. 2008. "'Neighborhood Effects' of Democratization in Europe." *Taiwan Journal of Democracy* 4(2): 29–45.

Besters-Dilger, Juliane. 2009. *Language Policy and Language Situation in Ukraine: Analysis and Recommendations*. Frankfurt am Main: Peter Lang.

Bever, Olga. 2010. "Linguistic Landscapes of Post-Soviet Ukraine: Multilingualism and Language Policy in Outdoor Media and Advertising." *The University of Arizona Campus Repository*. Retrieved: May 25, 2015 (http://hdl.handle.net/10150/194464).

Bilaniuk, Laada and Svitlana Melnyk. 2008. "A Tense and Shifting Balance: Bilingualism and Education in Ukraine." *International Journal of Bilingual Education and Bilingualism* 11(3–4): 340–72.

Blake, Charles and Stephen Morris. 2009. *Corruption and Democracy in Latin America*. Pittsburgh: University of Pittsburgh Press.

Bohara, Alok K., Neil J. Mitchell, and Carl F. Mittendorff. 2004. "Compound Democracy and the Control of Corruption: A Cross-Country Investigation." *Policy Studies Journal* 32(4): 481–99. doi: 10.1111/j.1541-0072.2004.00077.x.

Boskholov, Sergei. 2003. "Organized Crime and Corruption in Russia." *Demokratizatsiya* 3(3): 270–74.

Bova, Andriy and Robert J. Valliere. 1999. "The Population's Attitudes toward Bribery in Some Cities of Ukraine." *International Journal of Sociology* 29(4): 6–15.

Bowser, Donald. 2001. "Corruption, Trust, and the Danger to Democratization in the Former Soviet Union." *Corruption; Trust and Democratization in the Former Soviet Union*. Available at http://citeweb.info/20010517198.

Brown, Ed and Jonathan Cloke. 2004. "Neoliberal Reform, Governance and Corruption in the South: Assessing the International Anti-Corruption Crusade." *Antipode* 36(2): 272–94.

Brunetti, Aymo and Beatrice Weder. 2003. "A Free Press Is Bad News for Corruption." *Journal of Public Economics* 87(7–8): 1801–24. doi: http://dx.doi.org/10.1016/S0047-2727(01)00186-4

Bukovansky, Mlada. 2002. "Corruption Is Bad: Normative Dimensions of the Anti-Corruption Movement." Department of International Relations, Australian National University. Unpublished Working Paper.

Čábelková, Inna and Jan Hanousek. 2004. "The Power of Negative Thinking: Corruption, Perception and Willingness to Bribe in Ukraine." *Applied Economics* 36(4): 383–97. doi: 10.1080/00036840410001674303.

Carothers, Thomas. 2002. "The End of the Transition Paradigm." *Journal of Democracy* 13(1): 5–21.

Copsey, Nathaniel. 2005. "Popular Politics and the Ukrainian Presidential Election of 2004." *Politics* 25(2): 99–106.

D'Anieri, Paul. 2005. "What Has Changed in Ukrainian Politics?: Assessing the Implications of the Orange Revolution." *Problems of Post-Communism* 52(5): 82–91.

Darden, Keith A. 2001. "Blackmail as a Tool of State Domination: Ukraine under Kuchma." *East European Constitutional Review* 10:67.

Davidonis, Ramunas. 2001. "The Challenge of Belarus, and European Responses." The Institute for Security Studies, Western European Union, Unpublished Occasional Paper.

Davis, Kevin E., Benedict Kingsbury, and Sally Engle Merry. 2010. "Indicators as a Technology of Global Governance." *NYU Law and Economics Research Paper* (10–13): 10–26.

della Porta, Donatella and Alberto Vannucci. 1997. "The 'Perverse Effects' of Political Corruption." *Political Studies* 45(3): 516–38. doi: 10.1111/1467-9248.00094.

Diamond, Larry Jay. 2002. "Thinking About Hybrid Regimes." *Journal of Democracy* 13(2): 21–35.

DiMaggio, Paul J. and Walter W. Powell. 2012. "The Iron Cage Revisited: Institutional Isomorphism and Collective Rationality in Organizational Fields [1983]." *Contemporary Sociological Theory*: 175.

Diuk, Nadia. 2014. "Euromaidan: Ukraine's Self-Organizing Revolution." *World Affairs* 176(6): 9–17.

Doig, Alan, Stephanie McIvor, and Robin Theobald. 2006. "Numbers, Nuances and Moving Targets: Converging the Use of Corruption Indicators or Descriptors in Assessing State Development." *International Review of Administrative Sciences* 72(2): 239–52.

Dowley, Kathleen M. and Brian D. Silver. 2002. "Social Capital, Ethnicity and Support for Democracy in the Post-Communist States." *Europe-Asia Studies* 54(4): 505–28.

Dryomin, Viktor. 2004. "Organized Crime and Corruption in Ukraine as a System Phenomenon." *Publication Series-European Institute for Crime Prevention and Control*: 49–59.

Eke, Steven M. and Taras Kuzio. 2000. "Sultanism in Eastern Europe: The Socio-Political Roots of Authoritarian Populism in Belarus." *Europe-Asia Studies* 52(3): 523–47. doi: 10.1080/713663061.

Feduta, Aleksandr. 2005. *Лукашенко: Политическая Биография*. Moscow: Referendum Press.

Feng, Yi. 1997. "Democracy, Political Stability and Economic Growth." *British Journal of Political Science* 27(03): 391–418.

Fimyar, Olena. 2010. "Policy Why (S): Policy Rationalities and the Changing Logic of Educational Reform in Postcommunist Ukraine." In *Post-socialism Is Not Dead: (Re) reading the Global in Comparative Education*. Book series: International Perspectives on Education and Society, Vol. 14: 61–91.

Fineman, Stephen. 1996. "Emotional Subtexts in Corporate Greening." *Organization Studies* 17(3): 479–500.

Finkel, Evgeny and Yitzhak M Brudny. 2012. "No More Colour! Authoritarian Regimes and Colour Revolutions in Eurasia." *Democratization* 19(1): 1–14.

Fisman, Raymond and Roberta Gatti. 2002. "Decentralization and Corruption: Evidence across Countries." *Journal of Public Economics* 83(3): 325–45. doi: http://dx.doi.org/10.1016/S0047-2727(00)00158-4.

Fournier, Anna. 2002. "Mapping Identities: Russian Resistance to Linguistic Ukrainisation in Central and Eastern Ukraine." *Europe-Asia Studies* 54(3): 415–33.

Frank, Björn and Günther G. Schulze. 2000. "Does Economics Make Citizens Corrupt?" *Journal of Economic Behavior & Organization* 43(1): 101–13.

Friedland, Roger and Robert R. Alford. 1991. "Bringing Society Back In: Symbols, Practices and Institutional Contradictions." Pp. 232–63 in *The New Institutionalism in Organizational Analysis*, edited by W. Powell and P. Dimaggio. Chicago: University of Chicago Press.

Fritz, Verena. 2007. *State-Building: A Comparative Study of Ukraine, Lithuania, Belarus and Russia*. Budapest: Central European University Press.

Gerber, Jurg. 2000. "On the Relationship between Organized and White-Collar Crime: Government, Business, and Criminal Enterprise in Post-Communist Russia." *European Journal of Crime Criminal Law and Criminal Justice* 8(4): 327–42.

Gerber, Theodore P. and Sarah E. Mendelson. 2008. "Public Experiences of Police Violence and Corruption in Contemporary Russia: A Case of Predatory Policing?" *Law & Society Review* 42(1): 1–44.

Gibson, James L. 1996. "A Mile Wide but an Inch Deep (?): The Structure of Democratic Commitment in the Former USSR." *American Journal of Political Science* 40(2): 396–420.

Ginsburg, Tom and Tamir Moustafa. 2008. *Rule by Law: The Politics of Courts in Authoritarian Regimes*. New York: Cambridge University Press.

Gleason, William. 2001. "Ukrainian Higher Education in Transition: Perspectives and Policy Implications." *Demokratizatsiya* 9(3):434.

Gorbachev, Nikolai N., Sergei N. Malchenko, and Siarhei A. Zenchanka. 2006. "The Implementation of International Standards into the Education Process in Belarus." *International Journal of Foresight and Innovation Policy* 2(2): 175–83.

Grødeland, Åse B., Tatyana Y. Koshechkina, and William L. Miller. 1998. "'Foolish to Give and yet More Foolish Not to Take' – In-depth Interviews with Post-Communist Citizens on Their Everyday Use of Bribes and Contacts." *Europe-Asia Studies* 50(4): 651–77.

Graham, Loren R. 1993. *Science in Russia and the Soviet Union: A Short History*. New York: Cambridge University Press.

Granovetter, Mark. 1985. "Economic Action and Social Structure: The Problem of Embeddedness." *American Journal of Sociology*: 481–510.

Gray, Cheryl and Daniel Kaufman. 1998. *Corruption and Development*. Washington, DC: The World Bank.

Grossman, Gregory. 1977. "The 'Second Economy' of the USSR." *Problems of Communism* 26(5): 25–40.

Gupta, Sanjeev and George T. Abed. 2002. *Governance, Corruption, and Economic Performance*. Washington, DC: International Monetary Fund.

Gupta, Sanjeev, Hamid Davoodi, and Rosa Alonso-Terme. 2002. "Does Corruption Affect Income Inequality and Poverty?" *Economics of Governance* 3(1): 23.

Hale, Henry E. 2005. "Regime Cycles: Democracy, Autocracy and Revolution in Post-Soviet Eurasia." *World Politics* 58(1): 133–65.

Hallak, Jacques and Muriel Poisson. 2007. "Academic Fraud, Accreditation and Quality Assurance: Learning from the Past and Challenges for the Future." *Report: Higher Education in the World 2007: Accreditation for Quality Assurance: What Is at Stake?* Global University Network for Innovation. doi: https://upcommons.upc.edu/bitstream/handle/2099/8108/hallak_poisson.pdf

Hankivsky, Olena. 2006. "Imagining Ethical Globalization: The Contributions of a Care Ethic." *Journal of Global Ethics* 2(1): 91–110.

Hannan, Michael T. and John Freeman. 1984. "Structural Inertia and Organizational Change." *American Sociological Review* 49(2): 149–64.

Haran, Olexiy. 2011. "From Viktor to Viktor: Democracy and Authoritarianism in Ukraine." *Demokratizatsiya* 19(2): 93.

Hellman, Joel, Geraint Jones, and Daniel Kaufmann. 2000. "'Seize the State, Seize the Day': State Capture, Corruption, and Influence in Transition." The World Bank, Unpublished Working Paper.

Hendley, Kathryn. 1999. "Rewriting the Rules of the Game in Russia: The Neglected Issue of the Demand for Law." *East European Constitutional Review* 8(4): 89–95.

Herzfeld, Thomas and Christoph Weiss. 2003. "Corruption and Legal (in) Effectiveness: An Empirical Investigation." *European Journal of Political Economy* 19(3): 621–32. doi: http://dx.doi.org/10.1016/S0176-2680(03)00018-1

Hindess, Barry. 2005. "Investigating International Anti-Corruption." *Third World Quarterly* 26(8): 1389–98.

Hoffmann, Lutz and Felicitas Möllers. 2012. *Ukraine on the Road to Europe*. New York: Springer.

Hofstede, Geert. 1980. "Culture and Organizations." *International Studies of Management & Organization* 10(4): 15–41.

Holmes, Stephen. 2012. "Fragments of a Defunct State." *The London Review of Books*, January 5, pp. 23–25.

Hopkin, Jonathan. 2002. "States, Markets and Corruption: A Review of Some Recent Literature." *Review of International Political Economy* 9(3): 574–90.

Humphrey, Caroline. 2000. "Rethinking Bribery in Contemporary Russia." Pp. 216–41 in *Bribery and Blat in Russia: Negotiating Reciprocity from the Middle Ages to the 1990s*, edited by S. Lovell, A. V. Ledeneva, and A. Rogachevskii. New York: St. Martin's Press.

Humphrey, Caroline. 2002. *The Unmaking of Soviet Life: Everyday Economies after Socialism*. Ithaca, NY: Cornell University Press.

Jackall, Robert. 1988. "Moral Mazes: The World of Corporate Managers." *International Journal of Politics, Culture, and Society* 1(4): 598–614.

Jain, Arvind K. 2001. "Corruption: A Review." *Journal of Economic Surveys* 15(1): 71–121.

Jamieson, Alison. 2001. "Transnational Organized Crime: A European Perspective." *Studies in Conflict and Terrorism* 24(5): 377–87.

Janmaat, Jan Germen. 2000. "Nation-Building in Post-Soviet Ukraine: Educational Policy and the Response of the Russian-Speaking Population." *Netherlands Geographical Studies*. Royal Dutch Geographical Society Faculty of Social and Behavioral Sciences Universiteit van Amsterdam, Utrecht/Amsterdam. Unpublished Dissertation.

Janmaat, Jan Germen and Nelli Piattoeva. 2007. "Citizenship Education in Ukraine and Russia: Reconciling Nation-Building and Active Citizenship." *Comparative Education* 43(4): 527–52.

Javorcik, Beata S. and Shang-Jin Wei. 2009. "Corruption and Cross-Border Investment in Emerging Markets: Firm-Level Evidence." *Journal of International Money and Finance* 28(4): 605–24.

Johnston, Michael. 2005. *Syndromes of Corruption: Wealth, Power and Democracy*. New York: Cambridge University Press.

Jong-Sung, You and Sanjeev Khagram. 2005. "A Comparative Study of Inequality and Corruption." *American Sociological Review* 70(1): 136–57.

Jowitt, Ken. 1983. "Soviet Neotraditionalism: The Political Corruption of a Leninist Regime." *Europe-Asia Studies* 35(3): 275–97.

Karatnycky, Adrian. 2005. "Ukraine's Orange Revolution." *Foreign Affairs* 84(2): 35–52.

Karklins, Rasma. 2005. *The System Made Me Do It: Corruption in Postcommunist Societies*. Armonk, NY: M. E. Sharpe.

Kaufmann, D., A. Kraay, and M. Mastruzzi. 2006. "Measuring Corruption: Myths and Realities." The World Bank, Unpublished note.

Kaufmann, Daniel, Joel S. Hellman, Geraint Jones, and Mark A. Schankerman. 2000. "Measuring Governance, Corruption, and State Capture: How Firms and Bureaucrats Shape the Business Environment in Transition Economies." *World Bank Policy Research Working Paper* (2312).

Kennedy, David. 1999. "International Anti-Corruption Campaign." *Connecticut Journal of International Law* 14: 455.

Khmelko, Valeri and Andrew Wilson. 1998. "Regionalism and Ethnic and Linguistic Cleavages in Ukraine." Pp. 60–80 in *Contemporary Ukraine: Dynamics of Post-Soviet Transformation*, edited by T. Kuzio. Armonk, NY: M. E. Sharp.

Khondker, Habibul Haque. 2006. "Sociology of Corruption and 'Corruption of Sociology': Evaluating the Contributions of Syed Hussein Alatas." *Current Sociology* 54(1): 25–39.

Knack, Stephen. 2006. "Measuring Corruption in Eastern Europe and Central Asia: A Critique of the Cross-Country Indicators." *Policy Research Working Paper Series*.

Kopissky, B. and N. Listopad. 1996. "Belarus." Pp. 99–104 in *Relations between State and Higher Education*, edited by R. Veld and H.-P. Fiissel. Hague, the Netherlands: Kluwer Law International.

Korosteleva, Elena. 2012. "Questioning Democracy Promotion: Belarus' Response to the 'Colour Revolutions'." *Democratization* 19(1): 37–59.

Kostadinova, Tatiana. 2012. *Political Corruption in Europe: Politics after Communism*. Boulder, CO: Lynne Rienner.

Kovtun, Olena and Sheldon Stick. 2009. "Ukraine and the Bologna Process: A Case Study of the Impact of the Bologna Process on Ukrainian State Institutions." *Higher Education in Europe* 34(1): 91–103.

Krawchenko, Bohdan. 1997. *Administrative Reform in Ukraine: Setting the Agenda*. Budapest: Local Government and Public Service Reform Initiative.

Kremen, Vasyl, Stanislov Nikolajenko, and Michael Stepko. 2006. *Higher Education in Ukraine*: UNESCO-CEPES.

Kubicek, Paul. 2005. "The European Union and Democratization in Ukraine." *Communist and Post-Communist Studies* 38(2): 269–92.

Kulyk, Volodymyr. 2011. "Language Identity, Linguistic Diversity and Political Cleavages: Evidence from Ukraine." *Nations and Nationalism* 17(3): 627–48.

Kurczewski, Jacek. 2004. "Is a Sociology of Corruption Possible?" *Polish Sociological Review* 146: 161–81.

Kuzio, Taras. 1996. "National Identity in Independent Ukraine: An Identity in Transition." *Nationalism and Ethnic Politics* 2(4): 582–608.

Kuzio, Taras. 2002. *Ukraine: State and Nation Building*. New York: Routledge.

Kuzio, Taras. 2005. "From Kuchma to Yushchenko Ukraine's 2004 Presidential Elections and the Orange Revolution." *Problems of Post-Communism* 52(2): 29–44.

Kuzio, Taras. 2006a. "Everyday Ukrainians and the Orange Revolution." Pp. 45–68 in *Revolution in Orange: The Origins of Ukraine's Democratic Breakthrough*. Washington, DC: Carnegie Endowment for International Peace.

Kuzio, Taras. 2006b. "Civil Society, Youth and Societal Mobilization in Democratic Revolutions." *Communist and Post-Communist Studies* 39(3): 365–86.

Kuzio, Taras. 2007. "Oligarchs, Tapes and Oranges: 'Kuchmagate' to the Orange Revolution." *Journal of Communist Studies and Transition Politics* 23(1): 30–56.

Kuzio, Taras. 2011. "Political Culture and Democracy: Ukraine as an Immobile State." *East European Politics & Societies* 25(1): 88–113. doi: 10.1177/0888325410388410.

Kuzio, Taras. 2015. "Ukraine: Leaving the Crossroads." Pp. 481–512 in *Central and East European Politics: From Communism to Democracy*, edited by S. L. Wolchik and J. L. Curry. Lanham, MD: Rowman & Littlefield.

Lalountas, Dionisios A., George A. Manolas, and Ioannis S. Vavouras. 2011. "Corruption, Globalization and Development: How Are These Three Phenomena Related?" *Journal of Policy Modeling* 33(4): 636–48.

Lambsdorff, Johann Graf. 2005. "Consequences and Causes of Corruption: What Do We Know from a Cross-Section of Studies?" *The Open Access Publication Server of the ZBW*. Retrieved: December 18, 2012 (www.econstor.eu/bitstream/10419/55031/1/684238772.pdf).

Lane, David. 2008. "The Orange Revolution: 'People's Revolution' or Revolutionary Coup?" *The British Journal of Politics & International Relations* 10(4): 525–49.

Lauth, Hans-Joachim. 2000. "Informal Institutions and Democracy." *Democratization* 7(4): 21–50.

Ledeneva, Alena V. 1998. *Russia's Economy of Favors: Blat, Networking and Informal Exchange*. New York: Cambridge University Press.

Ledeneva, Alena V. 2006. *How Russia Really Works: The Informal Practices That Shaped Post-Soviet Politics and Business*. Ithaca, NY: Cornell University Press.

Ledeneva, Alena V. 2008. "Blat and Guanxi: Informal Practices in Russia and China." *Comparative Studies in Society and History* 50(1): 118–44.

Lennhag, Mi. 2011. "5. Understanding Post-Soviet Petty Corruption. Informal Institutions, Legitimacy, and State Criticism." *Informal Relations from Democratic Representation to Corruption. Case Studies from Central and Eastern Europe* 8.

Lenzi, Mark. 2002. "Lost Civilization: The Thorough Repression of Civil Society in Belarus." *Demokratizatsiya* 10(3): 401.

Levin, Mark, and Georgy Satarov. 2000. "Corruption and Institutions in Russia." *European Journal of Political Economy* 16(1): 113–32. doi: http://dx.doi.org/10.1016/S0176-2680(99)00050-6

Levitsky, Steven and Lucan Way. 2010. *Competitive Authoritarianism: Hybrid Regimes after the Cold War*. New York: Cambridge University Press.

Libman, Alexander and Anastassia Obydenkova. 2013. "Communism or Communists? Soviet Legacies and Corruption in Transition Economies." *Economics Letters* 119(1): 101–3.

Linz, Juan José. 2000. *Totalitarian and Authoritarian Regimes*. Boulder, CO: Lynne Rienner Publishers.

Lipset, Seymour Martin and Gabriel Salman Lenz. 2000. "Corruption, Culture and Markets." Pp. 112–24 in *Culture Matters: How Values Change Human Progress*, edited by L. J. Harrison and S. P. Huntington. New York: Basic Books.

Lonkila, Markku. 1997. "Informal Exchange Relations in Post-Soviet Russia: A Comparative Perspective." *Sociological Research Online* 2(2).

Lunyachek, V. 2011. "Problem of Education System Development of Ukraine in Time of Crisis." *Public Policy and Administration* 10(1): 67–78.

Magocsi, Paul R. 2010. *A History of Ukraine: The Land and Its Peoples*. Toronto: University of Toronto Press.

Markovska, Anna. 2007. "The Bitter Pill of a Corrupt Heritage: Corruption in Ukraine and Developments in the Pharmaceutical Industry." Pp. 127–47 in *Crime Business and Crime Money in Europe: The Dirty Linen of Illicit Enterprise*, edited by P. C. van Duyne, A. Maljevic, M. van Dijck, K. von Lampe, and J. Harvey. Nijmegen, The Netherlands: Wolf Legal Publisher.

Marples, David R. 1999. *Belarus: A Denationalized Nation*, Vol. 1. Amsterdam, The Netherlands: Taylor & Francis.

Marples, David R. 2006. "Color Revolutions: The Belarus Case." *Communist and Post-Communist Studies* 39(3): 351–64.

Marples, David R. and Frederick V. Mills. 2014. *Ukraine's Euromaidan: Analyses of a Civil Revolution*, Vol. 138. New York: Columbia University Press.

Martin, Roderick. 2006. "Segmented Employment Relations: Post-Socialist Managerial Capitalism and Employment Relations in Central and Eastern

Europe." *The International Journal of Human Resource Management* 17(8): 1353–65.

Mauro, Paolo. 1997. *Why Worry about Corruption?* Vol. 6. Washington, DC: International Monetary Fund.

Mauro, Paolo. 2004. "The Persistence of Corruption and Slow Economic Growth." *IMF Staff Papers*: 1–18.

McFaul, Michael. 2002. "The Fourth Wave of Democracy and Dictatorship: Noncooperative Transitions in the Postcommunist World." *World Politics* 54(2): 212–44.

McMann, Kelly. 2014. *Corruption as a Last Resort: Adapting to the Market in Central Asia*. Ithaca, NY: Cornell University Press.

McPherson, Chad Michael, and Michael Sauder. 2013. "Logics in Action Managing Institutional Complexity in a Drug Court." *Administrative Science Quarterly*: 0001839213486447.

Miller, Arthur H. and Ola Listhaug. 1999. "Political Performance and Institutional Trust." Pp. 204–16 in *Critical Citizens: Global Support for Democratic Government*, edited by P. Norris. New York: Oxford University Press.

Miller, William L., Åse B. Grødeland, and Tatyana Y. Koshechkine. 1998. "Are the People Victims or Accomplices?" *Crime, Law and Social Change* 29(4): 273–310.

Miller, William L., Ase B. Grødeland, and Tatyana Y. Koshechkina. 2001. *A Culture of Corruption? Coping with Government in Post-Communist Europe*. Budapest: Central European University Press.

Mitter, Wolfgang. 1992. "Education in Eastern Europe and the Former Soviet Union in a Period of Revolutionary Change: An Approach to Comparative Analysis." *Oxford Studies in Comparative Education* 2(1): 15–28.

Mobarak, Ahmed Mushfiq. 2005. "Democracy, Volatility, and Economic Development." *Review of Economics and Statistics* 87(2): 348–61.

Montinola, Gabriella and Robert W. Jackman. 2002. "Sources of Corruption: A Cross-Country Study." *British Journal of Political Science* 32(1): 147–70.

Moran, Jonathan. 2001. "Democratic Transitions and Forms of Corruption." *Crime, Law and Social Change* 36(4): 379–93.

Morris, J. and A. Polese. 2014. "Informal Health and Education Sector Payments in Russian and Ukrainian Cities: Structuring Welfare from Below." *European Urban and Regional Studies*. doi: 10.1177/0969776414522081.

Morris, Stephen D. and Joseph L. Klesner. 2010. "Corruption and Trust: Theoretical Considerations and Evidence from Mexico." *Comparative Political Studies* 43(10): 1258–85. doi: 10.1177/0010414010369072.

Moser, Michael. 2013. *Language Policy and Discourse on Languages in Ukraine under President Viktor Yanukovych*, Vol. 122. New York: Columbia University Press.

Ng, David. 2006. "The Impact of Corruption on Financial Markets." *Managerial Finance* 32(10): 822–36.

Oliver, Christine. 1991. "Strategic Responses to Institutional Processes." *Academy of Management Review* 16(1): 145–79.

Onuch, Olga. 2014. "Who Were the Protesters?" *Journal of Democracy* 25(3): 44–51.

Osipian, Ararat L. 2007. "Corruption in Higher Education: Conceptual Approaches and Measurement Techniques." *Research in Comparative and International Education* 2(4): 313–32.

Osipian, Ararat L. 2008a. "Corruption and Coercion: University Autonomy Versus State Control." *European Education* 40(3): 27–48.

Osipian, Ararat L. 2008b. "Political Graft and Education Corruption in Ukraine: Compliance, Collusion, and Control." *Demokratizatsiya: The Journal of Post-Soviet Democratization* 16(4): 323–44.

Osipian, Ararat L. 2009. "Corruption Hierarchies in Higher Education in the Former Soviet Bloc." *International Journal of Educational Development* 29(3): 321–30.

Osipian, Ararat L. 2012. "Education Corruption, Reform, and Growth: Case of Post-Soviet Russia." *Journal of Eurasian Studies* 3(1): 20–29. doi: http://dx.doi.org/10.1016/j.euras.2011.10.003.

Osipian, Ararat L. and Alexandr L. Osipian. 2006. "Why Donbass Votes for Yanukovych: Confronting the Ukrainian Orange Revolution." *Demokratizatsiya* 14(4): 495.

Osyka, Igor. 2003. "Anti-Corruption Policies in the Ukraine." In *Criminal Finances and Organising Crime in Europe*. Nijmegen: Wolf Legal Publishers.

Paldam, Martin. 2002. "The Cross-Country Pattern of Corruption: Economics, Culture and the Seesaw Dynamics." *European Journal of Political Economy* 18(2): 215–40. doi: http://dx.doi.org/10.1016/S0176-2680(02)00078-2.

Park, Hoon. 2003. "Determinants of Corruption: A Cross-National Analysis." *Multinational Business Review* 11(2): 29–48.

Parusinski, Jakub. 2010. "Ukraine's Higher Education Institutions: Fighting Isolation." *European Focus* 7: 1–8.

Pathak, Saurav, Emanuel Xavier-Oliveira, and André O. Laplume. 2015. "Entrepreneurship in Transition Economies: The Role of Corruption and Individual Attributes." *Journal of Balkan and Near Eastern Studies* 17(4): 427–46.

Peng, Mike W. 2003. "Institutional Transitions and Strategic Choices." *Academy of management Review* 28(2): 275–96.

Persson, Torsten, Gerard Roland, and Guido Tabellini. 1997. "Separation of Powers and Political Accountability." *The Quarterly Journal of Economics* 112(4): 1163–202.

Pleskovic, Boris. 2002. *Capacity Building in Economics Education and Research in Transition Economies*, Vol. 2763. Washington, DC: World Bank Publications.

Polese, Abel. 2008. "'If I Receive It, It Is a Gift; If I Demand It, Then It Is a Bribe': On the Local Meaning of Economic Transactions in Post-Soviet Ukraine." *Anthropology in Action* 15(3): 47–60.

Protsyk, Oleh and Andrew Wilson. 2003. "Centre Politics in Russia and Ukraine Patronage, Power and Virtuality." *Party Politics* 9(6): 703–27.

Puglisi, Rosaria. 2003a. "Clashing Agendas? Economic Interests, Elite Coalitions and Prospects for Co-Operation between Russia and Ukraine." *Europe-Asia Studies* 55(6): 827–45.

Puglisi, Rosaria. 2003b. "The Rise of the Ukrainian Oligarchs." *Democratization* 10(3): 99–123.

Rehn, Alf and Saara Taalas. 2004. "'Znakomstva I Svyazi' (Acquaintances and Connections) – Blat, the Soviet Union, and Mundane Entrepreneurship." *Entrepreneurship & Regional Development* 16(3): 235–50.

Reid, Anna. 2000. *Borderland: A Journey through the History of Ukraine*. New York: Basic Books.

Riabchuk, Mykola. 2007. "Ambivalence or Ambiguity? Why Ukraine Is Trapped between East and West." Pp. 70–88 in *Ukraine, the EU and Russia*, edited by S. Velychenko. New York: Palgrave Macmillan.

Rivkin-Fish, Michele. 2005. "Bribes, Gifts and Unofficial Payments: Rethinking Corruption in Post-Soviet Russian Health Care." Pp. 47–64 in *Corruption: Anthropological Perspectives*, edited by D. Haller and C. Shore. Ann Arbor, MI: Pluto.

Roberts, Ken, Colette Fagan, Levan Tarkhnishvili, E. Ivaschenko, and A. Abidekian. 2000. "Employment and Social Mobility: Evidence from Armenia, Georgia and Ukraine in the 1990s." *European Journal of Education* 35(1): 125–36.

Rose, Richard and Doh Chull Shin. 2001. "Democratization Backwards: The Problem of Third-Wave Democracies." *British Journal of Political Science* 31(2): 331–54.

Rose-Sender, S. K., M. E. A. Goodwin, M. Boersma, and H. Nelen. 2010. "Linking Anti-Corruptionism and Human Rights: A Dangerous Addition to the Development Discourse." Pp. 221–39 in *Maastricht Series on Human Rights*, edited by M. Boersma and H. Nelen. Maastricht, The Netherlands: Maastricht University Press.

Rothstein, Bo. 2011. *The Quality of Government: Corruption, Social Trust, and Inequality in International Perspective*. Chicago: University of Chicago Press.

Round, John, Colin C. Williams, and Peter Rodgers. 2008. "Corruption in the Post-Soviet Workplace: The Experiences of Recent Graduates in

Contemporary Ukraine." *Work, Employment & Society* 22(1): 149–66. doi: 10.1177/0950017007087421.

Round, John and Colin Williams. 2010. "Coping with the Social Costs of 'Transition': Everyday Life in Post-Soviet Russia and Ukraine." *European Urban and Regional Studies* 17(2): 183–96.

Rousso, Alan and Franklin Steves. 2007. "The Effectiveness of Anti-Corruption Programs: Preliminary Evidence from the Post-Communist Transition Countries." *International Handbook on the Economics of Corruption*: 247.

Sampford, Charles John, Arthur Henry Shacklock, Carmel Connors, and Fredrik Galtung. 2006. *Measuring Corruption*. Aldershot, UK: Ashgate.

Sampson, Martin W., III. 1987a. "Cultural Influences on Foreign Policy." Pp. 384–405 in *New Directions in the Study of Foreign Policy*, edited by C. F. Hermann, C. W. Kegley Jr., and J. N. Rosenau. Boston: Allen and Unwin.

Sampson, Steven L. 1987b. "The Second Economy of the Soviet Union and Eastern Europe." *Annals of the American Academy of Political and Social Science* 493: 120–36. doi: 10.2307/1046198.

Sampson, Steven. 2005. "Integrity Warriors: Global Morality and the Anti-Corruption Movement in the Balkans." Pp. 103–30 in *Corruption: Anthropological Perspectives*, edited by D. Haller and C. Shore. London: Pluto Press.

Sampson, Steven. 2010. "The Anti-Corruption Industry: From Movement to Institution." *Global Crime* 11(2): 261–78.

Sasse, Gwendolyn. 2001. "The 'New' Ukraine: A State of Regions." *Regional & Federal Studies* 11(3): 69–100.

Schipani-Aduriz, Andres and Alyaksandr Kudrytski. 2005. "Banana Revolutions and Banana Skins." *Transitions Online: Regional Intelligence*. doi: www.tol.org/client/article/14432-banana-revolutions-and-banana-skins.html

Schnytzer, Adi and Tatiana Andreyeva. 2002. "Company Performance in Ukraine: Is This a Market Economy?" *Economic Systems* 26(2): 83–98.

Shaton, Galina. 2009. "Academic Freedom in Belarus." *Social Research: An International Quarterly* 76(2): 615–18.

Shaw, Marta A. 2013. "Flawed Implementation or Inconsistent Logics? Lessons from Higher Education Reform in Ukraine." *European Education* 45(1): 7–24.

Shaw, Philip, Marina-Selini Katsaiti, and Brandon Pecoraro. 2015. "On the Determinants of Educational Corruption: The Case of Ukraine." *Contemporary Economic Policy* 33(4): 698–713.

Shelley, Louise. 1998. "Organized Crime and Corruption in Ukraine: Impediments to the Development of a Free Market Economy." *Demokratizatsiya* 6(4): 648–63.

Shelley, Louise. 2006. "Organized Crime Groups: 'Uncivil Society.'" Pp. 95–109 in *Russian Civil Society: A Critical Assessment*, edited by A. B. Evans Jr., L. A. Henry, and L. M. Sundstrom. New York: M. E. Sharpe.

Shen, Ce and John B. Williamson. 2005. "Corruption, Democracy, Economic Freedom, and State Strength a Cross-National Analysis." *International Journal of Comparative Sociology* 46(4): 327–45.

Shlapentokh, Vladimir. 2013. "Corruption, the Power of State and Big Business in Soviet and Post-Soviet Regimes." *Communist and Post-Communist Studies* 46(1): 147–58. doi: http://dx.doi.org/10.1016/j.postcomstud.2012.12.010.

Silitski, Vitali. 2005. "Preempting Democracy: The Case of Belarus." *Journal of Democracy* 16(4): 83–97.

Smith, Daniel Jordan. 2010. *A Culture of Corruption: Everyday Deception and Popular Discontent in Nigeria*. Princeton, NJ: Princeton University Press.

Solomon Jr., Peter H. and Todd S. Foglesong. 2000. "Two Faces of Crime in Post-Soviet Ukraine." *East European Constitutional Review* 9: 72.

Stapenhurst, Rick and Sahr John Kpundeh. 1999. *Curbing Corruption: Toward a Model for Building National Integrity*. Washington, DC: World Bank Publications.

Stefes, Christoph H. 2007. "Measuring, Conceptualizing, and Fighting Systemic Corruption: Evidence from Post-Soviet Countries." *Perspectives on Global Issues* 2(1): 1–16.

Stetar, Joseph, Oleksiy Panych, and Bin Cheng. 2015. "Ukrainian Private Universities: Elements of Corruption." *International Higher Education* (38): 13–15.

Steves, Franklin and Alan Rousso. 2003. "Anti-Corruption Programmes in Post-Communist Transition Countries and Changes in the Business Environment, 1999–2002." Working Paper No. 85, *European Bank for Reconstruction and Development*. doi: www.ebrd.org/downloads/research /economics/workingpapers/wp0085.pdf

Streeck, Wolfgang and Kathleen Thelen. 2005. *Beyond Continuity: Institutional Change in Advanced Political Economies*. Oxford: Oxford University Press.

Sundakov, Alexander. 2001. *Public Sector Reforms in Ukraine: On the Path of Transformation*. Local Government and Public Service Initiative. doi: http://old.icps.com.ua/files/articles/32/18/nl_eng_20010219_0097.pdf

Sung, H. E. 2004. "Democracy and Political Corruption: A Cross-National Comparison." *Crime, Law and Social Change* 41(2): 179–93. doi: 10.1023 /b: cris.0000016225.75792.02.

Swidler, Ann. 1986. "Culture in Action: Symbols and Strategies." *American Sociological Review* 51(2): 273–86.

Tanzi, Vito. 1998. "Corruption around the World: Causes, Consequences, Scope, and Cures." *Staff Papers – International Monetary Fund* 45(4): 559–94.

Tavits, Margit. 2010. "Why Do People Engage in Corruption? The Case of Estonia." *Social Forces* 88(3): 1257–79. doi: 10.1353/sof.0.0288.

Thornton, Patricia H. and William Ocasio. 1999. "Institutional Logics and the Historical Contingency of Power in Organizations: Executive Succession in the Higher Education Publishing Industry, 1958–1990" *American Journal of Sociology* 105(3): 801–43.

Treisman, Daniel. 2000. "The Causes of Corruption: A Cross-National Study." *Journal of Public Economics* 76(3): 399–457.

Treisman, Daniel. 2007. "What Have We Learned about the Causes of Corruption from Ten Years of Cross-National Empirical Research?" *Annual Review of Political Science* 10: 211–44.

Tudoroiu, Theodor. 2007. "Rose, Orange, and Tulip: The Failed Post-Soviet Revolutions." *Communist and Post-Communist Studies* 40(3): 315–42. doi: http://dx.doi.org/10.1016/j.postcomstud.2007.06.005

Urra, Francisco Javier. 2007. "Assessing Corruption: An Analytical Review of Corruption Measurement and Its Problems: Perception, Error and Utility." *Edmund A. Walsh School of Foreign Service*. doi: http://unpan1.un.org/intradoc/groups/public/documents/APCITY/UNPAN028792.pdf

Uslaner, Eric M. 2008. *Corruption, Inequality, and the Rule of Law: The Bulging Pocket Makes Life Easy*. New York: Cambridge University Press.

Van Rijckeghem, Caroline and Beatrice Weder. 2001. "Bureaucratic Corruption and the Rate of Temptation: Do Wages in the Civil Service Affect Corruption, and by How Much?" *Journal of Development Economics* 65(2): 307–31. doi: http://dx.doi.org/10.1016/S0304-3878(01)00139-0

Varese, Frederico. 2000. "Pervasive Corruption." Pp. 99–111 in *Economic Crime in Russia*, edited by A. Ledeneva and M. Kurkchiyan. London: Kluwer Law International.

Vaughan, Diane. 1998. "Rational Choice, Situated Action, and the Social Control of Organizations." *Law and Society Review* 32(1): 23–61.

Vaughan, Diane. 1999. "The Dark Side of Organizations: Mistake, Misconduct, and Disaster." *Annual Review of Sociology* 25: 271–305.

Wallace, Claire and Rossalina Latcheva. 2006. "Economic Transformation Outside the Law: Corruption, Trust in Public Institutions and the Informal Economy in Transition Countries of Central and Eastern Europe." *Europe-Asia Studies* 58(1): 81–102.

Wanner, Catherine. 2010. *Burden of Dreams: History and Identity in Post-Soviet Ukraine*. University Park: Pennsylvania State University Press.

Way, Lucan A. 2005a. "Authoritarian State Building and the Sources of Regime Competitiveness in the Fourth Wave: The Cases of Belarus, Moldova, Russia, and Ukraine." *World Politics* 57(2): 231–61.

Way, Lucan A. 2005b. "Rapacious Individualism and Political Competition in Ukraine, 1992–2004." *Communist and Post-Communist Studies* 38(2): 191–205.

Weick, Karl E. 1995. *Sensemaking in Organizations*, Vol. 3. Thousand Oaks, CA: Sage Publications, Inc.

White, Stephen and Ian McAllister. 2009. "Rethinking the 'Orange Revolution.'" *Journal of Communist Studies and Transition Politics* 25(2–3): 227–54.

Wigell, Mikael. 2008. "Mapping 'Hybrid Regimes': Regime Types and Concepts in Comparative Politics." *Democratisation* 15(2): 230–50.

Williams, Colin C. and John Round. 2008. "Retheorizing the Nature of Informal Employment: Some Lessons from Ukraine." *International Sociology* 23(3): 367–88.

Williams, Colin C., Olga Onoschenko, J. Morris, and A. Polese. 2013. "The Diverse Livelihood Practices of Healthcare Workers in Ukraine." Pp. 21–34 in *The Informal Post-Socialist Economy: Embedded Practices and Livelihoods*, edited by J. Morris and A. Polese. London: Routledge.

Wilson, Andrew. 2005a. *Ukraine's Orange Revolution*. New Haven: Yale University Press.

Wilson, Andrew. 2005b. *Virtual Politics: Faking Democracy in the Post-Soviet World*. New Haven: Yale University Press.

Wilson, Jeanne L. 2010. "The Legacy of the Color Revolutions for Russian Politics and Foreign Policy." *Problems of Post-Communism* 57(2): 21–36.

Wolczuk, Kataryna. 2000. "History, Europe and the 'National Idea': The 'Official' Narrative of National Identity in Ukraine." *Nationalities Papers* 28(4): 671–94.

Wright, Joseph. 2008. "Do Authoritarian Institutions Constrain? How Legislatures Affect Economic Growth and Investment." *American Journal of Political Science* 52(2): 322–43.

Xin, Xiaohui and Thomas K. Rudel. 2004. "The Context for Political Corruption: A Cross-National Analysis." *Social Science Quarterly* 85(2): 294–309.

Yang, Mayfair Mei-hui. 1994. *Gifts, Favors, and Banquets: The Art of Social Relationships in China*. Ithaca, NY: Cornell University Press.

Zakaria, Fareed. 2003. *The Future of Freedom: Illiberal Democracy at Home and Abroad*. New York: W. W. Norton & Co.

Zaloznaya, Marina. 2012. "Organizational Cultures as Agents of Differential Association: Explaining the Variation in Bribery Practices in Ukrainian Universities." *Crime, Law and Social Change* 58(3): 295–320.

Zaloznaya, Marina. 2013. "Beyond Anti-Corruptionism: Sociological Imagination and Comparative Study of Corruption." *Comparative Sociology* 12(5): 705–51. doi:10.1163/15691330-12341281.

Zlobina, T. 2007. "Cultural Markers of Ukrainian Public Space. Mixture and Instability: The City of Lviv Case." European Humanities University Center for Advanced Studies and Education (CASE), Unpublished Working Paper.

Zon, Hans van. 2005. "Political Culture and Neo-Patrimonialism under Leonid Kuchma." *Problems of Post-Communism* 52(5): 12–22.

INDEX

CAMBRIDGE STUDIES IN LAW AND SOCIETY

Books in the Series

Diseases of the Will
Mariana Valverde

The Politics of Truth and Reconciliation in South Africa: Legitimizing the Post-Apartheid State
Richard A. Wilson

Modernism and the Grounds of Law
Peter Fitzpatrick

Unemployment and Government: Genealogies of the Social
William Walters

Autonomy and Ethnicity: Negotiating Competing Claims in Multi-Ethnic States
Yash Ghai

Constituting Democracy: Law, Globalism and South Africa's Political Reconstruction
Heinz Klug

The Ritual of Rights in Japan: Law, Society, and Health Policy
Eric A. Feldman

The Invention of the Passport: Surveillance, Citizenship and the State
John Torpey

Governing Morals: A Social History of Moral Regulation
Alan Hunt

The Colonies of Law: Colonialism, Zionism and Law in Early Mandate Palestine
Ronen Shamir

Law and Nature
David Delaney

Social Citizenship and Workfare in the United States and Western Europe: The Paradox of Inclusion
Joel F. Handler

Law, Anthropology and the Constitution of the Social: Making Persons and Things
Edited by Alain Pottage and Martha Mundy

Judicial Review and Bureaucratic Impact: International and Interdisciplinary Perspectives
Edited by Marc Hertogh and Simon Halliday

Immigrants at the Margins: Law, Race, and Exclusion in Southern Europe
Kitty Calavita

Lawyers and Regulation: The Politics of the Administrative Process
Patrick Schmidt

Law and Globalization from Below: Toward a Cosmopolitan Legality
Edited by Boaventura de Sousa Santos and Cesar A. Rodriguez-Garavito

Public Accountability: Designs, Dilemmas and Experiences
Edited by Michael W. Dowdle

Law, Violence and Sovereignty among West Bank Palestinians
Tobias Kelly

Legal Reform and Administrative Detention Powers in China
Sarah Biddulph

The Practice of Human Rights: Tracking Law Between the Global and the Local
Edited by Mark Goodale and Sally Engle Merry

Judges Beyond Politics in Democracy and Dictatorship: Lessons from Chile
Lisa Hilbink

Paths to International Justice: Social and Legal Perspectives
Edited by Marie-Bénédicte Dembour and Tobias Kelly

Law and Society in Vietnam: The Transition from Socialism in Comparative Perspective
Mark Sidel

Constitutionalizing Economic Globalization: Investment Rules and Democracy's Promise
David Schneiderman

The New World Trade Organization Knowledge Agreements: 2nd Edition
Christopher Arup

Justice and Reconciliation in Post-Apartheid South Africa
Edited by François du Bois and Antje du Bois-Pedain

Militarization and Violence against Women in Conflict Zones in the Middle East: A Palestinian Case-Study
Nadera Shalhoub-Kevorkian

Child Pornography and Sexual Grooming: Legal and Societal Responses
Suzanne Ost

Darfur and the Crime of Genocide
John Hagan and Wenona Rymond-Richmond

Fictions of Justice: The International Criminal Court and the Challenge of Legal Pluralism in Sub-Saharan Africa
Kamari Maxine Clarke

Conducting Law and Society Research: Reflections on Methods and Practices
Simon Halliday and Patrick Schmidt

Planted Flags: Trees, Land, and Law in Israel/Palestine
Irus Braverman

Culture under Cross-Examination: International Justice and the Special Court for Sierra Leone
Tim Kelsall

Cultures of Legality: Judicialization and Political Activism in Latin America
Javier Couso, Alexandra Huneeus and Rachel Sieder

Courting Democracy in Bosnia and Herzegovina: The Hague Tribunal's Impact in a Postwar State
Lara J. Nettelfield

The Gacaca Courts and Post-Genocide Justice and Reconciliation in Rwanda: Justice without Lawyers
Phil Clark

Law, Society, and History: Themes in the Legal Sociology and Legal History of Lawrence M. Friedman
Robert W. Gordon and Morton J. Horwitz

After Abu Ghraib: Exploring Human Rights in America and the Middle East
Shadi Mokhtari

Adjudication in Religious Family Laws: Cultural Accommodation, Legal Pluralism, and Gender Equality in India
Gopika Solanki

Water on Tap: Rights and Regulation in the Transnational Governance of Urban Water Services
Bronwen Morgan

Elements of Moral Cognition: Rawls' Linguistic Analogy and the Cognitive Science of Moral and Legal Judgment
John Mikhail

A Sociology of Transnational Constitutions: Social Foundations of the Post-National Legal Structure
Chris Thornhill

Mitigation and Aggravation at Sentencing
Edited by Julian Roberts

Institutional Inequality and the Mobilization of the Family and Medical Leave Act: Rights on Leave
Catherine R. Albiston

Authoritarian Rule of Law: Legislation, Discourse and Legitimacy in Singapore
Jothie Rajah

Law and Development and the Global Discourses of Legal Transfers
Edited by John Gillespie and Pip Nicholson

Law against the State: Ethnographic Forays into Law's Transformations
Edited by Julia Eckert, Brian Donahoe, Christian Strümpell and Zerrin Özlem Biner

Transnational Legal Process and State Change
Edited by Gregory C. Shaffer

Legal Mobilization under Authoritarianism: The Case of Post-Colonial Hong Kong
Edited by Waikeung Tam

Complementarity in the Line of Fire: The Catalysing Effect of the International Criminal Court in Uganda and Sudan
Sarah M. H. Nouwen

Political and Legal Transformations of an Indonesian Polity: The Nagari from Colonisation to Decentralisation
Franz von Benda-Beckmann and Keebet von Benda-Beckmann

Pakistan's Experience with Formal Law: An Alien Justice
Osama Siddique

Human Rights under State-Enforced Religious Family Laws in Israel, Egypt, and India
Yüksel Sezgin

Why Prison?
Edited by David Scott

Law's Fragile State: Colonial, Authoritarian, and Humanitarian Legacies in Sudan
Mark Fathi Massoud

Rights for Others: The Slow Home-Coming of Human Rights in the Netherlands
Barbara Oomen

European States and Their Muslim Citizens: The Impact of Institutions on Perceptions and Boundaries
Edited by John R. Bowen, Christophe Bertossi, Jan Willem Duyvendak and Mona Lena Krook

Environmental Litigation in China
Rachel E. Stern

Indigeneity and Legal Pluralism in India: Claims, Histories, Meanings
Pooja Parmar

Paper Tiger: Law, Bureaucracy and the Developmental State in Himalayan India
Nayanika Mathur

Religion, Law and Society
Russell Sandberg

The Experiences of Face Veil Wearers in Europe and the Law
Edited by Eva Brems

The Contentious History of the International Bill of Human Rights
Christopher N. J. Roberts

Transnational Legal Orders
Edited by Terence C. Halliday and Gregory Shaffer

Lost in China? Law, Culture and Society in Post-1997 Hong Kong
Carol A. G. Jones

Security Theology, Surveillance and the Politics of Fear
Nadera Shalhoub-Kevorkian

Opposing the Rule of Law: How Myanmar's Courts Make Law and Order
Nick Cheesman

The Ironies of Colonial Governance: Law, Custom and Justice in Colonial India
James Jaffe

The Clinic and the Court: Law, Medicine and Anthropology
Edited by Tobias Kelly, Ian Harper and Akshay Khanna

A World of Indicators: The Making of Government Knowledge through Quantification
Edited by Richard Rottenburg, Sally E. Merry, Sung-Joon Park and Johanna Mugler

Contesting Immigration Policy in Court: Legal Activism and Its Radiating Effects in the United States and France
Leila Kawar

The Quiet Power of Indicators: Measuring Governance, Corruption, and Rule of Law
Edited by Sally Engle Merry, Kevin Davis and Benedict Kingsbury

Investing in Authoritarian Rule: Punishment and Patronage in Rwanda's Gacaca Courts for Genocide Crimes
Anuradha Chakravarty

Contractual Knowledge: One Hundred Years of Legal Experimentation in Global Markets
Edited by Grégoire Mallard and Jérôme Sgard

Iraq and the Crimes of Aggressive War: The Legal Cynicism of Criminal Militarism
John Hagan, Joshua Kaiser and Anna Hanson

Culture in the Domains of Law
Edited by René Provost

China and Islam: The Prophet, the Party, and Law
Matthew S. Erie

Diversity in Practice: Race, Gender, and Class in Legal and Professional Careers
Edited by Spencer Headworth and Robert Nelson

A Sociology of Transnational Constitutions: Social Foundations of the Post-National Legal Structure
Chris Thornhill

Shifting Legal Visions: Judicial Change and Human Rights Trials in Latin America
Ezequiel A. González Ocantos

The Demographic Transformations of Citizenship
Heli Askola

Criminal Defense in China: The Politics of Lawyers at Work
Sida Liu and Terence C. Halliday

Contesting Economic and Social Rights in Ireland: Constitution, State and Society, 1848–2016
Thomas Murray

Buried in the Heart: Women, Complex Victimhood and the War in Northern Uganda
Erin Baines

Palaces of Hope: The Anthropology of Global Organizations
Edited by Ronald Niezen and Maria Sapignoli

CPSIA information can be obtained
at www.ICGtesting.com
Printed in the USA
LVOW04*1226160517
534715LV00009B/57/P

9 781107 184312